Encountering
Global Environmental Politics

To Rosanna,

You never know

what will happen!

Hah!

Mike

31 Jany 2003

Encountering Global Environmental Politics

Teaching, Learning, and Empowering Knowledge

Edited by
Michael Maniates

ROWMAN & LITTLEFIELD PUBLISHERS, INC.
Lanham • Boulder • New York • Oxford

ROWMAN & LITTLEFIELD PUBLISHERS, INC.

Published in the United States of America
by Rowman & Littlefield Publishers, Inc.
A Member of the Rowman & Littlefield Publishing Group
4720 Boston Way, Lanham, Maryland 20706
www.rowmanlittlefield.com

PO Box 317, Oxford, OX2 9RU, United Kingdom

British Library Cataloguing in Publication Information Available

Library of Congress Cataloging-in-Publication Data

Encountering global environmental politics : teaching, learning,
and empowering knowledge / edited by Michael Maniates.
   p. cm.
   Includes bibliographical references and index.
   ISBN 0-8476-9541-7 (cloth : alk. paper)—ISBN 0-8476-9542-5 (pbk. : alk.
paper)
   1. Environmental responsibility—Study and teaching (Higher) 2.
Global environmental change—Study and teaching (Higher) 3.
Environmental policy—Study and teaching (Higher) 4. Environmental
protection—International cooperation   I. Maniates, Michael.
GE195.7 .E53   2003
363.7'0071—dc21   2002009975

Printed in the United States of America

♾ ™ The paper used in this publication meets the minimum requirements of
American National Standard for Information Sciences—Permanence of Paper for
Printed Library Materials, ANSI/NISO Z39.48-1992.

Contents

Foreword

It's almost midnight and still close to one hundred degrees in the steamy Punjabi town of Bhatinda. Waiting for our train on a dusty platform, my daughter and I talk quietly with our Indian guide, Afsar Jafri. Nearby, destitute people sleep on the bare concrete. We've spent the day with Jafri talking to local farmers about environmental devastation and the epidemic of farmer suicides here in India's breadbasket.

Weary myself and aware that this young man has chosen to devote his life to reversing these alarming trends, I ask, "How do you keep going?"

"I do what I do because it is the only way *I* can survive," he answers calmly, and on many occasions since, I've pondered the meaning of his words.

Jafri, a recent Ph.D. in agronomy, had gathered considerable knowledge in his twenty-nine years. Much of it is about how bad things have become in India, where Green Revolution technology is backfiring and Gene Revolution advocates proffer yet another quick fix fraught with danger. But this knowledge has not overwhelmed him, even in circumstances far more dire than we in the industrial West typically encounter.

But what did Jafri mean? And how is it that he remained empowered despite the depth of his knowledge of the problems? Now, the notion that knowledge could *ever* be other than empowering is anathema to me. Yet, if I'm honest with myself, I know part of me long feared that if I told others how *really* bad I think things are they would throw up their hands in despair, in defeat.

So I welcome *Encountering Global Environmental Politics* in part because it forces me to examine this unexamined fear and enables me to learn from the insightful educators Dr. Maniates brings together in this book to ask, what ensures that knowledge empowers?

The search for answers, I believe, begins with our assumptions about our basic nature. The prevailing thought system, now going global, makes no bones about who we humans are. It throws up to us a view of ourselves as narrowly ego-driven and materialistic—what I have come to see as a shabby caricature that belies our rich complexity as well as a commonsense look at evolution. An alternative view, argued by many anthropologists, is that *Homo sapiens* simply would not have survived without two particularly deep needs—for effectiveness in the larger world and for connection with others. On the need for agency, social philosopher Erich Fromm felt so strongly that he rephrased Descartes to sum up our sense of self thusly: "I am, because I effect."

If true, then knowledge seeking isn't optional—it is essential to meeting our deepest needs. That night at the train station, Jafri was telling us that he engaged in this trying work for *himself*. Knowledge that he was gaining about environmental and social devastation in the Punjab was empowering, not disempowering, because he was conscious of his need for effectiveness in the world and using his knowledge to meet his own need.

So we need not protect ourselves from the bleak news of planetary decline nor prod ourselves with it either. We needn't guilt trip ourselves about some pay back demanded by virtue of our privilege. We have only to create environments in which educators and students alike can come to hear—through the clatter of opposing messages—and to trust their own yearning for effectiveness in the larger world and for connection with others.

Responding to our own needs, trusting them, we become free to empower ourselves with knowledge.

In my case, it took awhile to get there; in fact, it took my entire formal education! I love to agitate my hosts of university-sponsored lectures by saying that I started learning for the first time once I left graduate school. Looking back, it is easy to see why. And that it needn't have been that way.

In college I tried to please professors. Actually, I tried to trick them into not discovering I was actually the dumb Texas female I believed myself to be. My approach to seeking knowledge was disempowering; it was not a pathway for acting on my deeper needs but what I grasped in desperation to avoid exposing my true self.

Then, in my mid-twenties, something changed. Afraid of ending up never knowing why I was here on this little planet at all, I took a deep breath and made a personal vow: I won't do anything else to save the world until I understand how what I am doing relates to the underlying causes of deepening suffering, until I can explain to myself why I had chosen one path and not another.

That meant I had to stop. I had no structure, no external identity. Yikes! But soon a funny thing—novel to me—began to happen. I started listening. I started listening to myself, and I was astounded to discover that there were questions coming from inside me. Questions I had to answer. Questions that ultimately drew me to the U.C. Berkeley agricultural library, a large basement catacomb, where I developed a research technique that has served me for thirty years. I call it "following my nose."

Some of you may recall that era, the late 1960s, a time of alarming predictions about the inevitability of famine. Could it be that humans have actually lost the race and overrun the earth's capacity? I had to figure this out for myself. I let one question lead to the next and unearthed information that would forever change my life: Not only is there enough food in the world to feed everyone but enough to make us all overweight.

To discover my own questions required wandering, allowing each question to lead me to the next. The value of such open-ended intellectual exploration was the first lesson I learned about empowering knowledge. It allowed me to see what my teachers missed, not because I was smarter or had more data, but because I listened to my own questions and let them lead me wherever they would. I had the advantage as well of starting at square one, whereas those advanced in the field had long ago leapt over it.

Ultimately, I became aware of an even more important aspect of empowering knowledge. My question-to-question approach began to create for me a new "frame of orientation," as Fromm calls it: The mental and emotional structure to which we attach new learning and the lens determining what we can see of the world. It's what Einstein was getting at when in 1926 he wrote, "it is theory which decides what we can observe."

One's frame of orientation—or what I call our mental map—determines, I believe, whether knowledge is either empowering or disempowering. If we unwittingly absorb and convey only the mental map of the dominant culture—one telling us we've finally arrived, happily or not, at the end of history, one assuring us that global corporate capitalism is humanity's culminating social system because it best suits our selfish nature—then, I believe, it's difficult to see how knowledge can empower.

The reason is simple. Power, from the Latin *posse*, to be able, suggests our capacity to act, but the dominant mental map tells us our sphere of action is strictly limited. We can act as consumers in the marketplace, or, a few of us at least, as experts behind the scenes. Whereas, to pull our now global civilization back from the environmental and social precipice, we must act as *citizens*. There is scarce room in the dominant map for citizens. By citizens I mean people aware of their deep need for effectiveness as cocreators of their world; people who understand democracy not merely as a structure of government but as a way of life. By citizens in its fullest sense, I therefore mean people aware that, while none of us come to democracy fully equipped, we can learn the collaborative arts of democracy just as we learn any art, whether it be ballet or basketball.

This crisis—the crisis of a *missing culture of democracy*—is the real one, the crisis beneath all our monumental environmental and other global concerns. In such an era—in a time when the dominant map constricts us, yet the crises facing us are of unprecedented magnitude—I believe no

social role is more critical than that of educator. And that is why I am
delighted by Dr. Maniates's vision that created this book. To me, empowering educators are those helping themselves and students listen both to
the deep need for effectiveness and to our own authentic questions.

Knowledge is empowering, then, as it becomes a process of building—
question by question—new frames of orientation that are life serving
because they acknowledge our need to be effective, to be citizens in the
fullest sense of the word. Such a teaching and learning experience by its
very nature begins to dissolve the dominant map telling us we're merely
selfish materialists, for in it we experience ourselves not as passive consumers of information but as creators of knowledge.

Frances Moore Lappé

Preface

If a picture is worth a thousand words, the cover photos for this book could fill a chapter. Taken over five weeks from late January to early March of 2002, they show the rapid disintegration of a Rhode Island–sized piece of the Larsen B ice shelf of Antarctica. Experts say that the now obliterated ice shelf was 12,000 years old with a thickness approaching 700 feet (240 meters). Its sudden collapse is unprecedented in the modern age. Global warming, driven largely by the combustion of fossil fuels, is the likely culprit, and the crumbling of the ice shelf may be far from over.

Photos like these are startling, to say the least. They underscore the previously unimaginable possibility that human society is now encountering any number of critical environmental thresholds of global magnitude. These thresholds are unnerving for at least two reasons. First, they are hard if not impossible to definitively identify. We know they are out there but we cannot point to a discrete line in the sand. Second, once such thresholds are crossed there is no turning back. The damage, often surprising in both its extent and speed, is typically irreversible, at least on any time scale we're used to thinking about. The Larsen B ice shelf reminds us that, as a global community, we're flirting with irreversible change and nasty surprise, and that the time to worry and to act is here and now, not in some distant future.

The problem with worrying and acting, especially in response to mega-events like the collapse of a chunk of Larsen B, is that the first tends to undermine the second. We worry more and more about large-scale environmental change and can, as a result, feel paralyzed and insignificant. Resisting this paralysis is supremely difficult, yet making the leap from knowledge to action is essential if together we are to fashion a future that makes sense. Doing so demands an often elusive faith in our power to change the world and the nerve to act in ways that can seem risky or wild.

Cultivating the faith and nerve we need to act on our growing knowledge of global environmental degradation is the primary focus of this book. It is a product of several years of work by many gifted people, not the least of whom are the authors of the chapters that follow. For their enduring belief in this project and their patience with its sometimes glacial pace they have my deepest thanks. Special thanks go to Geoff Dabelko, Marc Levy, and Jennifer Knerr. Geoff was a stalwart advocate of this volume from its inception. Without his many years of encouragement and advice this project would surely have met the same fate as that Rhode Island–sized piece of Larsen B ice. Marc Levy reviewed an early outline of this volume and, with enthusiasm and grace, made several useful suggestions and steered it, and me, to Jennifer Knerr at Rowman & Littlefield. Ms. Knerr's early and strong support of the project elicited similar backing at a critical time from Allegheny College, my home institution. For valuable review and development of this work I also thank Jehanne Schweitzer, production editor at Rowman & Littlefield, and copyeditor Leslie Evans. Allegheny College provided helpful financial support at the end of project for which I am also grateful.

In ways I'd poorly appreciated at the outset, shepherding this project from its earliest stages to the volume you now hold required its own brand of faith and nerve. Kathy, Sarah, and Hannah are my wellsprings of both, and to them I dedicate this book, with love, gratitude, and joyful anticipation of the struggles to come.

1

❖

Of Knowledge and Power

Michael Maniates

What moron said that knowledge is power? Knowledge is power
only if it doesn't depress you so much that it leaves you in an immo-
bile heap at the end of your bed.

—Paula Poundstone, comedian (1997: 80)

I run an e-mail discussion list of almost two hundred people, mostly college and university professors who teach courses in global environmental politics, peace studies, and international environmental problems.
I confess to having started the list for rather selfish reasons: of all the
classes I teach (I am a professor of political science and environmental
science at a liberal arts college), my course in global environmental politics has always been the most vexing. There is so much material to cover
and so little time, and the topics I do get to can jump from natural science
issues like the intricacies of the carbon cycle and the chemistry of stratospheric ozone, to heady social science subjects like theories of international diplomacy or network analyses of transnational nongovernmental
organizations. My students, typically an eclectic bunch, always seem willing to tackle the subject. At first. But as the semester wears on, fatigue
sets in. They become demoralized, I think, by the deeply interdisciplinary
quality of the course (just when they have one topic figured out, another
comes along from an entirely different vantage point) and sometimes confused by the variety of often arcane theories of global governance. The
core themes of any course in global environmental politics, moreover, are
no walk in the park: wrestling with the details of mounting global environmental degradation and social injustice, the seeming inability of
nation-states to cope with transboundary environmental ills, and the

1

slowness with which needed change appears to occur is depressing stuff indeed. A valued colleague likes to say that, in any given semester, "the best courses are those that go downhill slowly." You'd think he taught global environmental politics on a regular basis.

And so, prodded by my own feelings of classroom clumsiness, I launched the "teaching global environmental politics" e-mail list as a forum for how to better teach the subject.[1] That was several years ago. The list has since grown, its geographic reach has spread to the far corners of the planet, and it has been blessed by the active participation of many of the brightest minds in the field. The insight, advice, and narratives posted to it have made me, and others too, a better teacher and scholar of the politics of global environmental ills. Thankfully, the list has always been episodic. Days, sometimes weeks, will go by without a single message, and then someone will post a question or comment or problem, and bam! . . . there will be a dozen responses inside a day or two. And then the thing goes quiet again. It's the perfect list for people who already get too much e-mail.

Of all the postings to and exchanges on the list, though, the most memorable for me is a discussion string of a few years back. A professor of political science and relative newcomer to the classroom wrote of her frustration with the apathy and passiveness of her students. She explained that she became a professor, and developed a course in global environmental politics, because she wanted to contribute to the resolution of environmental ills by informing and motivating a new generation of environmental scholars and activists. But her teaching, she feared, was doing more to reinforce students' sense of the impossibility of change and the inevitability of ecocollapse, than anything else. What was she doing wrong, she asked our little cyber-community? What might she do differently?

The response was quick and large. Professor after professor, from large universities to small colleges, responded that they too faced a similar classroom dynamic, and that they often felt frustrated and small. Newspaper reports and surveys that document a broad distrust among undergraduates of formal political institutions and elected leaders, and chronicle their deepening doubts about our collective ability to make a dent in the big problems looming before us, are not just words on a page. They are real and incarnate in the very students who make their way into classes on international studies and global environmental politics, according to the flurry of e-mailed replies.[2] Despite all the Ph.D.'s in our electronic community, nobody on the list had much to say about what to do about the problem. When confronted by student passivity and seeming apathy, professors confessed to feeling as helpless as their pupils. They wanted their teaching to make a difference. But they were reconciling themselves to the seeming fact that they were working with a generation more interested (in the face of genuinely scary problems) in making the best of a bad situation than in walking the riskier, less illuminated road of changing the rules of the game.

This dynamic of retreat is not limited to the students of the professors on my e-mail list. Journalist Ross Gelbspan tells a similar story in his book *The Heat Is On* (1998: 172) as he describes a series of three seminars on the global environment held in the mid-1990s at Harvard Medical School. The first seminar meeting was packed, the second session was only half full, and the third was barely attended. Dr. Daniel Goodenough, the organizer of the seminar, queried his students about their tailspinning attendance and, according to Gelbspan, the students' "responses were identical. The material was compelling, they said, but it engendered overwhelming personal reactions. The problems were so great—and the ability of the students to affect them so remote—that they could deal with their feelings of frustration and helplessness and depression only by staying away."

Nor is this dynamic confined to classes that grapple solely with *global* environmental ills. A few years back, I was team teaching a course in introductory environmental science with a fellow member of the environmental science department. The course is your standard undergraduate introduction to environmental problems: it cuts across the natural and social sciences, and humanities too; and it challenges students to explore the physical cause-and-effect relationships that manifest themselves as environmental degradation and to think critically about the struggles for power and influence that underlie most environmental problems. Near the end of a very productive semester, my colleague divided the class of about forty-five students into smaller issue groups (energy, water, agriculture, etc.) and asked each to develop a rank-order list of responses or solutions to environmental threats specific to that issue. He then brought the class back together, had each group report in, and tabulated their varied solutions. The fourth most recommended response was to ride a bike rather than drive a car. Number three on the list was to recycle. The second most preferred action was "to plant a tree," and the top response was, again, "to plant a tree" (the mechanics of tabulating student preference across the issue groups permitted a singularly strong preference to occupy two slots).

When we asked our students why, after thirteen weeks of intensive study of environmental problems, they steered away from solutions that would involve collective action aimed at changing policy and modifying institutions, they shrugged. Sure, we remember studying these kinds of approaches in class, they said, but such measures were, well, fuzzy, messy, and, above all, idealistic. In the face of mounting and complex problems, they seemed to be saying, it is better to do something you know will make a very small change ("plant a tree!" "ride a bike!" "recycle a jar!") than contemplate citizen action beyond the level of individual life-style choices whose impact would be, at best, uncertain.[3]

E-mailing professors, burnt-out Harvard students, tree-planting environmental studies undergraduates wary of broader social forces: these stories are far from special. They surface whenever higher education focuses on the environmental crisis and the politics it spawns. I'm betting that you can tell a similar tale or two, drawn from the classroom hours you have logged as a teacher or student. If you can't, this book probably won't hold much relevance for you. But if you can, then you may find yourself agreeing with the twin premises of this volume.

The first is that, despite differences in training, age, experience, politics, taste in music, and tendencies toward dress, teachers *and* students of global environmental problems are in the same boat. We both make our way to the academy expecting, in part, that our scholarly work will some-how advance the common good—and we work with one another out of this faith. Isn't knowledge empowering, and don't we believe that more education is critical to a transition to an environmentally sustainable world? We consequently pour our energies into courses meant to educate about environmental ills and foster sustainability—but sometimes, by semester's end, the dynamic of retreat is in full gear, and courses for which we had high hopes end up eroding our hope and diminishing our sense of power to act productively upon the world. Knowledge, as Paula Poundstone reminds us at the start of this chapter, does not always mean power.

The second premise is that teachers and students are not very good at talking with one another about this process of disenchantment and "feel-ing small" *as it unfolds in the classroom.* Members of my e-mail list exchanged ideas with one another but not with their own students. Dr. Goodenough at Harvard Medical School interrogated his students, but only after their dwindling numbers at his seminar series became too stark to ignore. My colleague and I accidentally discovered that we were rein-forcing student cynicism about the possibility of broad-based social change—but by the time we figured out what was going on, it was too late to engage them in meaningful conversation.

The environmental studies and political science classroom is a busy place, with all manner of topics up for discussion. So why the relative silence on how our study of global environmental ills undermines our hope for the future and our individual sense of agency? The reasons prob-ably aren't complicated. Students surely find it difficult to let on, in the middle of a class for which they had high hopes, that they are feeling depressed or overwhelmed. To do so might reveal an intellectual inade-quacy or appear to inappropriately challenge the professor. How, moreover, does a student single-handedly create an opening for such discussion without sounding, well, whiny? ("Excuse me, Professor, but I found last night's reading to be particularly disempowering. May I be excused for a good cry down the hall?" isn't very promising.) On the other side of the lectern, professors are reluctant to confess their disappointment or frustration. Doing so might further demoralize students or open the floodgates of student criticism and could easily come off as churlish or condemnatory. Professors, moreover, are often unable to sense (or, perhaps, choose not to acknowledge) their students' disaffection until the very end of the semester, when it is too late to do anything about it (recall my experience in my introductory environmental studies course), so preoccupied are they with getting through the course material.

Imagine, instead, if professors and students consciously grappled with the dynamics of retreat in the midst of their substantive engagement with the politics of global environmental ills. Professors would learn a thing or two about the fears and motivations and political sensibilities of their students, in ways that could only make them better teachers. Students would find themselves reexamining their assumptions about civic participation, social change, and personal responsibility in the face of frank talk by their professors; and they could bring this reexamination to bear on future courses in political science and environmental studies, and on their larger lives as citizens. Both would come to see that they have more in common than one might first think: a shared faith in education to better the world, a wish to make a difference, deep concerns about global environmental trajectories, and vulnerability to feelings of insignificance and futility. Students and teachers would probably cover less material in such a course; there would undoubtedly be wandering conversation that would steal time away from lecture periods. But what good is knowledge without power? Why, in the end, would we choose to teach and learn about global environmental problems, if not to discover within us ways to contribute to their resolution?

RISKY BUSINESS

Jump-starting this process of discovery demands an additional layer of classroom discussion and inquiry, one that rides above the normal curriculum and raises questions about why we study the material we do, how that study influences our perceptions of the future and our own power in the world, and what we could do differently in our study to strengthen our capacity as analysts and our will as citizens. Have you ever had the experience of being intensely engaged in some activity—talking with a friend, giving a lecture, reading a book, camping in the mountains—only to suddenly experience a part of yourself reflecting on the activity in some detached way, distinctly separate from whatever it is you're doing? (Professor friends tell me that this happens to them rather frequently when they're lecturing; it happens to me.) This sort of "floating above it all to watch, comment, and assess" experience—one that is strategically employed, collectively shared, periodically assessed, and used in tandem with conventional classroom material—is what we need more of in the global environmental politics classroom.

The chapters in this volume (together with their editorial introductions and concluding "Questions for Reflection and Discussion") are about fostering this "looking down from above" experience. They are meant to complement traditional exploration of the bread-and-butter topics of the global environmental politics classroom. Some chapters, you will find, speak more directly to students. Others tilt toward the professor's ear. Each is from an accomplished teacher-scholar in the field. They together seek to draw teacher and student into conversation about the struggle for influence and power occasioned by the emergence of global environmental problems, and about how the classroom can become a site of preparation for understanding *and* engaging this struggle.

Such conversation is not without risk. It requires an openness between student and instructor uncommon to most upper-division courses in environmental studies and political science. Discussion about what we, teacher and student, together expect of education and university life and of what brings us to a study of global environmental politics becomes unavoidable, and this poses dangers to junior faculty working with impatient students who expect just the facts or find such broader stage-setting conversation to be uncomfortable or threatening. It also calls for a heightened tolerance of syllabus slippage: conversation cannot be channeled or predicted by a syllabus authored weeks if not months before the course begins, no matter how diligent the professor. If course organization (i.e., how tightly did the course conform to the schedule laid out in the syllabus?) is a significant factor in course evaluations, committing to classroom conversation about the teaching and learning of course material is begging for trouble. Such conversation presumes, moreover, real classroom interest in sustaining a spirit of collaboration, one that would inspire students to learn how teachers of the subject think and inspire teachers to consider deeply how students react to course material. All this makes for a demanding classroom, one sustained by real relationships and a commitment to explore our common aspirations and fears. It is a classroom to which we would return not because we have to, or should, but because of how it challenges and sustains us.

This book is organized with these risks and demands in mind. Part I (The Classroom: Four Walls, Many Possibilities) presents two chapters, one by Paul Wapner (chapter 2), the other by William Ayers (chapter 3). Wapner and Ayers are two sides of a coin: Wapner speaks to students, while Ayers raises important issues for teachers, but do not assume that Wapner's words are meant only for students and that Ayers speaks only to teachers. To explore and identify their common ground and shared agenda in the classroom, teachers *and* students of global environmental politics should read both chapters together, compare their reactions, and wrestle with the challenges raised by each.

Part II (Knowledge That Empowers: Relearning the Basics of Global Ecopolitics) is the most conventional chunk of the book. Its five chapters focus on accepted *conceptual* pillars of global environmental politics, but twists them to provoke classroom reflection and debate. Lamont Hempel (chapter 4) and Ken Conca (chapter 5) ask us to reconsider some of the central habits and concepts that frame coursework in the field. In doing so, they provide a bridge from the general conversation in Part I about the meaning of teaching and learning, to the thorny challenges of global environmental politics that occupy the remainder of this volume. Peter Taylor (chapter 6) unpacks the "tragedy of the commons" framework that infuses almost any inquiry into environmental degradation. Geoffrey Dabelko and Richard Matthew argue (in chapter 7) for renewed appreciation of security issues in our explorations of international environmental challenges. And I return in chapter 8 to connect classroom inquiry into global climate change with ideas of able citizenship and classroom simulations.

By contrast, Part III (Education Expanded: Paths Are Made by Walking) challenges accepted *procedural* routines that infiltrate the college classroom. B. Welling Hall begins (in chapter 9) with a discussion of theory plays, and Tom Princen and Karl Steyaert continue in the vein of innovative classroom practice with their discussion (chapter 10) of a water politics simulation. Matthew Auer considers (in chapter 11) how teachers and students of global environmental politics can best tap the Internet, and his advice will prove useful to courses that model Howard Warshawsky's "consultancy group" approach (described in chapter 12) to learning and teaching in international politics. Nancy Quirk follows with a comprehensive, forward looking exploration (in chapter 13) of service-learning at the university.

Resist the temptation to categorize this final section as merely a collection of activities that students and their instructors might adopt in their own classes. Each chapter can serve this purpose, to be sure, but there's more—each is also making claims about what's wrong with contemporary global environmental politics education, about what kinds of remedies present themselves, and about how and why these remedies usefully oppose an education that would depress and disempower. These chapters deserve to be read, digested, and debated even if the exercises and simulations they describe are not adopted, for they advance prescriptions for how we should situate ourselves in the classroom if we expect to leave it more invigorated then when we entered.

You will discover well before this final batch of chapters that, as a supplemental textbook for courses in global environmental politics and environmental studies, this collection isn't for everyone. Instructors reluctant to trim course content to free up space for reflective conversation will experience this text as a distraction—and risk-averse students who understand their education as a commodity to be consumed rather than as a potentially life-changing experience will find the volume to be even more annoying. To their credit, the thirteen chapters here do not tidily lead the reader through a connect-the-dots landscape of ultimate, easily testable truths. It is an intentionally messy collection, one that raises as many questions as it answers, at times sending contradictory messages with equal intensity—all in the service of firing passion, fueling debate, and equipping the students of today for the demands of citizenship that even now press upon them.

Why isn't this debate and passion already commonplace in the global environmental politics classroom? Earlier, I suggested that an understandable reluctance among students and teachers to confess to their disappointment or disaffection was to blame. Surely another reason is logistical: many lecture-centric courses don't naturally accommodate conversation. Another is habit and custom: many instructors are not accustomed to facilitating such discussion (in part because students, after years of socialization in nonconversational, sometimes regimented classrooms do not expect or appreciate it).

Another important reason, though, flows not from habit or convention, but rather from assumptions about education and expertise that infuse contemporary notions of sustainability and, by extension, courses in global environmental problems and politics that adopt sustainability as an organizing theme. Before moving on, it would be useful to explore the constraints these often unrecognized assumptions impose on our classroom practice.

EDUCATING FOR SUSTAINABILITY?

Much time has passed since the release of the 1987 Brundtland Commission's *Our Common Future* (World Commission on Environment and Development 1987), but the report's popularization of sustainability and sustainable development continues to frame our understanding of environmental problems and the politics they spawn. Like the environmental analyses that precede it, the report argued that the world was headed in the wrong direction. Unlike its predecessors, however, *OCF* called for a new kind of international cooperation and technology transfer that would foster robust economic growth, reduce global inequity, and restore damaged environmental systems. For the Brundtland Commission, economic growth was good, even necessary, *if* it was the right kind of growth. But getting the right kind of growth would be no easy matter. Required were far reaching policies whose adoption implicitly demanded a new kind of citizen, one able to grasp the fundamentals of environmental risk and global economics, who could be counted on to support government policies that might challenge commonly accepted ideas about progress, prosperity, and the good life. (One example might be a rising tax on gasoline—our new citizen would take a hit in the pocketbook but would cheerfully accept the tax for its dampening effect on oil consumption and its spur to energy conservation and renewable energy technologies.) Achieving this oxymoronic sustainable growth was, for the Commission, as much an educational enterprise as a technical one, as much about the formation of a knowledgeable citizenry as the marshalling of elite support and scientific expertise.

But what kind of education? Ideas about sustainability espoused by the Commission, and other major actors of global environmental policymaking, embrace a top-down, technocratic approach to environmental problem-solving (William Clark called it "planetary management" in his influential 1989 essay). It is not surprising, then, that education for sustainability, as conventionally understood, focuses on two goals: (1) convincing people that we face real environmental crises, and (2) getting them to go along with initially painful but ultimately desirable policy measures devised and implemented by highly trained experts. If people are taught about the severity of ecosystem damage and the concomitant risks to human well-being, the thinking goes, they will be more likely to tighten their belts and change their lifestyles in support of national and international policies devised to arrest the damage. Applied to the nuts and bolts of the classroom, this dominant perspective says the following to college and university instructors looking to make a difference: Teach in a way that rigorously conveys to students accurate information about the "environmental problematique" and instill in them a touch of informed technocratic professionalism.[4] Some students—the best and the brightest—could then go forth with their understanding of things global and environmental to devise, within the confines of corporate or government bureaucracy, effective policies for security, prosperity, and sustainability. The rest, armed by their education, would be ready to fulfill the duties of informed citizenship, which in practice has meant (see, for example, Sennett 1977 or, more recently, Sandel 1996) supporting—

through the enlightened use of the ballot box—policies and programs framed to maintain economic growth.

This approach dominates today's teaching and learning about global environmental politics, perhaps to our collective detriment. A top-down, expert-oriented, planetary management style of problem-solving that imagines education as a vehicle for producing a compliant citizenry might make sense if global environmental problems were straightforward, unambiguous, and simple, and therefore lent themselves to clear and credible policy prescriptions. But they are not. Complexity, ambiguity, and uncertainty are the calling cards of these global problems. Persistent uncertainties about the workings of complex environmental systems cloud the ability of the scientific community to speak in a single political voice; the transboundary, intergenerational components of global environmental ills defy neutral technocratic management; and the very nature of the sustainability debate calls into question the desirability of exponential economic growth managed by professional economists. Old guideposts and old ways of teaching and learning about them may not apply.

Muddling towards sustainability, in other words, is messy work—it means, at times, coloring outside the lines, in imaginative, unanticipated ways, which is what Professor Kai Lee of Williams College surely had in mind when he observed that "sustainable development cannot be reduced to a recipe because we have neither a list of ingredients nor a kitchen" (1993: 199). This suggests that education for sustainability, rather than training experts and rewarding passive acceptance of facts, should be about reproducing this messiness in the classroom (at least some of the time) in order to acclimate students conditioned by years of sitting in neat rows and raising their hands before speaking to the topsy-turvy work awaiting them. (You now see why, a few paragraphs back, I suggested that this volume's strength lies in its reluctance to connect the dots and point to simple truths.) Under this alternative view, higher education should be training students to patiently cope with ambiguity, to systematically evaluate conflicting expert claims about the state of the environment, to dissect the ways in which competing interests mask risk and highlight uncertainty to their advantage, to cultivate a passion for civic engagement, and to roll up their sleeves and set to work on local and regional causes of environmental decline that sum to global environmental degradation.

Yet most courses at the academy, in particular courses in global environmental problems and politics, do not happily embrace messiness. There is usually too much material to move through to tolerate, much less invite, the inefficiencies that come with spontaneous conversation and serendipitous learning. ("Was the organization and conduct of the course sufficiently messy to challenge you?" would be a wonderful question on end-of-term class evaluations, but don't hold your breath.) The classroom lecture still reigns, even though it models for students a passive deference to expertise and fosters a reluctance to rock the boat or break free of contemporary norms that occupy the core of our environmental problems.

At one level, perhaps this is to be forgiven, considering how far the academy has come in such a short period of time. After all, as recently as the late 1980s, despite growing attention to large-scale environmental threats (tropical deforestation, for example, or the degradation of stratospheric ozone), few college courses grappled with the global ecopolitics of sustainability. Most students emerged from four or six or even ten years of higher education with little exposure to ideas of sustainability and effective environmental policymaking, even if they actively sought it. More often then not, a bachelor's degree signaled an active ignorance of the environmental choices being debated and made at the national and international level. North Carolina State's Marvin Soroos spoke for many when he argued, in 1991, that professors of political science and international studies had best begin teaching about sustainability if they harbored any hope of "prepar[ing] students for the historically unprecedented challenges that their generation will face." Soroos passionately argued his case. It was not clear at the time if anyone was listening.

What a difference a decade makes. As I write these words (in mid-2002), the college curriculum has never been greener. In those two disciplines where the global politics of environmental futures are most systematically explored—political science and international studies—more classes exploring the struggle for sustainability are offered than ever before. The number of U.S. undergraduate programs in environmental science and studies has doubled in the final years of the 1990s (Maniates and Whissel 2000), and more texts on global environmental politics were published these last ten years than in the preceding fifty. By almost any measure, higher education rose to Soroos's challenge.

That's the good news. The downside is that while college administrators and university professors were greening the curriculum (albeit a curriculum dominated by the tidy classroom lecture), young people were bringing to the academy a growing skepticism about the possibilities for lasting social change. As Ted Halstead—a political analyst and "Gen X" member himself—observes (1999), it is not so much that the undergraduates populating college campuses are disinterested in the larger world or less hopeful than their predecessors for a better future. It is just that they are more consumed by the practical, more concerned about fitting in and finding a job, more conscious of the divide between idealism and making a living. For many, college has become less a wellspring of knowledge, power, or wisdom than a source of vocational insurance. Go to class, get decent grades, don't take chances and maybe, just maybe, there will be a job waiting at the end of the conveyor belt; this, arguably, is how higher education is increasingly perceived by those who consume it. Reports that reveal record levels of felt powerlessness among first-year American college students[5] no longer surprise.

The result is a slow-motion collision between the recent greening of the curriculum, with its naïve hope that more knowledge about global ills will make students feel powerful, and a deepening "browning" of college students' sense of the politically possible. Already wary of the future before they come to college, students drawn into a green curriculum are inclined to see the glass as half empty, not half full. Their studies easily allow them to confirm that which they already suspect: global prospects for peace and prosperity are diminishing; few leaders appear to command the power or wisdom to do much about it; existing bureaucratic and technocratic institutions, organized as they are around ideas of the state and the primacy of economic growth, are hopelessly archaic; individuals are powerless in the face of these forces; and life will probably get worse before it gets better. The outcome is what this chapter has called the dynamic of retreat: we teach, we learn, we withdraw, we become (even more) detached, and we focus on doing good by engaging in largely apolitical, and thus ultimately ineffective, acts of buying recycled paper or planting a tree in our backyard. As Professor David Orr of Oberlin College notes (1994), we are history's most highly educated people and yet remain passively remote from political efforts to wrestle environmental problems to the ground.

The answer is not to stop teaching and learning about the environmental challenges before us. Rather, it is time to explore different twists on the environment-oriented curriculum—different shades of green, if you will. My bias, and that of the contributors to this volume, is clear. We are suspicious of lecture-centric courses that are wonderfully efficient at communicating the harsh facts about planetary health but unavoidably reproduce a top-down, planetary-manager process of experts who know the answers and communicate them to passive, increasingly overwhelmed citizens. We believe that the recent greening of the curriculum, while laudatory, cannot be fully effective until it comes to grips with two things: the understandable detachment of undergraduates and the inherent messiness and ambiguity of sustainability. We'd hope that courses like those in global environmental politics would thus experiment with less regimented styles of classroom practice that open up opportunities for experimentation and reflection and acclimation to ambiguity, without abandoning the substantive core of the field. Indeed, in the place of lecture after lecture after lecture, we imagine a more conversational and collaborative classroom, one where teacher and student periodically step back to assess together the personal and political impact of their shared classroom work. This volume will have succeeded if, in your classes on global environmental ills and sustainable development, it stimulates useful conversation about how we might together make our way from a perilous present to a future of which we can be proud.

QUESTIONS FOR REFLECTION
AND DISCUSSION

1. What do you make of this "dynamic of retreat"? Have you observed or been a part of it? And do you find my explanation of its root causes to be credible and complete?

2. Have you ever been part of a classroom experience where, in the midst of the term, a frank discussion between teacher and students occurred about what was working well in class and what wasn't? What that a productive moment? What forces, other than those described in this chapter, might work against such frank talk?

3. This chapter is implicitly critical of how teachers and students imagine their part in the pursuit of knowledge. Teachers are taken to task for too easily embracing the predictability and efficiency of the classroom lecture. And students, I suggest, are so conditioned to raise their hand and sit quietly and remain passive that they probably find the familiar tedium of classroom lectures strangely comforting. What portions and how much of this critique of students and teachers do you find to be fair, and what aspects of it, in your view, are overdrawn? Support your response with your own experiences and observations of classroom practice, and your own assessment of what the undergraduate classroom should ultimately be trying to achieve.

4. Fostering sustainability will require imagination, an attitude of risk taking, a willingness to make mistakes, and a certain degree of spontaneity and chutzpa. Can undergraduate courses in global environmental problems and politics really foster these attributes? And if they can, should they, even if this means that less material may be covered in class?

5. A wide variety of assessments of college students point to a growing political disaffection on campus. As Ted Halstead points out in his "The Politics of Generation X" essay, undergraduates increasingly skeptical of formal political institutions are putting their conscience to work by engaging in practical, hands-on service projects, like planting trees or volunteering in soup kitchens or helping out with recycling drives. The problem with this, says Halstead, is that these individual actions don't have much effect on larger political priorit-

ies and processes, and the people who practice them are doomed to political irrelevance. Perhaps you'll have time to read his essay. But even if you don't, you can reflect on the collision between green and brown argument that closes out this chapter. It maintains that teaching politically disaffected college students about environmental problems and politics will, absent concerted effort to the contrary, drive students towards small acts of kindness that address the unjust outcomes of existing patterns of power, influence, and behavior rather than taking up the far more messy and unpredictable work of altering the patterns themselves. What do you make of this argument? Does it speak to your experience within higher education?

NOTES

1. Learn more about The Project on Teaching Global Environmental Politics, of which the e-mail list is a part, by going to webpub.alleg.edu/employee/m/mmaniate/GepEd/geped.html and following the links to the list. If you have trouble making a connection, e-mail me at mmaniate@allegheny.edu for assistance.

2. At work here is a fundamental suspicion of collective action and a shift toward safer, less ambiguous, quick payback community service and service learning initiatives. On students' suspicion of politics as conventionally practiced, see Halstead (1999), Loeb (1994), Sanchez (1998), and Sax, Astin, Korn, and Mahoney (1999). On the attractiveness of service learning and community service to students yearning to make a difference, see (in addition to Halstead) Eyler and Giles (1999). Levine and Cureton (1998) provide a mild corrective to the claim that undergraduates are predisposed against collective activism for institutional change. For a stronger counterargument, one that suggests a repoliticization of undergraduates in industrial North America, see Featherstone (2000). And for links between economic globalization and the decline of civic virtue and political engagement, see Barber (1998).

3. For more on how environmental studies education tends to individualize responsibility for the environmental crisis, see Maniates (2002a) and references therein.

4. For a provocative overview of how schooling has done just this, see Postman (1996). For more detail, see Bellah et al. (1991) (especially chapter 5), Mary Clark (1989), and Maniates (1993).

5. See, for example, the annual *The American Freshman* report produced by UCLA's Higher Education Research Institute. Executive summaries of recent reports are available at the Institute's Web site at www.gseis.ucla.edu/heri/heri.html.

I

THE CLASSROOM
Four Walls, Many Possibilities

2

✪

Ecological Thinking

Studying Global Environmental Politics
with a Wild Mind and a Mindful Heart

Paul Wapner

If politics, as it is sometimes said, is the art of the possible, then global environmental politics (GEP) is nothing less than the struggle for an environmentally sustainable future in the face of rapid growth in human population, economic activity, technological power, and global inequity. College courses that explore the field do not easily lend themselves to tried and true student strategies of rote memorization, practiced regurgitation, and passive inquiry ("will this be on the exam?"): the issues on the table are too sweeping, the stakes are too high, and the rewards of careful thinking and critical debate are too great. A "wild mind" is more consistent with the demands of the subject; that, and an ability to stretch oneself in unexpected, sometimes uncomfortable ways. To understand first the destructive global collision between natural and social systems that is occurring all around us, and then to analyze systematically the resulting political struggles, and then to discern the paths we might best walk in the face of burgeoning threats to the integrity of vital ecological processes—all this is a tall order indeed. And yet most college level courses in global environmental politics ask nothing less of their students and instructors.

"We are not," as Dorothy once observed to Toto, "in Kansas anymore." Doing well in the GEP classroom, as either a student or an instructor, calls for a different way of learning and knowing. This is precisely the message that Paul Wapner, a professor at American University and an accomplished analyst of global civil society, delivers in this chapter. At one level, Wapner's urgings read

as a primer for the student of global environmental politics who is looking to do more than go through the motions. At another level, though, they challenge both students and their instructors to reflect—together, perhaps aloud—about how our stance toward the GEP classroom might foster a certain wildness that would do justice to the art of the possible.—M.M.

L iving in a way that protects the environment is a perennial challenge. We know, for example, that the first farmers of ancient Mesopotamia used methods of agriculture that ruined the land, and that similar acts of environmental degradation took place throughout ancient Greece and Rome. More recently we've learned that native Americans—long hailed as ecological stewards—used forms of agriculture that dramatically altered the soil and species of the American West. Ecologically benign living seems to be an anomaly. Looking back over human history, one sees a steady pattern of human abuse of the earth as people try to live out their lives.

While ecological well-being is a longstanding challenge, something new has taken place over the last few decades to raise the stakes. Human population has skyrocketed: while putting the first billion people on earth took from the beginning of time to about 1830, the latest billion was added in only the last twelve years. This is an astounding phenomenon, and it has great repercussions for the environment. More people means greater impact on the earth's natural systems. At present, it means that the earth must support the needs and wants of over six billion people. Additionally, humans have perfected technologies that allow us to use the earth's resources and produce wastes at accelerating rates. This means that we can cut down trees, catch fish, and use petroleum faster than the earth can replenish such resources, and that we can generate pollution faster than the earth can absorb it. Taken together, increased numbers of people and greater technological capability are pressing the earth's ecological services and, in the extreme, are compromising the very biophysical infrastructure that supports life on earth.

The immense impact of human action on the earth has moved environmental issues from the strict domain of natural science to the realm of public, political concern. Politics is fundamentally about organizing collective life. It is about the virtues that are possible and the problems that arise when human beings live together. Environmental degradation has reached a point that the quality—if not the very long-term possibility—of human life is at stake. Environmental protection, then, has become a first-order political enterprise. Safeguarding the ecological integrity of the earth calls for *reorganizing* ourselves to respect the planet's biophysical imperatives and finding realistic and humane ways of doing so.

The study of *global* environmental politics attempts to understand contemporary environmental challenges at the most comprehensive level. It reflects upon the dynamics that animate current environmental abuse, the mechanisms available to redirect widespread behavior, and the scenarios for a more environmentally sustainable future. It concentrates on the global level of collective life—for environmental affairs are fundamentally nonnational in character and ultimately affect the earth's biophysical well-being—and looks to international as well as intranational action as sources of response.

This chapter provides some guideposts for studying global environmental politics. It assumes that students are intrigued by contemporary environmental challenges and works to highlight ways of thinking, reading, and writing about global environmental politics. One of the major obstacles to environmental protection is that very few people are educated in the dynamics of global politics and the processes of the earth's ecosystem. This is not because people have not tried to master both disciplines but rather because doing so involves understanding moving targets. Economic, social, cultural, and political changes are taking place at increasingly rapid speeds, and each of these (not to mention their interactions) has profound effects on the environment. Moreover, our knowledge of ecosystems is accelerating as new methods of investigation and scientific collaboration emerge. The study of global politics must make sense of these changes and provide frameworks for evaluating and analyzing them. Furthermore, it must offer some vision of how to advance global environmental protection. There are no hard and fast rules for doing so—the discipline is young and tools are still being forged—but we can identify a number of ways to educate ourselves toward such an endeavor.

WILD MIND AND THEORETICAL
UNDERSTANDING

One of the virtues of a new discipline is that the path of inquiry is relatively untrodden. This is true of global environmental politics. While there are tentative schools of thought in the discipline and increasing amounts of relevant information, the enterprise itself is new enough that the basic categories of analysis are still being fashioned. There is a tremendous need to chart out the intellectual terrain. Global environmental politics is consequently *an interactive discipline*—we partially create it as we find insightful ways to understand global environmental issues. The best way to engage the subject, therefore, is to cultivate what could be called a "wild mind." Wild mind denotes an intellectual attitude that is willing to address issues outside of established categories. It suggests a way of seeing the world that is marked by excitement and passion and by a form of inquiry that is courageous enough to proceed without reliable conceptual maps. Most of all, wild mind means a commitment to freeing our own intellect and exploring where our thoughts take us rather than worrying about replicating the ideas of others.

Ironically, one of the things college students often neglect to do in school is to think. We can become so busy reading books and articles and listening to our professors and puzzling out what the instructor wants us to know and say that we tend to forget that education includes developing one's critical faculties and insights. Mark Twain's declaration that he never let his schooling get in the way of his education stands as a reminder of what we should embrace and what we should avoid as we move through our college years.

Professors often assume that simply exposing students to other people's thoughts will generate an ability for students to think on their own. While there is much truth to this—riding the wave of another's thought is one of the most exhilarating and inspiring intellectual experiences—a flat out acceptance of this view can constrain student thinking by suggesting that our own thoughts are unworthy of serious reflection. As students, we are trained to think of our minds as capable of reflecting only upon our personal lives; other types of thoughts such as our own political or social or scientific ideas are seen merely as speculations. In the study of global environmental politics, perhaps more than other disciplines, this attitude is a liability and the educational forces that foster it an impediment. Our own thoughts are crucial to figuring out our present condition and to imagining better futures. No one has a monopoly over ecological wisdom, and no one has absolute political insight. Humanity has struggled over what "ecological right livelihood" might mean for so long that the historical record itself underlines the poverty of much conventional knowledge and opinion. Global environmental politics is a discipline that is constantly calling out for critical reflection and conceptual creativity. Wild mind, even though it clashes with the conventional norms of higher education, is essential to these activities.

While necessary, wild mind is not sufficient for unraveling the complexities of global environmental politics. Wild mind provides the attitude but does not offer the means of generating creative, critical insight, for it leaves out the social dimension of creative activity. Great ideas—while conceptualized and expressed by courageous and free-spirited thinkers—do not emerge out of the blue but arise in a cultural context in which thinkers are ruminating over similar puzzles. The Michelangelos and Einsteins of our world always operate within traditions of thought. Their creativity expresses itself insofar as they master the thinking of others working in their respective fields and arrive at novel ways of seeing the world that both build upon and transcend earlier insight. We have all met people who come up with ideas that they themselves think are significant; we have all known people who claim to have come up with a major breakthrough in some area of contemporary life. The problem with these people, from the perspective of creativity, is that they often fail to appreciate how their ideas fit into or relate to existing perspectives. Genuine creativity is not simply a personal musing but an idea that is valuable enough to others to become part of our collective understanding. As students of global environmental politics, we do not want to reinvent the wheel (or the United Nations). Rather, we want to understand contemporary situations and make enough sense of existing knowledge to push thought one step farther. The ability to push comes from our wild mind; our understanding of which direction to push comes from our immersion in the discipline.

How does one effect such an immersion? How does one become proficient in the study of global environmental politics? The most reasonable answer is to read as much as possible about global environmental politics and to talk to as many people as possible about it. But this skirts the question. How does one do *that*? How does one make sense of the growing literature on environmental issues and integrate understanding from diverse sources? The best way to do this, as I see it, is to cultivate a theoretical orientation to our work. To think theoretically involves abstraction. It requires looking at particular instances of things and conceptualizing the general character they all share. Plato talked about this in terms of the "forms." He believed that everything in the material world had an immaterial "formal" existence that captured the essence of a thing. Thus, while there are individual dogs called Rover, Fido, and Spot, Plato would say that there is also something called "dogness" itself that each of these animals share and that to know dogness provides a genuine understanding of the essence of each individual dog. The same type of abstraction is involved with studying global environmental politics. It is, in fact, essential.

When we read any text that describes the host of environmental ills, often we soon become numb from the overload of information. Frequently we read things like: six of the first eight months of 1998 were marked by all-time high global temperature records, or that the percentage of overexploited marine fish species jumped from zero in 1950 to 70 percent today, or that the population of Pakistan is projected to increase from 148 million to 357 million people, surpassing the United States by 2050 (Brown et al. 1999). While knowing these things is essential, we need to think for a moment and ask ourselves what they mean and how we can make them intellectually useful. If we memorized every fact we read about environmental conditions we'd be geniuses. Assuming that most of us are not of that caliber, we need some way to organize our thinking, some format to distill the meaning of things, some tool to help clue us into the most meaningful facts. Theoretical abstraction provides such a mechanism. It calls on us not to remember exactly how many months global temperatures were above historical records but to understand that global warming is a genuine possibility and that evidence suggests we are already witnessing the phenomenon. Likewise, it allows us to forget the exact percentage of overexploited fisheries and simply understand that humans are catching fish faster than the oceans can replenish them. The idea is to see trends and to understand particular instances and examples that make up the trend. This does not mean we take specific facts at face value—we must always strive to evaluate their accuracy. It implies, rather, that we work to develop a capacity to see the big picture of what is being communicated.

Many may see such an approach as cheating, as somehow ignoring or slighting the "real" facts. This might be true if an education in global environmental politics were merely about memorizing empirical phenomena. The discipline is more than this, however. Yes, it is important to remember key facts on particular issues that one is trying to master or that seem to express the fundamental character of a given problem. In fact, this is crucial. But a more fundamental task of our work is to see the broad patterns, to understand the general character of global environmental affairs. Once we do this, we can then consider various bits of empirical data and ask how they speak to the exact issues we are trying to unravel.

This has implications for the way we read texts. When reading a book or article we should resist becoming overwhelmed by the wealth of empirical information. We shouldn't take it as our task to memorize all the facts and figures. Rather, we should read the facts as instances of broader issues and solidify those issues clearly in our minds. Moreover, we should see specific facts as evidence for or illustrations of broader points that individual authors are trying to make, and we must then form a clear conception of the author's point. Most articles or books seek to express a point of view, an orientation, an argument. As students, we need to catch on to these; we need to understand the substantive content of what is being expressed. Without this, there is no framework with which to make sense of the host of facts and figures presented. Having said this, it is also important to point out that we must still take empirical data seriously—we must evaluate stated facts and know how to retrieve their details when it comes time to do research or develop an argument. But this is done as part of developing a theoretical perspective.

The focus on theoretical abstraction is also relevant to listening to (and composing) lectures. Empirical facts are brought to bear to provide evidence for particular points of view. Without marshaling facts, ideas are unjustified in that they find no real-world confirmation. Lecturers, like authors, must present evidence and thus often pepper their talks with empirical information. This information is important and worthy of remembering. But it is more worthwhile to focus on the overall points being made rather than to memorize specific facts. Put differently, we must try to grasp the essence of the facts and to appreciate how they relate to the lecturer's overall argument and to other relevant phenomena with which we are familiar. This enables us to evaluate critically what we are listening to.

Notwithstanding this emphasis, theoretical abstraction cannot stand on its own. Wild mind must come back to integrate the abstraction into our own understanding and to provide meaning. The meaning of *meaning* is to be part of something that is itself a part of something greater. A star assumes meaning, for example, within a constellation, within its relationship to the other stars. Likewise, we make sense of facts and arguments as they relate to other ideas we might have. The key is that it is *our* mindframes and stocks of information and commonsense that provide the meaning. We are the ones to make the connections, to place information into a context and appreciate the pattern of conceptual relationships. This requires, to a certain extent, taking information personally. When faced with new information, we need to ask ourselves: What does this mean to me? How does it matter, given what I already know about the world? Where does it fit into my existing understanding of global environmental politics? And, if it doesn't fit in easily, we must ask if the new information requires a fundamental rethinking of our conventional categories of meaning (a situation addressed in the following section). In short, we must always be working to make sense of what we come in contact with. And the best way to do this with regard to global environmental politics is to combine wild mind and theoretical abstraction.

NORMATIVE THOUGHT

Politics is different from biology or physics. When natural scientists study a wave in the ocean, for example, they ask certain questions about it. What is its velocity? How much water is involved? Does its motion correlate with the moon? These are empirical questions. While students of politics ask empirical questions, they usually ask normative ones as well. They want to know not only what happened or what is going on but also what *should* have happened and what *should* take place in the future. Put differently, students of politics are concerned not only with the way the world *is* but also with the way it *should* be. This makes political analysis quite tricky.

Foremost, it requires us to know that there are no correct answers to political questions—normative queries cannot be answered definitively one way or the other. Rather, as political scientists, we are forced into making judgments about politics. Think for a moment about climate change. Let us assume that most scientists agree that carbon dioxide and other greenhouse gases are being released into the atmosphere at increasing rates and that this may cause global temperatures to rise. And, let's assume further that many believe this will result in rising sea levels, shifting climatic zones, and erratic, dangerous weather patterns. This still doesn't solve the problem of what should be done. Should we work to prevent or prepare for further climate change? Should all countries contribute equally to protection efforts, or should responsibility be distributed in a different manner? Are market mechanisms the best way to address change or is government action? These are the kinds of questions that are presently being debated, and they have no obvious answers. Nevertheless, we are required to make judgments about them. We need to evaluate the pros and cons of certain courses of actions and arrive at a decision. Again, this decision will not be Right (with a big *R*) but will be right in terms of reflecting our values and concerns.

As students of global environmental politics, we must realize that the political world is made up of judgments and thus our analysis is always a matter of interpreting and evaluating not truths per se but decisions that have been made. Furthermore, we must recognize that we too must make judgments about environmental affairs. We too must deliberate not simply about what has already taken place but about what should take place in the future. And, as would be expected, this involves bringing our own political orientations to the task.

Whether we acknowledge them or not, we all possess certain values and care about some things more than others. This is what it means to be human, and as Aristotle reminds us, humans are uniquely political beings. As students and teachers of global environmental politics, we cannot get away with hiding or being ashamed of our politics. We must instead draw upon them to formulate our judgments. Thus, we must bring our politics into the classroom and into the dialogue we have with the books and articles we read. To be sure, we should not be ideologues and, with closed ears, insist that our perspective is always superior—an act that would drown out alternative perspectives and thus deny us a genuine educational and political experience. Rather, the GEP classroom calls us to use our politics like software: employ them to make sense of conflicting points of view and to formulate political prescriptions but be willing to alter them as our minds change in the face of new information, persuasive arguments, and newfound understandings.

Some of us may be frightened to bring our politics into the classroom or other discussions involving global environmental politics. We may feel that our views are so out-of-step with those of our professors or fellow students that to express them would invite ridicule, condemnation, and perhaps biased evaluation. My sense is that such fear is misplaced. Academic inquiry is about open discussion with the expectation that people will disagree—many times vehemently—about certain things. This makes discussion worthwhile. In fact, the healthiest contribution to academic inquiry is to invite disagreement because only by debating diverse perspectives can people arrive at sound judgments. When we openly and constructively disagree with our professors or fellow students, we are actually playing an important part in the study of global environmental politics. When we bring our politics to the classroom or similar arenas, our intent is not to do battle. Political discussions, to repeat, are not about ideologues warring over words. Rather, our aim is to enlighten each other, and this calls for an ability to listen as well as talk.

Our politics need to be amenable to change. The way to ensure that this is possible and that we can develop more insightful political positions is to be—to use an old-fashioned word—honest. That is, we need to give a good argument its due and not simply dismiss it because it contradicts or questions our own view. For although we all hold political positions, this does not mean that all positions are equally valid. Some positions are better justified than others and our task is to develop sound political orientations. This happens when our positions are tested by being exposed to contrasting points of view and as various perspectives are able to meld in conversation to produce new understandings. This is the nature of political discussion and academic inquiry. We aim not to arrive at truth but to make sound judgments. The best way to do this is to engage in a dialogue with ourselves and others and constantly readjust ourselves and persuade others to readjust themselves as a result. (As an aside, by remaining open to others and considering alternative points of view, one immediately wins credibility for one's own views.)

A final consideration has to do with developing the ability to make political judgments. How do we engender the capacity to discriminate? How do we cultivate the skill of valuing one set of affairs over another? The political theorist Michael Oakshott (1962) believes that the skill of political deliberation is handed down from generation to generation and that some people are simply better equipped with the ability than others. He feels that political ability is like an inherited trait belonging to certain well-situated people. My own view is that all of us have a political dimension to ourselves that can be exercised and developed. That is, the skill of political judgment is something to be cultivated and nurtured rather than inherited. But how does one do so? How does one develop discrimination? Although it may sound circular, the best way is to *practice* decision making and debate—i.e., make lots and lots of decisions and present them for scrutiny and critical appraisal by others.

Have you ever met someone who is always willing to go along with other people's opinions? These are the people who, when asked what movie they would like to see, respond by saying, "Whatever you want to see." These are the people who always "go with the flow" and feel that social graces demand that they always agree with others. The best way to develop political judgment is not to be one of those people. We need to be people who take positions, make decisions, come up with opinions. This, of course, doesn't mean that we must get our way all the time or always impose our views on others; rather, it means that we at least know what we feel or have a sense of the best course of action as we see it. The more we make decisions for which we are accountable, the better we become at making them. We practice weighing alternatives and, more importantly, choosing among them. The normative side of global environmental politics demands that we make judgments. Practicing the art of decision making in all facets of our lives will enable us to hone this skill.

TRANSNATIONALISM

Wild mind, theoretical abstraction, and normative judgments can and should be used to engage all things political. Their usefulness is not limited to global environmental politics, though these practices do take on particular applications when it comes to GEP. The discipline of GEP directs us to look at all levels of political life and understand how actions on and across these levels both contribute to environmental degradation and can be enlisted in the service of environmental protection. Our bold, analytic, and discriminating minds must operate in this setting.

One of the first things we notice about environmental issues is that they ignore political boundaries. Air, water, shifting soils, and migrating animals fail to recognize where one country ends and another begins: birds do not put on the brakes (or produce passports) as they arrive at a border; air does not situate itself only above certain territories. As students of global politics, then, we must expand our focus. We are so used to thinking in terms of our own country that we often assume that political problems are wholly defined and best addressed within the province of our own territory. This habit makes sense in that most of our everyday lives revolve around domestic events. This is especially the case in the United

States, where mass entertainment and news tend to be domestically focused. The transboundary character of the earth's natural systems scrambles this orientation.

Global environmental politics, to speak plainly, requires that we think across state boundaries. It demands that we recognize the fluidity of environmental issues and force our minds to expand to correlate with natural patterns rather than forcing natural systems to fit into political preconceptions. A large part of this involves thinking globally, that is, imagining the earth as a whole as our unit of analysis rather than a given state or even group of states. Such an injunction is, of course, no surprise: we have grown up on bumper stickers telling us to think and worry globally. But neither is it simple, even if we are increasingly surrounded by slogans encouraging it. It involves an extreme amount of abstraction. It requires us to rise above anything we can immediately experience and propel our minds to visualize the broadest of patterns—the planet itself.

You can get a sense of how tricky this is by staring at a globe. Ever since the Apollo space mission produced pictures of the earth as a blue-green ball hanging in space, the globe as a depiction of the earth has become all too familiar. We are accustomed to seeing globes everywhere (and have come to understand them as the mascot of the environmental movement). But does a globe give us an accurate picture of the planet? Does it enable us to gain a sense of the whole? Does it allow us to see the entire planet as an integrated unit? On the one hand, globes do provide an image that encourages global thinking. They enable us to see the whole, and this goes a long way toward lifting ourselves out of our narrow domestic focus. On the other hand, however, most globes undercut a genuinely global perspective by emphasizing political boundaries while hiding ecological ones. They circumscribe countries with different colors and suggest that what really matters goes on within or across state boundaries. Indeed, most of us use globes to understand where countries are in relation to each other and to plot coordinates around the planet's spherical shape. We do not use them to appreciate the ecological dimensions of the earth.

The other thing about globes is that they present the earth as an inanimate object. The earth appears, as Aristotle said, as a mere rock in the universe. This flies in the face of what most people now understand as the living quality of the earth. The planet's carbon, water, and other cycles are fundamental to the earth's character and yet their swirling, changing dynamics are undepictable in the form of a constructed globe. Globes suggest that the earth is a dead piece of matter on which plants, animals, and microbes live and which humans can manage, rather than a functioning whole of which life is an integral part. Ironically, globes bleach out much necessary information for thinking globally.

Notwithstanding the difficulty of thinking globally, it demands our effort. One of the great follies of modern times is the fixation on our own territorial community while ignoring or underappreciating other areas of the earth. When, for example, London faced an air pollution problem in the early part of the twentieth century, part of its response was to build higher smokestacks so that pollution would drift away from the city ("the solution to pollution is dilution"). We find the same move being made today when communities export their wastes or draw resources from other areas without due compensation or concern (Wapner 1997). Behind such moves is the implicit sense that areas outside our own immediate territory are unworthy of environmental concern. Most of us identify with our home country and imagine environmental dynamics taking place solely within its borders—but the study of global environmental politics demands something more from us. It asks that we let go of this identification, at least for analytical purposes, and see the transboundary interconnections that animate ecological phenomena. When we do this and genuinely think globally, we begin to look at the host of sources of environmental harm and the complex political systems that must be reconciled, coordinated, and enlisted in the service of environmental protection. When we rise to the global level, we begin to appreciate the scale and magnitude of the challenge of global environmental well-being. We also begin to generate concern at a level of political life for which no single country is responsible and address the task of global environmental governance.

Although thinking globally is essential—and, arguably, uniquely mandatory for the study of global environmental politics—our job is not finished after we expand our minds to the highest level of abstraction. Regional and local dynamics are as much a part of consideration. Environmental problems do not just happen but originate within given territories. Every car driven, every field irrigated, and every riverbed fished can potentially contribute to large-scale, long-term ecological damage. The dynamics of such activities take place in specific locales. Global environmental politics must take these locales into account and must appreciate the complex interfacing between local areas and regional and global conditions. Here the issue is still a matter of abstraction but one a bit more easily amenable to the human mind. The move to abstraction is less severe but equally necessary.

Given the requirement to think both locally and globally, some suggest that we orient ourselves "glocally" (see Hempel's book [1996a], and his complementary chapter later in this volume). This means that we maintain the dual analytical focus up and down, as it were, when working to understand global environmental politics. To put it differently, the discipline of global environmental politics requires that we expand our minds to the furthest reaches of abstraction—to the entire earth itself—and then home them in back toward our local experience. It calls on us to delink our knowledge about environmental challenges from the political units that so strongly grab our attention and loyalty. Global environmental politics asks us to play an important mind game—one that sees everything but doesn't lose sight of what is in front of our eyes. This is the intellectual challenge at the heart of the discipline.

THE SELF

A glocal perspective directs us to multiple layers of collective life. It asks that we consider the small actions of our own neighborhoods as well as the cumulative effects of all neighborhoods in the earth's ecosystem. It has limitations, however, insofar as it focuses attention only on collective life. While environmental issues arise largely through our interactions with others—i.e., through our economic, social, and cultural practices and transactions—they also result from individual habits and activities that we undertake in the privacy of our own separate lives. As we live through our days, we make thousands of decisions that influence the environment. How we eat, travel, entertain, and employ ourselves affects environmental quality. In studying global environmental politics, we must be mindful of the ecological ramifications of our individual decisions. Doing so is less an option than a necessity, for it ultimately provides a sense of meaning to our studies.

When we think about all the decisions in our day-to-day lives, we must remember that they are not made in a vacuum. We are subject to structural constraints that set the parameters for our choices. For instance, when most of us go to buy an automobile, we must choose a car that runs on fossil fuel and gets between ten and thirty miles per gallon. This represents a structural impediment to environmental well-being. Such constraints make it impossible for us *not* to contribute to environmental degradation in the decision to buy a car. (We could, of course, choose not to buy a car and generally this would represent a more environmentally benign option, but many of us are caught in another structural impediment—the utter lack of reliable public transportation—that makes "car consumption" a necessity.) But, even while we are destined to degrade the environment by buying a car, we still have choices—as to which models are more energy efficient and pollute less and how often we intend to drive—that *do* affect the environment. That is, the decisions we make in the interstices of structural arrangements are environmentally meaningful and demand our attention. Structural factors, in other words, do not determine everything about human action; we all enjoy a degree of individual freedom and, when it comes to environmental issues, this freedom is an additional aspect of politics. To be sure, our individual decisions will not ensure global environmental well-being; they will, however, contribute to any widespread effort to minimize human impact on environmental quality.

Global environmental politics involves both structural constraints and individual decision making. It is about analyzing the way economic, political, and social structures set up the parameters of our choices and the incentives that animate individual choice within these parameters. Individual decision making is part of the discipline because, although it is private, it has public effect. Even the most intimate decisions—like how many children we choose to have or whether we eat meat—affect wider ecological circles (McKibben 1998). Part of our job as students of global environmental politics is to be aware of the role individual choice has in environmental quality. We need to be mindful that the dynamics of environmental degradation do not begin and end with institutions like the state and corporations but include the actions of individuals as they choose their way through their lives. Moreover, and just as significant, we need to recognize the power of structural constraints and place them on the agenda for meaningful political change.

That the self is part of global environmental politics is not only an additional point of focus; it also stands as an entryway into fully grasping the discipline. We can use our experience as a point of contact with the broader dynamics of global environmental issues. For instance, when we study the politics of climate change, it is instructive to examine our own energy use and ask ourselves what it would take for us to change our behavior. Would we best respond to greater governmental legislation, new informal codes of conduct, or market mechanisms that allow us to save money in the act of environmental protection? Additionally, when we study biodiversity protection, it is worth exploring our own relationship to the natural world and asking ourselves what it would take to change it in the service of environmental well-being. In short, to bring the material of global environmental politics home, we can invest ourselves in our studies, and this can serve as the litmus test for significance and relevance.

Examining the self raises a final question about the purpose of education. Many times we find ourselves excited by the material we encounter in classes and wishing to find ways to incorporate our new understandings into our lives. As a professor of environmental politics, I often have students approach me wanting to know how they can fold environmental concerns into their life plans by becoming environmental professionals. Responding to such requests is always tricky because it has to do with the most personal dimensions of a student's life in the sense that charting out a life plan is a matter of identifying and integrating one's most cherished values and one's most enjoyable endeavors. For me, it seems essential that we choose life paths that reflect a combination of what we care about and what we like to do. Too often we do things because we think we need to do them. For example, I know of many who work professionally for environmental causes because they feel it is a moral responsibility to do so but seem unfulfilled in their activities. While I am grateful to such people for their moral sensitivity and political commitment, I often wonder if both they themselves and the environmental movement would be better off if they found a more comfortable fit between what they do for a living and who they are.

The interesting thing about all political issues, but especially environmental ones, is that the forces at work are manifold, and thus there are various ways into an issue. There are many factors that create political issues and a panoply of appropriate responses. This is because the forces that govern us are not simply governmental but also economic, social, and cultural. Consequently, if one cares about a particular issue one need not simply become a lobbyist or policymaker—one could also fruitfully be a businessperson, teacher, writer, or entertainer. This is especially the case with environmental issues in that they arise not simply through governmental action nor can they be sufficiently addressed solely through acts of governments. Other dimensions of collective life—cultural, social and economic—are as responsible and represent important mechanisms for addressing environmental issues.

So, as we try to fashion professional trajectories for our lives, it is essential that we do not try to fit ourselves into those vocational boxes that are explicitly or most immediately environmental, if that feels uncomfortable. Rather, we might explore the whole mix of who we are and search for vocations that will allow us to express the multiple and most meaningful dimensions of our personalities. This will enable us to be more effective at, and to find greater satisfaction in, what we do for a living. Pursuing such a life path will not, hopefully, mean that we forget our political commitments but rather, if we fully invest ourselves as students of politics, it means finding ways to fold our political concerns into our vocations. For those turned on to environmental issues, it means finding creative ways to integrate environmental concerns into our work, whatever our occupation, and striving to express those concerns in politically effective ways.

I mention the issue of environmental commitment and life goals to highlight a final way to get the most out of the study of global environmental politics. The discipline exposes us to some pretty frightening material and calls on us to learn much about natural and social systems. In this way, undergraduates and their professors are both students of the discipline; though at different stages in our intellectual development, we are all working hard to make professional and personal sense of an unprecedented and unpredictable set of evolving ecological and political dynamics. If we struggle with this material with an eye toward how the issues can become a part of our lives, rather than as a set of substantive issues that we must master simply to do well in our courses, we can more deeply penetrate environmental politics. Thinking about how our own lives dovetail with environmental issues can, moreover, provide us with a sense of what is really at stake with regard to global environmental politics. Having a sense of what environmental challenges mean for us as individuals, community members, and human beings, as well as for the well-being of the world and the earth and its other species, can go a long way toward making us responsible students and citizens of the world.

QUESTIONS FOR REFLECTION AND DISCUSSION

1. Professor Wapner often uses the word *we* when talking about the challenges and rewards of studying global environmental politics. His wording implies that professors and students of GEP, because they're both "working hard to make professional and personal sense of an unprecedented and unpredictable set of evolving ecological and political dynamics," must collaborate in unusual ways if their study of GEP is to be rewarding and successful. What do you make of this argument? Why? What does it imply about how we might best approach, in practical and specific ways, a course on global environmental politics?

2. *Politics* is used in overlapping but often different ways in this chapter. What does Wapner mean when he uses the term, and which of these varied meanings are most important to understand and retain?

3. Henry David Thoreau once claimed that "in wildness is the preservation of the world." (Thoreau is often misquoted by people who inadvertently replace "wildness" with "wilderness.") In view of looming global environmental challenges, do you think Thoreau to be right, wrong, or both?

4. Has your education been about fostering a "wild mind"? And do current practices of schooling reward such a thing? To what extent is it possible, wise, and fair for those charged with facilitating your understanding of global environmental politics to ask you to develop a wild mind?

5. Wapner's understanding of the GEP classroom is distinctive and challenging: it imagines a wild mind, limited preoccupation with details, immersion into broader theoretical frameworks, open but

respectful disagreement and conflict, and ongoing practiced decision making. Given the constraints and prevailing practices of higher education, can students and their instructors be reasonably expected to practice what Wapner preaches? More to the point, should they? Do these elements persuasively promise to enhance our grasp of global environmental politics?

6. The end of the chapter suggests a provocatively encouraging cycle: If students invest themselves in a study of global environmental politics (what is meant, by the way, by this word *invest*?), they will be pushed to examine their own beliefs and practices. And if they examine their "self," their time in academe will take on new meaning and purpose. This in turn will prompt students, among other things, to become more actively engaged in their studies—to cultivate, in other words, something of a wild mind. On the basis of your experience with the classroom, do you find this cycle to be plausible? Is it worth cultivating in politics courses? Why? How?

7. Shouldn't so much of what Professor Wapner shares in this chapter be common knowledge and commonly practiced? Why isn't it?

3

❂

Teaching as an
Ethical Enterprise

William Ayers

Are teachers of global environmental politics engaged in morally charged work? To be true to their profession, must instructors fire in students a felt urgency to change the world? Are the best instructors those who conform to student expectations, or those who upset the applecart of classroom complacency? Must teaching, and learning too, be a labor of love? And what might this have to do with the study and practice of global environmental politics?

These are good questions all. Yet they are strangers to classroom conversation—they seem somehow inappropriately subjective or personal. This is unfortunate. Paradoxical as it may seem, time spent talking about the teaching process, though it may take away from focused discussion of the details of one global environmental ill or another, lays the foundation for scrutiny of a set of questions that sit at the core of GEP—questions about the ability of education to foster a sustainable society; about the easy roles we assume as teachers or students, roles that may undermine our ability to put our knowledge to good use; and about the essential ethical elements of our studies. If, as Paul Wapner claims in the previous chapter, a "wild mind" is essential to our inquiry into global environmental politics, how can we fail to step back, if for just a moment, and reflect upon the ambiguous and fluid role of teacher and, by extension, student too?

In the remarkable chapter that follows, William Ayers aims to teach teachers a thing or two about their craft, though he writes in a way that invites fruitful eavesdropping by students. His chapter, with its claims about "ethical practice" and "changing the world"—and its biting distinction between schooling and education—offers a safe harbor in which student and teacher might together reflect on the moral challenges that infuse the classroom.—M.M.

T here is a telling passage in Naguib Mahfouz's *Palace of Desire* (1991), the epic tale of a traditional family from the old quarter of Cairo, swept by the storms of custom in conflict with modernism, faith in a collision with knowledge, imperialist thrust exploding upon nationalist response. Kamal, the teenage son, is invited by his father to tell him which branch of the university he would like to attend. Without hesitation, Kamal responds enthusiastically that he wishes to enroll in the teachers' college. The father replies scornfully that teaching is "a miserable profession which wins respect from no one. . . . It's an occupation uniting people who have modern education with the products of traditional religious education. It's one utterly devoid of grandeur or esteem. I'm acquainted with men of distinction and with civil servants who have flatly refused to allow their daughters to marry a teacher" (Mahfouz 1991: 48–49).

Yet Kamal perseveres. He has faith in the intrinsic value of learning, in the life of the mind, and in the pursuit of truth. He tentatively suggests that in advanced nations—in Europe, for example—teaching is esteemed. The father notes, "You live in this country. Does it set up statues in honor of teachers? Show me a single sculpture of a teacher" (Mahfouz 1991: 53).

THE NATURE OF TEACHING

What is teaching, after all? Anyone who has practiced it can attest that it is more than the life of the mind, more than the calm, contemplative pursuit of truth. Kamal's vision is surely naive. Is teaching a calling to shake the world? Well, hardly. We know that teaching is excruciatingly complex, idiosyncratic, backbreaking, mind boggling, exhausting, and wrenching. Yet Kamal is onto something in both intuitions. His idealism points—against the hard and cynical realism of his father and much of the world—to the possibility of teaching as something more. While he is nursing a dream, his illusion cloaks an unimpeachable fact: teaching at its best requires heart and mind, passion and intellect, intuition, spirit, and judgment. Great teaching is an act of love.

This essential, central truth of teaching is often overlooked, many times by teachers themselves and almost always by the larger public. I sometimes find myself at parties with lawyers, for example, engaging in casual chitchat:

LAWYER: What do you do?
ME: I teach kindergarten. It's the most intellectually demanding thing I've ever done.

This always causes a head-snap as the lawyer tries to reconcile three words: teach, kindergarten, intellectual. Yet the effect is short lived.

LAWYER: (*composing a pitying look*) That must be very interesting.

Reaching for an even grander rejoinder, I try this:

LAWYER: What do you do?
ME: I teach kindergarten, the most intellectually demanding thing I've ever done. If you ever are bored with making six figures and want to make a positive difference in children's lives, you ought to think of a career change. Join me.

I seldom get that far, rarely piquing enough interest for another round. The lawyer moves on, and I am left feeling a bit like Kamal—naive, reprimanded, adrift in an indifferent world with my pathetic little dreams of teaching. Yet, like Kamal, I am not entirely wrong, either. So, in what way is teaching intellectual work? How is teaching an ethical enterprise?

THE CHALLENGE OF TEACHING

A primary challenge for teachers is to see each student as a three-dimensional creature with hopes, dreams, aspirations, skills, and capacities; with body, mind, heart, and spirit; with experience, history, and future. This knotty, complicated challenge requires patience, curiosity, wonder, awe, and humility. It demands sustained focus, intelligent judgment, inquiry, and investigation. Every judgment is contingent, every view partial, every conclusion tentative. The student is dynamic, alive, in motion. Nothing is settled once and for all. The student grows and changes in unpredictable ways. Yesterday's need is forgotten, and today's claim is all-encompassing and new. This intellectual task is of serious and huge proportion.

As difficult as this challenge seems, it is made tougher and more intense because teachers typically work in institutions of hierarchy and power, command and control. All too often, the habit of labeling kids by their deficits is commonsense and commonplace. The language of schools is a language of labeling and reduction; it lacks the spark and imagination of true education. The thinking teacher must look beneath and beyond labels.

Another basic challenge to teachers is to stay alert to the world and the concentric circles of context in which they live and work. Teachers must know and care about shared experiences. Their calling, after all, is to shepherd and enable the callings of others. Teachers, then, invite students to become somehow more capable, more thoughtful and powerful in their choices, more engaged in a culture and a civilization. How do we warrant that invitation? How do we understand this culture and civilization?

Teachers choose how to see the world, what to embrace or reject, whether to support or resist this or that directive. As teachers choose, the ethical emerges. Baldwin (1988: 4) noted:

> The paradox of education is precisely this—that as one begins to become conscious one begins to examine the society in which he is being educated. The purpose of education, finally, is to create in a person the ability to look at the world for himself, to make his own decisions. . . . But no society is really anxious to have that kind of person around. What societies really, ideally, want is a citizenry which will simply obey the rules of society. If a society succeeds in this, that society is about to perish.

Teachers are the midwives of hope or the purveyors of determinism and despair. Here, for example, are two quite different teachers at work.

In *Beloved*, Toni Morrison's (1987) novel of slavery, freedom, and the complexities of a mother's love, "schoolteacher," a frightening character with no other name, comes to Sweet Home with his efficient, scientific interest in slaves and makes life unbearable for the people there. Schoolteacher is a disturbing, jarring character for those of us who think of teachers as caring and compassionate people. Indeed, schoolteacher is cold, sadistic, and brutal. He and others like him are significant props in an entire system of dehumanization, oppression, and exploitation.

Toward the end of Amir Maalouf's *Samarkand* (1994: 234), a historical novel about the life of Omar Khayam, a British schoolteacher in the old Persian city of Tabriz explains an incident in which he was observed weeping in the marketplace. When the people saw him crying, they figured that he "had thrown off the sovereign indifference of a foreigner. . . . If they had not seen me crying, they would never have let me tell the pupils that this Shah was rotten and that the religious chiefs of Tabriz were hardly any better."

Both teachers show us that teaching occurs in context and that pedagogy and technique are not the wellsprings of moral choice. Teaching becomes ethical practice when it is guided by an unshakable commitment to helping human beings reach the full measure of their humanity and a willingness to reach toward a future fit for all—a place of peace and justice.

In *A Lesson before Dying*, Ernest Gaines (1993) created a riveting portrait of a teacher locked in struggle with a resistant student, wrestling as well with his own doubts and fears about himself as a teacher and as a person and straining against the outrages of the segregated U.S. South. Grant Wiggins has returned with considerable ambivalence to teach in the plantation school of his childhood. He feels trapped and longs to escape with another teacher Vivian to a place where he might breathe more freely, grow more fully, achieve something special. The story begins in a courtroom with his aunt and her lifelong friend Miss Emma sitting stoically near the front. Emma's godson Jefferson has been convicted of murder. The public defender, pleading for Jefferson's life, calls him a "cornered animal" who struck "quickly out of fear, a trait inherited from his ancestors in the deepest jungle of blackest Africa" (Gaines 1993: 78). Miss Emma is devastated, particularly because Jefferson was called an animal. She wants Wiggins to visit Jefferson, to teach him.

Wiggins resists: "'Yes, I'm the teacher,' I said. 'And I teach what the white folks around here tell me to teach'" (Gaines 1993: 13). More than this, Wiggins is shaken by the challenge and the context (Gaines 1993: 31):

> I'm supposed to make him a man. Who am I? God? . . . What do I say to him? Do I know what a man is? Do I know how a man is supposed to die? I'm still trying to find out how a man should live. Am I supposed to tell someone how to die who has never lived? . . . Suppose I was allowed to visit him, and suppose I reached him and made him realize that he was as much a man as any other man; then what? He's still going to die. . . . So what will I have accomplished? What will I have done? Why not let the hog die without knowing anything?

Wiggins is haunted by the memory of his own former teacher, a bitter and jaded man. The former mentor's message is that nothing a teacher does in these circumstances can make a difference. Worse, Jefferson himself is wracked with hopelessness; he is uncooperative and resistant. Wiggins begins by simply visiting Jefferson, being there, speaking sometimes, but mostly just sitting in silence. He encourages Jefferson to think of questions and write down his thoughts. He walks with Jefferson and talks to him (Gaines 1993: 191–92):

> I teach, but I don't like teaching. I teach because it is the only thing that an educated black man can do in the South today. . . . That is not a hero. A hero does for others. . . . I am not that kind of person, but I want you to be. . . . I want to show them the difference between what they think you are and what you can be. . . . You can do more than I can ever do. I have always done what they wanted me to do, teach reading, writing, and arithmetic. Nothing else—nothing about dignity, nothing about identity, nothing about loving and caring. They never thought we were capable of learning those things.

A Lesson before Dying is a teacher's tale. Though the circumstances are extreme, the interaction is recognizable. Every teacher appreciates the irony of teaching what we ourselves neither fully know nor understand.

Each can remember other teachers who counseled him or her not to teach, and each recognizes the resistant student who refuses to learn. Each can uncover moments of intense self-reflection, consciousness shifts, and personal growth brought on by attempts to teach.

Many teachers also know what it means to teach in the face of oppression, opposition, and obstinacy. When Jefferson writes in the journal, "i cry cause you been so good to me mr wigin and nobody aint never been that good to me an make me think im somebody" (Gaines 1993: 232), teachers recognize the sentiment.

Education, of course, lives an excruciating paradox precisely because of its association with and location in schools. Education is about opening doors, minds, and possibilities. School is about sorting, punishing, grading, ranking, and certifying. Education is unconditional; it asks nothing in return. School demands obedience and conformity as a precondition to attendance. Education is surprising, unruly, and disorderly, while the first and fundamental law of school is to follow orders. Education frees the mind, while schooling bureaucratizes the brain. An educator unleashes the unpredictable, while too many schoolteachers start with an unhealthy obsession with classroom management and linear lesson plans.

Working in schools—where the fundamental truths, demands, and possibilities of teaching are diminished and where the powerful ethical core of teachers' efforts is systematically defaced and erased—requires a reengagement with the larger purposes of teaching. When the drumbeat of our daily lives is all about controlling, managing, and moving the mob—conveying disembodied bits of information to inert beings propped at desks before us—the need to fight for ourselves and our students becomes imperative. Central to that fight is the understanding that there is no basis for education in a democracy except for a faith in the enduring capacity for growth in ordinary people.

The complexity of the teacher's task depends on its idiosyncratic and improvisational character. The teacher's work is about background, environment, setting, position, situation, and connection. Importantly, teaching is at its center about relationships with the person and the world. Teachers must assume a deep capacity, an intelligence, and a wide range of hopes, dreams, and aspirations in students. They must acknowledge, as well, obstacles to understand and overcome, deficiencies to repair, and injustices to correct. With this base, the teacher creates an environment for learning with multiple entry points for learning and multiple pathways to success. That environment must feature many opportunities to practice justice. Teachers must display, foster, embody, expect, demand, nurture, allow, model, and enact inquiry toward moral action. A classroom organized in this way follows a particular rhythm; questions focus on issues, problems, and action.

The question of what can be done is a daily challenge. Teachers must ask how to continue to speak the unhearable. How does self-censorship perpetuate the silence? The tension between aspiration and possibility is acute.

In her discussion of middle-class urban dwellers, Rich (1979) described three archetypes. One she called the "paranoiac"—this type lives in fear and suspicion of the world. The second she called the "solipsistic"—this type is privileged and blind to the horrors of many outside. Rich (1979: 54) posited a third possibility of love mixed "with horror and anger . . . more edged, more costly, more charged with knowledge." This recognition of the importance of human connections may be helpful for those of us who believe in a future for the city, children, and schools. Can we develop loving relationships? Can we develop that love in a struggle for human possibility and life itself?

WHAT OUGHT TO BE

Teaching as an ethical enterprise goes beyond presenting what already is; it is teaching toward what ought to be. It is more than moral structures and guidelines; it includes an exposure to and understanding of material realities, advantages and disadvantages, privileges and oppressions. Teaching of this kind might stir people to come together as vivid, thoughtful, and even outraged partners. Students, then, might find themselves dissatisfied with what had only yesterday seemed the natural order of things. At this point, when consciousness links directly to conduct and upheaval is in the air, teaching becomes a call to freedom.

The fundamental message of the teacher, after all, is that people can change their lives. Whoever you are, wherever you have been, whatever you have done, the teacher invites you to a second chance, another round, and perhaps a different conclusion. The teacher posits possibility, openness, and alternatives; the teacher points to what could be but is not yet. The teacher beckons you to change your path, and so the teacher's basic rule is to reach.

To teach consciously for ethical action adds a complicating element to that fundamental message, making it more layered, dense, and excruciatingly difficult to enact, yet at the same time more engaging, sturdy, powerful, and joyful. Teaching for ethical action demands a dialectical stance. The teacher must firmly fix one eye on the students. Who are they? What are their hopes, dreams, aspirations, passions, and commitments? What skills, abilities, and capacities does each one bring to the classroom? The teacher must, with the other eye, look unblinkingly at the concentric circles of context—historical flow, cultural surroundings, and economic reality. Teaching as an ethical enterprise is teaching that arouses students, engaging them in a quest to identify obstacles to their full humanity, the life chances of others, and their freedom. The teacher must then challenge them to move against those obstacles. The fundamental message the teacher for ethical action passes on to each student is "You must change the world."

QUESTIONS FOR REFLECTION
AND DISCUSSION

1. Does Ayers's understanding of what students are and what they should become mesh with your own? How? Why?
2. Education, say Ayers, lives with an "excruciating paradox," one that pits the freeing of the mind and the growth of the ordinary person against the imperatives of obedience and control and conformity. You've probably spent a fair amount of time in the belly of the beast of education—would you agree with Ayers's characterization of this "paradox"? And what does it have to do with the teaching and learning of global environmental politics?
3. "Teachers," writes Ayers, "invite students to become somehow more capable, more thoughtful and powerful in their choices, more engaged in a culture and a civilization." What might Ayers mean by "thoughtful and powerful," in particular "powerful"? How might the inherent nature of the global environmental politics classroom make it especially difficult for teachers to foster more "thoughtful and powerful" students? Should teachers, and the educational systems of which they're a part, really be concerned with fostering student engagement in "a culture and a civilization"? And what, within the context of your classroom or seminar space, would a teacher's invitation of this sort look like?
4. Should professors in fact "teach consciously for ethical action"? Should they in fact impart to their students the idea that "you must change the world"? If they do, isn't their objectivity and impartiality compromised? Would this not be tantamount to brainwashing, to turning students into miniature versions of the teacher?
5. A friendly critic of Ayers might argue that, given the complexity of global environmental politics and the sheer volume of information and skills that must be communicated to the student, conscientious teachers of the subject cannot afford to spend too much time thinking aloud with their students about the ethical responsibilities and

stances that might inform the GEP classroom. It is a question of efficiency and tradeoffs. As a student who expects through coursework to learn the nuts and bolts of GEP—or as an instructor who is often evaluated by students and peers on the basis of how much material is covered in a class—what do you make of this argument?

6. Ayers believes that "teachers are the midwives of hope or the purveyors of determinism and despair" for their students. But what about the reverse formulation? In classes that explore global environmental problems, aren't students the midwives of hope or the purveyors of determinism and despair for their instructors?

7. A helpful reviewer of an earlier draft of this book questioned the relevance of this chapter to the volume. What do you think? Was the chapter distracting, an unnecessary side trip down some intellectual alley? Or does it bear in useful and important ways on your learning and teaching of global environmental ills?

NOTE

This chapter originally appeared in *The Educational Forum* 63: 1 (Fall 1998: 52–57). Reprinted with permission.

II

KNOWLEDGE THAT EMPOWERS
Relearning the Basics of Global Ecopolitics

4

❖

Global Environmental Politics

Impediments, Frames,
and Tools

Lamont Hempel

When thinking about the college classroom, it is easy to fall into the dualistic construction of professor vs. student. The professor teaches, the student learns; the professor is expert, the student is novice. While both parties, in this view, are expected to bring energy and commitment to a course, both come to the classroom from very different places, with contrasting expectations, responsibilities, and agendas. They are different.

Such binary thinking has its place, but it risks obscuring shared assumptions, experiences, and insecurities that narrow the divide between student and profes- sor and that emerge, especially in interdisciplinary courses like global environ- mental politics, as impediments to understanding. One often cited example is our common classroom comfort with the professorial lecture. Professors embrace the lecture because of its predictability, efficiency, and familiarity. A Ph.D. armed with a lecture pretty much knows, walking into a classroom, what will transpire that day. The same obtains for students: though they may complain that lectures are boring or tedious, students embrace the lecture model of instruction for its familiarity, predictability, and efficiency. They know, when they see their profes- sor entering class with a lecture in hand, that no surprises—rude or otherwise— are in store. This despite the possibility (as a professor of mine long ago claimed) that lectures are the best way to transmit information from the instructor's notes to the notebook of the student, without going through the mind of either.

In this wide ranging and trenchant chapter, Lamont Hempel—now director of environmental programs at the University of Redlands—shines a light on the global environmental politics classroom and illuminates a set of prevailing practices and alternative frameworks that students and their teachers would be wise to carefully consider. He shows how teacher training and student expectations, working in tandem, fight against a rewarding and empowering investigation of global environmental ills—and he offers a synthesis of political economy and political ecology, together with a set of tools, as an antidote to comfortable classroom practice.—M.M.

S omewhere between instruction of the soul and destruction of the imagination lie the scattered pedagogical aims of secular higher education. In the best of circumstances, higher education informs, inspires, and integrates our thought processes; in the worst, it fosters insularity, cynicism, and resignation to problems that otherwise might yield to imagination and innovation. There are few academic quests that illustrate this contrast more powerfully than coursework in global environmental politics. The academic community's approach to environmental education has ranged from the deep green visions of ecotopians to the dark brown fears of catastrophists. In the conventional political science classroom, the response is usually guarded pessimism. Many students emerge from a course on global environmental politics with a strong, almost paralytic, sense of the limitations of collective action in a state-centric system. A few, perhaps buoyed by an instructor's enthusiasm, discover new reasons to be hopeful about the role of international regimes, nongovernmental organizations (NGOs), and innovative institutions in addressing global environmental problems. Most, however, find the proudly pessimistic,[1] power-centered, incremental outlook of mainstream political science to be much more acceptable, at least academically, than green globalism or the frayed idealism of the sustainable development movement. Ever fearful that they will be regarded by faculty and by their peers as naive or unsophisticated, today's students are likely to leave the classroom more cynical than when they entered.

EDUCATION AS INHIBITION:
A CHALLENGE TO PROFESSORS

Hank Jenkins-Smith (1990) has observed that the "most important institutional effect of policy analysis is its surprising tendency to inhibit political initiatives, thereby reinforcing the status quo." The study of global environmental politics may have the same kind of institutional effect on environmental initiatives. Thorstein Veblen would have called it a "trained incapacity" to effect major change. The pedagogical process involved here, however, is not so much one of intellectual *confinement* as it is academically approved *diversion* and specialization. This problem is so pervasive and familiar to social critics that most have stopped talking about its diagnosis. Fundamentally, the beliefs that structure our knowledge are rooted in objectivism (i.e., separation of facts from values), atomism (i.e., reducing the whole to its component parts—the justification for microspecialization), and universalism (i.e., universal laws governing reality). Reinforced by professionalized preferences for analytic depth over synthetic breadth, most learning continues to take place in curricular "stove pipes." What few efforts there are in higher education to build genuinely interdisciplinary bridges usually fail to overcome the countervailing incentive structures of departments for promotion and tenure within disciplines. As a consequence, it is difficult to find academic programs that provide students with a truly integrated learning experience.

In courses on global environmental politics, this failure is most evident in the lack of integration between environmental studies and the study of international politics. Most instructors of such courses, having been trained as political scientists, treat politics as the core subject and environment as an epiphenomenon. While this may seem only natural to the political scientist, it demonstrates a kind of instrumental thinking in which the adjective *environmental* comes to signify both a limitation, or qualification, and a valuation (i.e., something subordinate to politics). Students who make the academic mistake of treating the environment as the core subject often learn to their dismay that knowledge about ecosystems or carbon cycles, for example, matters much less in course preparation than knowledge about international politics, election cycles, and business cycles. Moreover, the greater the effort students make to integrate perspectives from the natural sciences and humanities with social science perspectives, the less time they will have to master what many of their instructors regard as the most important kind of environmental synthesis—the joining of political science and economics.

Theories of common pool resources and international political economy provide what many consider to be the cutting edges of teaching and research in global environmental politics. Although theories about the science, ethics, and politics of human population growth and material consumption are arguably more fundamental, they are widely dismissed as being too interdisciplinary and tangential to the study of politics and policy. Integrating approaches to population and consumption issues may be essential to the production of *useful* knowledge for most students, at least for those interested in real world environmental problems and opportunities, but it appears much less promising for the research aims of political science, economics, and, for that matter, the environmental sciences.

Consequently, global environmental scholars have become very skilled at measuring the gnats around the lightbulb while missing the elephant in the doorway. Instructors and their students tend to become preoccupied with the details of policy and trade actions that affect a particular natural resource or ecological service, while paying scant attention to the massive, cross cutting forces of human population growth and swelling per capita consumption that drive most of the policy and development issues they are investigating. A global birth-and-death cycle that results in the net addition of one billion people every twelve years warrants serious, bedrock examination in any course about global environmental politics. It is an inescapable part of almost every global issue worth covering. The same is true with respect to the "tyranny of expectations" (Maniates 2002b) associated with burgeoning per capita consumption levels, and the role that corporate capitalism and the revolutions in media marketing have played in this unsustainable consumption behavior. Such topics are every bit as legitimate in today's classroom as theories of interstate conflict and the mechanics of regime formation, yet they make most of us uneasy because they violate academic conventions and disciplinary objectives. Serious political scientists shun such broad, controversial, and low concept subjects, in part because we dislike the polemical terrain in which much of the relevant literature is mired and also, perhaps, because added attention to these areas might reveal more fully how our own lifestyles and consumption patterns contribute to the problems that we study.

Population and per capita consumption growth are clearly ubiquitous causes of most environmental problems but too obvious, unwieldy, and broad brush in nature to warrant serious and sustained treatment by most scholars. We can be grateful that modern physicists did not make the same judgment with respect to the force of gravity. Professors of global environmental politics and their students are presumably too sophisticated and academically refined to acknowledge the presence of this proverbial bull in the china shop. We seem content to examine the political and economic fragments of china scattered on the shop floor even as the bull of population and consumption continues its rampage. We know a great deal about the reconstruction of broken china, though our knowledge of bulls is sorely limited. After all, our professional status and rewards tend to flow from theoretical research in ceramics, not applied animal husbandry.

Many classroom teachers are understandably reluctant to introduce topics outside of their expertise or frames of reference that challenge their own outlooks, education, and training. According to Dryzek (1993), a frame of reference is "akin to a language or even a culture shared by a tribe of experts." The problem with applying frames of reference from political science, economics, and ecology to problems of regional and global environmental change is that most of us "experts" are ill-prepared to move from knowledge about *parts* to understanding of *wholes*. We are seldom willing to admit to ourselves, or to our students, just how limited our piece of the puzzle is for explaining the big picture. Moreover, our yearning for the expert's focused confidence may limit our curiosity about matters that lie outside our profession's recognized channels of specialization. As Harold Laski (1930: 102) observed, expertise can be a major obstacle to understanding:

> Expertise, it may be argued, sacrifices the insight of common sense to intensity of experience. It breeds an inability to accept new views from the very depth of its preoccupation with its own conclusions. It too often fails to see round its subject. It sees its results out of perspective by making them the center of relevance to which all other results must be related . . . It has, also, a certain caste-spirit about it, so that experts neglect all evidence that does not come from those who belong to their own ranks. Above all, perhaps, . . . the expert fails to see that every judgment he makes not purely factual in nature brings with it a scheme of values that has no special validity about it. He tends to confuse the importance of his facts with the importance of what he proposes to do about them.

Laski (1930: 106) goes on to observe, "The knowledge of what can be done with the results obtained in special disciplines seems to require a type of coordinating mind to which the expert, as such, is simply irrelevant." This "coordinating mind" is not so much a product of a broad liberal arts education or disciplinary convergence as it is one of transdisciplinary reconceptualization, usually encouraged by a process of mutual adjustment between two or more disciplines. The academic stretching that is required to integrate knowledge in this way is treated later in this chapter in a discussion of political economy and political ecology. In any event, it is only by relinquishing some academically safe turf—our cultivated zones of expertise—that we discover the promise of cross-disciplinary teaching and learning.

TURNING THE TABLES:
THE STUDENT AS OBSTACLE

So far, I have emphasized the constraints on learning imposed by academic institutions, disciplinary conventions, and cautious faculty members. Reluctance to deal with core issues or to mount cross-disciplinary efforts are readily explained as the legacies of graduate school indoctrination, professionalized social solidarity, and a peer review system that promotes narrow intellectual cloning over broad critical thinking. But a growing challenge to educating students about global environmental politics can be found in the resistance of students themselves to key elements of learning.

Most students I have encountered are not only unprepared by their educational backgrounds to tackle global environmental issues, they are unprepared (like their instructor) for the consequences of trying to do so within an American system of education. To the aforementioned challenge of *synthetic* thinking, in contrast to analytic thinking, must be added the challenge of learning within a multilingual, multicultural framework of instruction. Many very promising students, armed with a few powerful theories, statistical packages, and computer models but lacking any depth of exposure to world history, cultural diversity, or even basic comparative politics, have come to the self-serving conclusion that American hegemony—academically, if not geopolitically—obviates any need to learn about the experiences and perspectives of non-Western, even non-English-speaking, peoples. In their view, Western homogenization, economic globalization, and the supremacy of English as the language of business and diplomacy have rapidly combined to make immersion in other languages, cultures, and political systems unnecessary. Some students apparently believe that everything they need to know about Asia, Latin America, Europe, Africa, or elsewhere is available in English on the Internet. Cross-cultural and experiential approaches to learning are clearly discounted by this kind of thinking, and in the process something precious, though largely intangible, is lost.

I can think of no better device for teaching American students about global environmental challenges than placing them for at least one semester in a developing country, far away from the international hotels and the trappings of American-style comfort and privilege.[2] Impractical, yes, but extremely effective in many cases. The developing world, in my view, is where future scholars and diplomats should attempt to come to grips with the limits of markets, political institutions, and collective action in protecting the ecosphere. The standard textbook treatment of such issues is simply not adequate to this task and, worse yet, tends to reinforce the technocratic and hegemonic perspectives of conventional international relations pedagogy.

Neither the classroom nor the Internet can provide an acceptable substitute for experiential learning in an unfamiliar environment. But given the difficulty and expense of making such environments accessible to students, most instructors of global environmental politics are forced to fall back on the formerly tried-and-true classroom method of mixing key concepts and current events with historical case studies from exotic places. By combining a dash of cultural influence and a dollop of interest group politics, many case studies manage to convey a story about the struggle over natural resources and property rights that bears striking resemblance to the environmental contests taking place in the United States. One generally has to look to anthropology to find cases that emphasize fundamental differences in people's environmental perceptions and world views. Either way, the students, having grown up with the sound bite delivery of computer and television programmers, typically struggle to maintain concentration when presented with this material, especially in the absence of multimedia enhancements. For most students, environmental politics (unlike the environmental controversies themselves) is a dry subject, made drier by the academic imperative of rendering politics in terms of universal science, rather than as multicultural craft. By focusing on formal regime analysis rather than the perpetual clash of values over governance, many courses manage to skirt the fundamental issues that attracted students to environmental politics in the first place.

Some of my own students have thoughtfully objected to the classroom emphasis on conventional political actors and institutions, arguing that government capacity to address global environmental issues is less important than the growing power of multinational corporations, Hollywood film makers, or even, as one student put it, the producers of MTV, Nike ads, and Web site authoring tools. Although serious students continue to balance their television viewing time and Web entertainment with reading about resource regimes and game theory approaches to international cooperation, there is little doubt about which medium has more influence and holding power over their daily lives. The obvious implication for most instructors is that we will continue to have difficulties—increasing difficulties—holding the attention of students reared on interactive television and computer screens unless we modify our approach.

The classroom delivery that was popular in my own days as a student is still viable, but its emphasis on message over medium is no longer suitable for general education. Even pedagogies developed for students of the television age are becoming obsolete in the unfolding era of computer-television convergence. Increasingly, course planners are incorporating Web sites and cybercafes, interactive multimedia learning modules and simulations, and custom-made documentary films. Some are clearly more trendy than efficacious, but all speak to a pedagogical transformation that is well underway. Within a few years, numerous environmental documentary films and streaming videos will become available for home and classroom use via the Internet. My own environmental courses now feature several short documentaries I have made for the purpose of engaging students with hard hitting visual material. Their use as a pedagogical tool is discussed later in this chapter. Student demand for such products is strong, and will undoubtedly continue to be strong, even (especially?) if viewing them comes at the expense of lecture time.

Perhaps the biggest obstacle of all in student learning about global environmental challenges is a psychological one. Many students, not unlike their instructors, exhibit a combination of mulish cynicism and rational ignorance when it comes to internalizing knowledge about environmental affairs. Developing a sense of personal responsibility for environmental problems may place them at odds with the values of their peer group, or it may require changes in the high-impact lifestyles they practice or desire. Moreover, taking environmental messages to heart may place them at a competitive disadvantage in the job market or at least reduce the range of jobs they could perform with a clear conscience.

Honest and effective environmental education traces responsibility for environmental problems all the way to end users of nature and then provides hopeful options for reducing impacts. It goes to personal consumption patterns and promising ways to achieve more with less. The halfway approach of focusing on problems instead of opportunities and then assigning responsibility to loggers, land developers, auto makers, and so forth is part of a blame-game designed to keep most students feeling politically marginalized but comfortably disengaged from the subject matter.

I once pointed out to students seated around a mahogany seminar table that our discussion about tropical deforestation that day was not going to be entirely academic. College students seldom benefit from efforts to separate national and global environmental issues from their own personal lives. On the contrary, most students should be encouraged to internalize this kind of knowledge, but without overt preaching or haranguing from self-righteous instructors and without punishing standards of ecological virtue. While the Pogo declaration—"We have met the enemy and he is us!"—remains appropriate for every course on environmental issues, so does Edward Abbey's advice to become a "reluctant enthusiast, a part-time crusader, a half-hearted fanatic. Save the other half of yourselves for pleasure and adventure. It is not enough to fight for the land; it is even more important to enjoy it. While you can. While it is still there" (Abbey 1983: 57).

PERILS OF PEDAGOGY

Taken together, all of the aforementioned institutional, disciplinary, cultural, technological, and psychological obstacles constitute a formidable set of pedagogical challenges for instructors and students to confront in the learning process. A summary of some of the most important of these problems is presented in box 4.1. As an instructor of global environmental politics, I am acutely aware of how much easier it is to identify these pedagogical perils than to eliminate them from the classroom or from my lesson plans.

One of the hardest tasks in redesigning our pedagogy is to find consensus about what constitutes the irreducible minimum of concepts, theories, and approaches needed for the proper study of global environmental politics. I have already argued that greater emphasis on ecological literacy and less emphasis on the conventional wisdom of political science would be desirable, but I see no signs of consensus on this point. Given the overpowering trends toward greater microspecialization in graduate and professional education, it is hard to imagine how this task will become easier in the future.

Intemperate as it may seem, it is time to admit that most universities are failing badly to prepare college teachers who are environmentally informed and empowered to act. Tomorrow's teachers are being taught, for the most part, in "stove pipe" institutions with faculty cloning mechanisms appropriate for a bygone era. Experiential learning and extensive field research are barely tolerated in many places, and courses on actual teaching preparation are rare. In short, teaching is being shortchanged in order to perpetuate an intellectual caste system that caters to publishable forms of microspecialization, most of it in isolation from broad social and environmental needs. This is not an atmosphere in which the teaching of global environmental politics can thrive. Nor is it conducive to socializing students to the importance of personal engagement and accountability in making the world a better place.

There are of course many exceptions to this view of academia as a confederation of turfdoms, just as there are many scholars of global environmental politics who excel in teaching and motivating students. The point is that our pedagogy is embedded in a vast system of institutions whose prevailing standards are based on the professional and economic profit from research rather than the social profit from teaching. Instructors who attempt to challenge these standards with innovative courses quickly discover that their professional status may suffer; that appropriate textbooks and course materials may be harder to find and organize for class purposes; and that colleagues and even some students may complain about perceived shifts in emphasis from depth to breadth, from classroom to experiential learning, and from social science order to multidisciplinary chaos. Moreover, administrators may complain that it is harder to measure and certify learning of this type, not to mention that it may also be harder to convince parents that rising student tuition is justified in support of education that is broad-based, experiential, and experimental in form.

BOX 4.1. COMMON PROBLEMS ENCOUNTERED IN TEACHING AND LEARNING GLOBAL ENVIRONMENTAL POLITICS

Accenting the Negative

The subject matter is depressing for many students; some conclude that overwhelming forces are at work and, as a result, may experience a personal sense of powerlessness.

Overreliance on State-Centric Models

Many textbooks encourage the uncritical acceptance of the nation-state as the proper unit of analysis, treating it as the only viable source of transboundary environmental solutions.

Ecological Illiteracy

Most students and instructors lack basic education in ecology. Their knowledge of ecological concepts and processes (usually accompanied by a low level of science literacy) can be a major drawback in their understanding and analysis of environmental problems.

Microspecialization—Unidisciplinary Thinking

Closely related to ecological literacy problems is the tendency to view transboundary environmental problems within the narrow confines of a particular set of disciplinary explanations and tools, particularly those drawn from microeconomics and national security studies.

Cultural Provincialism

Most American students and faculty are not prepared to investigate environmental problems within the framework of a truly multilin-

Having identified some of the impediments to effective education in global environmental politics, it is appropriate to provide some practical means for overcoming them, in addition to the institutional reforms already suggested. Among the most useful measures are alternative course designs that promote fresh combinations of concepts and instruc-

gual, multicultural world—especially problems that are addressed in North–South terms.

Indivisible Ends—Divisible Means

The indivisible nature of many environmental problems requires a large-scale approach to problem solving, but the presence of high-action thresholds means that the politically favored approaches—usually incremental and small scale in nature—will end up looking tiny or futile in terms of the need for action. Students are often frustrated or depressed by studying problems that constantly loom larger than society's proposed solutions.

Information Overload

The explosion of relevant Web sites and databases offers exciting new research avenues but makes information management extremely taxing. Keeping up with the Internet flow of information is likely to be a daunting challenge for future scholars.

Analysis over Synthesis

Compartmentalization, reductionism, and the strict separation of science, politics, and ethics in many curricula insures that a trained incapacity for synthesis will be achieved. Heavy reliance on political economy approaches and natural resource economics as the principal tools of environmental policy analysis mitigates against holistic approaches.

Insulation from Personal Responsibility

Failure to link personal behavior, values, and lifestyles to environmental destruction, along with the tendency to keep the lessons generic and mostly free of normative content, prevents students from confronting ad hominem lessons about lifestyle choices and consumption patterns.

tional techniques. In general, the course-organizing reforms available to individual instructors are of two types: alternative frames of reference that enrich student comprehension of what is actually driving global environmental politics, and innovative tools of pedagogy that help students to apply insights and ideas derived from such frames of reference.

ALTERNATIVE FRAMES OF REFERENCE

Although the field of global environmental politics tolerates a wide range of teaching perspectives—including those of deep ecologists, ecofeminists, bioregionalists, social ecologists, resource economists, sociobiologists, and an assortment of post-positivist policy analysts and synthesists—classroom instruction tends to focus on conventional theories of state power and bargaining, as supplemented by theories of international political economy. Combining the best of both provides a powerful way to explain national responses to regional and global environmental problems. These theories typically reduce issues of international governance to the preferences of dominant state actors and to applications of structural power (e.g., Waltz 1979) or, in the case of political economy, to the microeconomic motives of Public Choice models. Although some attention is usually paid to alternative theories and explanations—institutional bargaining models (Young 1994), the role of decision cultures and social learning (Vernon 1993), the related roles of epistemic communities (Haas 1989), international organizations, and dominant social paradigms (Milbrath 1989)—the field remains firmly grounded—dare one say mired—in studying the behavior of nation-states and their role in the creation and solution of collective action problems.

The preoccupation with state power and utility-maximizing behavior in many global environmental politics courses is understandable, perhaps necessary, but by no means sufficient as an approach. Other theoretical approaches merit careful consideration. Among the most promising is that of political ecology. Unlike international political economy (IPE), which focuses primarily on the competitive relationships of nation-states, political ecology is fundamentally concerned with the asymmetrical interdependence of human communities and, by extension, nonhuman communities. It abandons the state-centric perspective and emphasizes the emerging roles of supranational and subnational actors and institutions, corporations, and mediating agents of culture and socialization that shape environmental problems and opportunities. Fundamentally concerned with the implications of interdependence for environmental sustainability, political ecology focuses primarily on services rather than goods. Its primary unit of analysis is typically a watershed, ocean, or biome, rather than a state or a market.

The political ecology approach represents a relatively new and untested field of inquiry, while the IPE perspective is derived from a massive and systematic flowering of literature and analysis that can be traced to Adam Smith's *Wealth of Nations* (1776), and perhaps further. Because of their rich possibilities for developing rival conceptions and explanations of global environmental politics, both of these frameworks warrant closer examination.

Political Economy

IPE frameworks deal with the ways in which incentive structures derived from resources, geography, and security arrangements combine with the personal self-interests of political leaders and the structural imperfections of markets to determine comparative advantage among nations. According to this perspective, failures and successes among international environmental regimes can be attributed to a combination of interest and exchange structures that shape and perpetuate the struggle for advantage among nations. International power is reflected in terms of trade, military capacity (either direct or via alliance formation), economic competitiveness, monetary policy, and the political interests that influence them.

In conventional political economy terms, a nation's power and wealth are positively related to its factor endowments—labor supply, natural resources, favorable climate, availability of capital, and so forth. When combined with information about cultural factors, intellectual capital, innovation rates, and political or military capacity, these endowment characteristics can reveal a great deal about a particular nation's policy preferences and political behavior and their implications for environmental quality. In the Middle East, for example, the key factor endowment for most of this century has been oil. In antebellum America, it was probably a combination of slavery, abundant farmland, and water-based transport (river, canal, and ocean). Improvements in factor endowments are commonly viewed as both instruments and as outcomes of economic development.

Regardless of the country or region, an understanding of the political economy of development or, in some cases, de-development, adds a critical dimension to the study of global environmental politics. IPE's contribution to this field of study is likely to grow with continued economic globalization. International trade, debt, the mobility of capital, and the expanding operations of multinational corporations can be expected to influence future global environmental politics and policy in significant ways, though the timing, direction, and intensity may be very difficult to forecast. The only safe predictions are that the effects of international investment patterns and national development strategies on natural resource consumption, land use, pollution levels, and the health of various ecological systems will grow, and these will in turn be amplified by population growth.

By exploring relationships among economies, polities, and governmental and nongovernmental actors, the IPE framework helps to focus attention on the *process* by which development takes place. It is only a short leap, pedagogically, to refocus this attention on the requisites of *sustainable* development.[3] Unfortunately, the IPE literature is very thin on the topic of sustainability. In fact, much of the literature celebrates the use of factor endowments that contribute to unsustainable development.[4] Although strengthened by synergies created in the joining of political science and economics, IPE reflects the weaknesses of both these disciplines in incorporating ecological precepts and ideas. In order to balance and deepen student understanding of global environmental politics, a political ecology framework can be used to supplement and, to some extent, challenge the conventional IPE approach.

Political Ecology

Political ecologists begin with the premise that economics is a subset of ecology, not the other way around. They hold that politics today is fundamentally about community and its governance through "intermestic" or "glocal" arrangements (Hempel 1996b). The ultimate goal of politics, from this perspective, is the peaceful achievement of just and sustainable communities.

If you cut through all the artifice of human development and hierarchy, the world appears as one giant ecosystem consisting of tens of thousands of human societies, coevolving imperiously with millions of other species, and spread across more than 14 major biomes (ecological regions), 207 terrestrial biogeographical provinces (ecoregions), and 40 marine faunal provinces. Community places, not states, shape the primary identities of the inhabitants. Biology, not economics, determines their ultimate fate.

The thousands of mapped lines crossing watersheds and subwatersheds, river basins, regional seas, forests, grasslands, deserts, mountain ranges, lakes, and other natural features all point to the incongruity between political and ecological boundaries. Resolving that incongruity in favor of ecosystem-based management, where practical, is a long-term objective of political ecologists. Their immediate objective, however, is to manage human activities that impair or threaten vital ecosystem services. Political ecologists understand that the successful management of human affairs requires careful attention to the operational imperatives of nonhuman nature. From political economists, they are learning that appropriate incentive structures will also be needed to achieve successful management. But even as the prospects improve for some kind of synthesis, both the political ecologist and the political economist are discovering entrenched state interests that constrain the sphere of action both above and below the national level.

Glocal Relations

From the political ecology perspective, the nation-state appears predominantly as an aggregation device for power and security. Increasingly, it is not only ecological factors that call into question state-centric boundaries, but economic forces as well. The world is becoming indivisible as an economy and, to some extent, as a polity. It is increasingly a transboundary realm—one in which peace, ecological integrity, and economic well-being can no longer be secured by the power and institutions of territorial sovereignty.

Despite this growing realization, however, governance continues to be organized and directed almost entirely by nation-states. The problem confronting this state-centric system is that most of today's critical environmental and economic challenges can be addressed more appropriately at the supranational and subnational levels of governance. From climate change and world trade to neighborhood revitalization and job creation, national governance appears increasingly inadequate, even anachronistic. In order to cope successfully with global change problems, local network opportunities, and expanding economic markets, our political institutions may have to become more glocal in design. Both global and local ends of the political spectrum may need to be strengthened to accommodate the changes in ecology, trade, and technology that have converged in the late twentieth century. The devolution of political authority and legitimacy from center to periphery in the United States and in many other parts of the world has fostered local empowerment, just as the development of the World Trade Organization, along with recent global environmental agreements, has tended to strengthen the prospects for limited experiments with supranational authority.

The reasons for experimenting with supranational authority seem to be straightforward, albeit politically unpopular. Environmental problems, along with many trade and human rights issues, are increasingly regional or global in scope and significance, yet governance remains sharply fragmented and territorial. Students are often more inclined to recognize and accept this perspective than are many of their instructors. They are typically less interested, however, in arguments to empower local communities.[5]

These arguments call for counterbalancing supranational authority, protecting the social fabric of technologically driven societies, facilitating social learning about bioregions and geographic places important for human identity formation, and improving government performance through enhanced civic involvement. By reestablishing the primacy of community in political life, the social and environmental sensibilities needed to manage the global reach of technology and capital are presumably more likely to emerge. Community revitalization is not only salutary for democracy; it may be essential as a counterforce for reducing the centripetal effects of technology. The ease with which billions of people can now communicate and trade with one another makes the comprehensible scale and sense of place afforded by local communities indispensable for balancing the freedom of global interaction with the responsibility of civic engagement.

Unfortunately—and alarmingly—this is a lesson that many students of global environmental politics are not prepared to grasp. Having shown an interest in the world at large and having been captivated by the promise of an electronic global village, many of these students regard local community-centered concerns as parochial and unexciting.

Despite their own international perspectives, instructors need to demonstrate that global environmental protection begins at the community and bioregional level—the level where complex living systems are most interdependent and vulnerable. Local watersheds, ecosystems, and microclimates are among the primary components of a bioregion, and their alteration by human activities is much easier to understand from the vantage point of local communities than from the macro perspective of global ecology. Moreover, if it is true that global threats to the environment require supranational policy responses, the offsetting empowerment of local communities may provide, as previously noted, needed checks and balances to reassure citizens interested in democracy that global environmental stewardship need not imply authoritarian forms of global government.

Asymmetrical Interdependence

The *political* essence of political ecology can be found in the concept of "skewed interdependence." Almost all political units today are interdependent with other units to some extent. What is striking about the new era we are entering is that most types of interdependence are growing as a result of advances in information technology and global communication, rapid growth in population and migration, heightened global risks of terrorism and nuclear proliferation, and accelerating rates of transboundary pollution and nonrenewable resource consumption. For some political scientists, the key feature of this interdependence is its asymmetry. Nearly all interdependency relationships tend to be stronger in one direction than another. Not surprisingly, those in the stronger position often fail to recognize their own forms of dependency. Today, however, the asymmetrical properties of interdependence are growing much stronger in some ways (e.g., gaps between rich and poor) and much weaker in others (e.g., greater parity in access to weapons technology that can disrupt or destroy societies). These differences in dependency—real or imagined—greatly influence the basic power and interest structures that govern competing political units. Some scholars, in fact, define power as a function of *asymmetrical interdependence* (e.g., Knorr 1977). These asymmetries also account for the basic inequities in the allocation rules that govern international trade, development, and the use of the global commons. Students of political ecology use this concept of interdependence to explain phenomena that a political economist might attribute to market forces and incentive structures.

By combining the political economy and political ecology frameworks, students can better grasp the dynamic interaction of the major forces at work in global environmental politics and policy. Against a background of increasing interdependence, this dual approach offers a powerful way to move back and forth between the science of incentives and the science of community. Most students, in my experience, are very receptive to this approach, even when it is presented at a broad, conceptual level. The problems arise with the instructor's feelings of inadequacy in teaching, in a nonsuperficial manner, multidisciplinary subjects that cross the boundary between the natural and social sciences. Political ecology, for example, has some important features in common with sociobiology. The stretch from political scientist to political economist is difficult enough without adding the challenge of biology and ecology. Hence, the real pedagogical challenge here is to reform graduate education in the relevant disciplines in such a way as to encourage more experimentation with cross-disciplinary teaching and research in the preparation of future faculty members.

INNOVATIVE TOOLS

Students and instructors who aspire to integrate politics, economics, and ecology in the classroom should not be without tools for doing so. Three tools I have found to be particularly helpful and relatively accessible for this task are (1) geographic information systems (GIS); (2) ecological footprint analysis; and (3) digital video libraries designed to support classroom teaching. Each in its own way is useful for introducing political ecology approaches and for engaging students, most of whom find it harder than did their parents to learn in conventional classroom settings.

GIS Applications

Computer-based tools of spatial analysis—geographic information systems—are capable of mapping the complex interplay of political economy-political ecology variables, using the vast geocoded data now available from high-resolution satellite remote sensing systems and from more conventional databases stored on the Internet. They provide a powerful means for envisioning the patterns locked in multiple layers of information.

Sophisticated desktop versions of GIS software are already bringing the worlds of geographers, planners, and environmental policy analysts much closer together. As regional and global databases improve, spatial analysis is likely to yield important new insights about global environmental politics and policy. Electronic atlases, thematic mapping, and dynamic GIS displays of human settlements are being keyed to literally thousands of environmental, economic, and sociopolitical indicators, allowing multiple overlays of massive amounts of data that can assist in genuine synthesis, as well as analysis. Many enterprising students in environmental policy already understand that proficiency in GIS may be just as important for their careers as proficiency in statistics or cost-benefit analysis. These and other powerful tools, like Web site authoring software, are being mastered by students at a rate that often puts their instructors to shame. This is one of the reasons why many us who were trained in the pre-desktop-computer days privately yearn for opportunities to retool and to educate ourselves about the uses and limitations of advanced information technologies.

Ecological Footprint Analysis

One of the most interesting tools for linking political ecology and political economy is ecological footprint analysis, developed by professor William Rees of the University of British Columbia, and extended by his former student Mathis Wackernagel (Wackernagel and Rees 1996). An ecological footprint is a measure of the load placed on the biosphere by a given population. Footprints are proportional to the combined population and per capita consumption levels of a community, state, or region. They are calculated in terms of the land and water appropriated for energy and resource consumption and for waste disposal. By allowing for trade-corrected consumption—the net appropriation of natural resources and ecological services from other countries and regions—footprint analysis opens useful avenues for discussion about ecological economics. It also helps students see connections between local activities and regional or global consequences. London, for example, has a footprint more than 120 times larger than its metropolitan area, most of it representing appropriated carrying capacity from abroad.[6] Students learn that the "ecological locations of human settlements no longer coincide with their geographic locations" (Wackernagel and Rees 1996: 29). Applying lessons from political economy, students also learn why per capita footprints in the United States are fourteen times larger than those of India (over 5.1 hectares/person in the United States, compared with 0.38 hectares/person in India), or why the Netherlands has one of the largest "ecological deficits" (1,900 percent) in the world.[7] Footprint analysis is also pedagogically useful as an inviting target for sensitivity analysis and classroom critiques. Because its creators have assumed greenhouse warming is a serious problem, their analysis is structured to amplify greatly the importance of carbon abatement and sequestration as quantifiable indicators of appropriated carrying capacity.

Digital Video Libraries

Although perceived as impractical by most instructors, the preparation of custom-made, short documentary films for use in the classroom is rapidly becoming both easy and affordable. In my own teaching, I employ a variety of 5–25 minute films that were made to supplement my regular teaching materials. Each film is edited and produced on a $2,000 digital studio computer, with features that would have cost over $200,000 as recently as the early 1990s and with operating requirements that can now be mastered by nonprofessionals in a few weeks of intensive use. Although excellent environmental documentaries are available commercially, they are typically longer and less relevant to my course aims than the highly focused projects that can be produced with a desktop digital studio. Besides, students have reported that instructor involvement in the film making gives the documentaries and accompanying discussions added interest and impact.

Having collected digital video footage of environmental subjects from different regions of the world and stored it on DV tape, I can develop selected lesson plans as storyboards, then capture and assemble relevant video segments, and in a matter of a few hours, create professional-looking short documentaries that provide an engaging face for the environmental controversies, actors, and institutions that I formerly presented as abstract lecture material. Instead of descriptive anecdotes, I present the sights and sounds of real environmental actors and conflicts. Although the custom video technique is not practical for everyday use and requires field research and access to digital imaging equipment, it is well suited for special presentations and occasional lectures that desperately need a visual hook. In my limited experience, custom videos developed around key concepts promote student engagement on a deeper level than anything else I have tried in the classroom. What seemed initially to be a student obstacle—short attention spans in class lecture and discussion—can also be seen as a teaching obstacle that yielded to a powerful new technology.

TOOLS AND HANDLES

The tools of GIS, footprint analysis, and digital video libraries add important dimensions to the teaching of global environmental politics and policy. Although all three promote a form of visual learning—an approach that some critics deplore as "candy for the mind of today's youth"—each can be well integrated with lecture and written text materials. Properly applied, these tools help students *envision* complex information, and thereby address a major challenge in any course dealing with the global environment.

Educational tools, however, need intellectual handles. The conceptual frameworks provided by political economy and political ecology offer what is arguably the longest and strongest pair of handles available to today's instructor of global environmental politics. At a minimum, these frameworks provide contrasting perspectives that stimulate student thinking in directions that appropriately call into question the disciplinary blinders used in much of higher education. Moreover, they point the way to what may be a productive synthesis of economic and ecological insights that can be incorporated into the study of politics and policy. Thus far, however, only the economic framework has gained entry to a large number of political science and international relations classrooms and publications. The problem of ecological illiteracy among many who study global environmental politics remains the single greatest obstacle to the development of a fully functional theory of political ecology.

With the increasing centralization of market coordination and the simultaneous decentralization of political authority, it is time to concentrate our learning and teaching more on matters of glocal governance and less on national government. As teachers, we need to understand how and why the emerging global market, the touchstone of political economists, and the community-centered polis, a defining feature of political ecologists, are affecting the environment and influencing global environmental policy. As students, we must acknowledge that topics or concepts that fail to immediately conform to our sense of the possible—the revitalization of local systems of cooperation and reciprocity, instead of reflexive reliance on supranational mechanisms of governance—are often among the most central to our evolution of a practical idealism. The importance of these two frameworks and their linkage through *glocal* institutions and politics is becoming more apparent with each new surge in trade, population, immigration, and telecommunications technology. By combining political economy and political ecology perspectives, students stand a much better chance of discovering and understanding the asymmetrical interdependencies that lie at the root of global environmental politics and policy.

QUESTIONS FOR REFLECTION
AND DISCUSSION

1. Several provocative assertions run throughout this chapter. Consider some or all of the following listed below. To what extent do you find them credible? Why? To what larger challenges or truths do they point? How could they be further tested and developed? And what relevance do they hold for your current exploration of global environmental ills?

   a. Political scientists shun broad and controversial topics such as overconsumption, population growth, or corporate merchandizing because of the polemical terrain that much of the relevant literature occupies and because study of these topics may uncomfortably implicate the wealthy. We consequently end up studying gnats around a lightbulb while ignoring the elephant in the doorway.

   b. Expertise sacrifices the insight of common sense to the intensity of experience. As such, it limits our curiosity about matters that lie outside our narrow comfort zone and explains somewhat the reluctance of college professors today to teach about the big issues that really count.

   c. The American system of education tends to tell students that they don't need to learn about the experiences and perspectives of non-Western or non-English-speaking peoples. Students who come to courses in global environmental issues are, therefore, rather clever but not terribly bright about the world.

   d. Students come to courses in environmental politics wanting to learn about the clash of values and interests and the larger controversies that tend to define political life. Professors of political science, because of their desire to be seen as keepers of a systematic science, steer clear of these controversies and instead focus on the development of universal theory rather than the fostering of multicultural craftsmanship.

   e. To return to the Edward Abbey quote, education should encourage students to be a "reluctant enthusiast, a part-time crusader, a half-hearted fanatic."

   f. Resolving global environmental ills requires a new focus on community processes of social reciprocity, local democracy, and environmental sustainability. Alas, students of today are so enamored of things global—the World Wide Web and globalization of culture—that this analytic focus on the local is lost. Professors of global environmental problems must work to overcome this deficiency on the part of their students. Yet many professors, by virtue of their training in *international* relations, fail to appreciate the importance of distinctly local solutions to global challenges. They may even feel inadequate to the task and hence fail to broach the subject.

2. What one or two additional assertions or arguments of note emerge from you reading of this chapter? Why do they jump out at you?

3. How might the two conceptual frameworks discussed by Hempel—political economy and political ecology—make sense of a global environmental problem like the depletion of the stratospheric ozone layer (see chapter 9) or the squeeze of the middle strata of sustainable consumers (see chapter 5)? Is one framework consistently superior to another when it comes to dissecting the politics of global environmental degradation? Or, as Hempel argues, are they best employed together, like two lenses in a pair of glasses?

4. A summary of Hempel's discussion might be: "It would seem that we come to understand the degradation of the globe's biosphere and our place in the process of degradation and the struggle for renewal in spite of, not because of, dominant educational practices and assumptions." Is this too strong? To what extent is it true? What now?

NOTES

1. The basis for this pessimism can be seen in popular accounts of political history. According to Hirschman (1991: 11, 43, 81), three basic theses about politics recur repeatedly in the popular understanding of history: the *futility* thesis, which holds that political reform is hopeless; the *perversity* thesis, which holds that political reform occurs but that it is usually counterproductive; and the *jeopardy* thesis, which holds that political reform can be beneficial, but it often places prior, and desirable, political accomplishments in jeopardy.

2. Fortunately, many students are sufficiently curious and adaptable to make such study abroad programs quite successful, though as income gaps between North and South increase, the perceived hardships and risks of studying in developing countries may reduce participation.

3. A starting point for this refocusing can be found in efforts to develop sustainability indicators, natural capital accounting schemes, and adjusted national income accounts (e.g., Van Dieren 1995; Daly and Cobb 1994).

4. Human population growth, which some argue is the "ultimate resource" (Simon 1987), is an example of a factor endowment that often impedes sustainable development. Political ecologists start with a different view of endowment characteristics and a different unit of analysis. Endowment is measured as a function of ecological wealth—for example, the availability of clean and affordable water or, more generally, a healthy biosphere (and, by extension, a stable climate). Such ecological assets are deemed to be just as valuable, ultimately far more valuable, than technological artifacts and other human creations.

5. When designed to promote cooperation for mutual benefit, local communi-

ties provide what Robert Putnam (2000) calls "virtuous circles" or self-reinforcing stocks of social capital: "cooperation, trust, reciprocity, civic engagement, and collective well-being." Although modern communities have been organized increasingly around the metaphor of the marketplace, they are understood more fruitfully in terms of the Greek ideal of the polis—"an entity small enough to have very simple forms of organization yet large enough to embody the elements of politics" (Stone 1988: 13). This distinction between market and polis represents one of the fundamental differences between political economy and political ecology.

6. Wackernagel and Rees (1996) measure appropriated carrying capacity by dividing consumption and associated waste processes into five categories—food, housing, transportation, consumer goods, services—and then calculating the amount of land area needed to support waste and resource consumption in each of eight land uses: land appropriated for fossil energy use, built environment, gardens, crop land, pasture, managed forest, untouched forest, and nonproductive areas.

7. Land needed for fossil-fuel energy development and associated carbon sequestration accounts for nearly half of the ecological footprint of some countries.

5

❂

Imagining the State

Ken Conca

Making our way to a sustainable world will surely be a political exercise, in that it will entail real struggle for power and influence, with winners and losers around issues that matter. But it will be much more than this too. Our capacity to envision alternative social arrangements, new mechanisms of global governance, and processes of education and implementation that mesh the local and global in ways that foster justice and environmental resilience will most certainly be tested. In this journey, imagination, to borrow from Albert Einstein's familiar assertion, may prove to be more important than knowledge.

Exploring the dimensions of political imagination, much less explaining why it may be important to do so, is almost impossible to do in the global environmental political classroom, largely because we lack undergraduate level essays that connect the imagination-limiting power of concepts we commonly employ to the core of global environmental analysis. In the chapter that follows, Ken Conca goes a long way toward filling this void. He appraises our evolving yet still-distorted understandings of the state and links the critical ability to imagine—to think outside the box—to the hard work of making sense of postsovereign theory. Conca's chapter will clear up student confusion about why the state is so central to the exploration of global environmental politics and why the study of global environmental politics must transcend state-centric analysis—and for this reason alone, it will be core reading for my courses in global environmental politics. But perhaps this chapter's greatest value flows from its no-nonsense challenge, to students and their teachers, to abandon cartoonish depictions of the state in favor of more nuanced understandings that can, in the author's words, truly confront "the great ecological crisis of contemporary world politics."—M.M.

THE EXAGGERATED DEATH OF
STATE-CENTERED TEACHING

R ead the first chapter of any popular introductory textbook on international relations and you are likely to find references to the "strange
new world" of the post–Cold War era or assertions that "We live in revo-
lutionary times."[1] Attend a convention of international relations scholars,
such as the annual conference of the International Studies Association,
and you will find a meeting theme such as "The New Agenda of World
Politics," "Beyond Sovereignty," or "Where to Next in International
Studies?" Titles such as these reflect the difficulties of finding patterns in
the international system since the end of the Cold War. But they indicate
a more fundamental change in outlook as well, in which the scholarly
enterprise of international relations has come to think about the state in
fundamentally new ways. Many scholars see the traditional idea of
states—as coherent, unified, sovereign actors in international relations—as irrelevant in a world of turbulent globalization; many others go
further, dismissing it as a cartoonish description of something that never
really existed at all. The old metaphors—of countries as strategically
minded thinkers engaged in a grand game of geopolitical chess or as sovereign billiard balls of similar form propelled by the logic of international
anarchy—have given way to more complex models in which the state
itself is a problematic notion. The modern state is seen as an incomplete,
fragile institution: riven with ethnic and sectarian conflict, beset by crises
of authority, ensnared by deepening transnational norms, powerless to
enforce the polite fiction of its sovereignty.

Yet, when I enter the classroom, I find that these tales of a postsovereign
era often exaggerate the extent to which our teaching and learning about
world politics has really changed. Borrowing from the American humor-
ist Mark Twain, I fear that when it comes to thinking aloud about global
environmental politics in the classroom, tales of the death of the state are
greatly exaggerated. Countries retain a powerful hold on our intellectual
imagination.

In several of my advanced undergraduate courses—not only on global
environmental politics but also on such postsovereign themes as the communications revolution or postcolonialism—I have observed a similar pattern. Early in the semester, we reflect dutifully on the problematic
character of sovereignty, the important role of nonstate actors, the incompleteness of the modern state's authority, the border-spanning reach of
transnational institutions and norms, and pollution's disdain for socially
constructed borders. Yet, as the semester proceeds, strong centripetal
forces push us back to a world in which countries are presumed to behave
as coherent, rational individuals with clear interests and unquestioned

authority. By the end of the semester, I find that my students and I are again conjuring a world of billiard balls and chess pieces, in which things happen because Brazil needs, China wants, or America refuses. In doing so, I fear that we too often fail to come to grips with the central issues of contemporary global environmental politics: the unaccountability of power in the contemporary world system, the deeply institutionalized and thoroughly transnationalized character of the forces that propel environmental destruction, and the inadequacy of state-based bargaining as a framework for addressing the health of the planet and its people. States are not irrelevant to these problems; indeed, a carefully detailed historical analysis of what states are, where they came from, and whose interests they tend to serve is essential to understanding the full scope of the challenges we face. The problem is not that we pay too much attention to the state but rather that in doing so we allow cartoonish ahistorical personified imagery to shape our view of what a state really is and how it behaves.

This chapter has three goals. The first is to explore why such images of the state endure in the face of so much postsovereign theorizing. The second goal is to draw out some of the consequences of using these images to think about global environmental problems. The third goal is to suggest several ways in which teaching and learning about global environmental politics can respond to this problem, so that a richer understanding of the state, its logic, and its limits may come into focus.

THE PERSISTENT PERSONIFICATION OF SOVEREIGN STATES

Each of the various intellectual disciplines that seek to explain aspects of human behavior has organized itself around a few core analytic concepts. In economics, for example, concepts such as the firm and the market are foundational. Economists may disagree about how firms will behave or markets will perform in a given context, but they tend to share an underlying notion of what these things *are*. Those who reject those underlying notions will probably not become economists and will probably be skeptical of the explanatory power of the economic paradigm. Similarly, anthropology has coalesced around the idea of culture, sociology around core concepts of society, modernization, and social stratification, and psychology around certain premises about the psyche and the self.

For the modern field of international relations, the foundational concept has been the state. But not just any notion of the state—"state" in this context refers to a coherent, autonomous, purposeful entity driven by certain fundamental goals and wielding certain basic forms of power.

Although there have always been skeptics, it is safe to say that most scholars and analysts working in the traditional field of international relations shared Hedley Bull's classic definition (1977: 8) in which states are entities that "possess a government and assert sovereignty in relation to a particular portion of the earth's surface and a particular segment of the human population." As Thom Kuehls (1996: 34) has explained it, in this view the "four pillars of the modern state" are government, sovereignty, territory, and population. Starting from this shared foundation of what the state is, and thus of what *all* states tend to be, international relations became a discipline that sought to explain the interaction among states, rather than encouraging critical inquiry into the essence of the state itself.

Unlike anthropology or economics, however, international relations has recently seen its central organizing concept subjected to the intellectual equivalent of a full frontal assault. For well over a decade now, the dominant trend in international relations theory has been to expose the allegedly fixed properties of sovereignty, territoriality, national identity, and governmental authority as incomplete and often tenuous social constructions. Where once we took the essence of states for granted, we now see the importance of studying the processes by which states and the interstate system are created, reproduced, and maintained. We also recognize that these acts of producing and reproducing the state are never easy, often violent, and in many cases becoming more difficult.[2]

Consider the dismantling of each of the four components of Bull's definition. The assertion of sovereignty? Studies of military intervention, postcolonialism, and economic globalization have exposed the contingent, partial, and fragmented character of state sovereignty.[3] Authoritative government? Research on the role of advocacy networks, international knowledge communities, and transnational social movements has challenged the assumption that states are coherent, authoritative actors.[4] A population with some semblance of a collective national identity? Inspection of migration processes, gender dynamics, and indigenous peoples reveals national identity to be not a fixed and immutable property of national populations but rather a constructed, shifting category that operates as a powerful but often brittle mechanism of social control.[5] Territory? The fixed, essential character of territory becomes questionable in a world of border-straddling ecosystems, transboundary pollutant flows, and deterritorialized global commons.[6] Given these insights, billiard ball and chess-playing metaphors—assuming as they do the centrality of governments, the separateness of societies, the fixed character of national interests, and the rationality of choice—are at best incomplete and at worst seriously distorting.

ROOTS OF THE PROBLEM

Why, then, do cartoonish notions about billiard balls and chess pieces persist in the classroom, at a time when the international relations paradigm from which they emanate has been disassembled so aggressively by such a wide range of theorists? One simple reason is the data that are available to us. Look at the appendices to an authoritative data source such as *World Resources*, the biennial publication of the World Resources Institute that so often informs classroom work in global environmental politics. The neat rows of nationally aggregated data reinforce a country level perspective on global problems, in which Argentina emits 117 megatons of carbon dioxide annually, India has set aside 4.4 percent of its land surface area in parks and protected areas, and Nigeria consumes, per capita, 7 gigajoules of commercial energy and 10 gigajoules of energy from traditional fuels.

Now try to draw a subnational or transnational picture of the same environmental impacts or problems. Instead of Argentina, how much does the border-straddling growth pole linking Sao Paulo and Buenos Aires contribute to global climate change? Instead of India, what is the scope of protected areas in a border-straddling watershed such as the Indus or Ganges? Instead of Nigeria, what are the different patterns of energy use by the various regions or communities within that strife-torn land? Such questions make at least as much sense from an ecological or social standpoint. Yet unlike national data, which can be easily uploaded, downloaded, dissected, regressed, and regurgitated, these subnational or transnational measures depend on fragmented; partial, hard-to-obtain bits of information, often supporting no more than order-of-magnitude guesses based on heroic assumptions. It may be that we keep coming back to the categories of Brazil, China, and the United States simply because that is what the data allow us to analyze.

Media coverage also reinforces the national level of analysis. Despite the powerful influence of transnational business lobbies and the growing ability of transnational social movement groups to participate directly in global governance, headlines from global conferences in Kyoto, Bonn, or Buenos Aires tell us that countries have unified positions on the issues and that those positions are what define outcomes. This distorted view is reinforced by the media's habit of covering global environmental politics as a disconnected series of meetings held in sovereign state forums such as the Stockholm Conference, the Earth Summit, or a conference of the parties to an interstate treaty. Nonstate actors appear in accounts of these events as small dogs nipping at the heels of their sovereign masters. Meanwhile, deeply border-negating processes of transnational lobbying, international coalition building, or socioeconomic integration that occur in the space between these periodic sovereignty-reinforcing gatherings go unnoticed and uncovered.

But the roots of the problem lie deeper than the academic and media templates used to create and frame information. Teaching in the field of international relations has also been slow to adjust to new theoretical understandings. At my university and most others, the basic introductory course in international relations draws a wide audience of students from many different majors. Most of these students will not go on to do advanced coursework in international relations. Rather than analyzing the latest theoretical insights, they are obtaining what might be termed a citizen's knowledge of world politics. But what are they learning? A quick review of popular introductory textbooks reveals that the sovereignty-challenging claims of the typical introductory chapter give way to pedestrian, country-centered analysis in the heart of the text. World history becomes synonymous with the origins of the European state system; Westphalia enjoys pride of place, followed quickly by the globalization of the family of nation-states in the twentieth century. Studying war and peace means analyzing interstate conflict, with a brief add-on asserting a rise in "ethnic conflict" and "state failure" since the end of the Cold War. Examining the global economy means looking at interstate cooperation under anarchy, to understand how states meet the challenge of managing their "interdependence" in a globalizing era.

Tellingly, themes related to nature, natural resources, ecology, and the transformation of the planet's places do not appear in any of the preceding analysis, with the exception of an obligatory passing reference to OPEC. Environmental issues and problems will be gathered in a highly futuristic chapter near the end of the textbook, easily skipped or skimmed if the instructor is falling behind the class syllabus. Worse, most of the emphasis in this textbook chapter will be on global population growth in poor countries and a few high-profile issues that lend themselves to interstate bargaining, such as the "global commons" of stratospheric ozone or climate. We should not be surprised that students with this foundation see world politics as an international system of free standing, autonomous, integrated national units joined in voluntary processes of bargaining and negotiation.

DISTORTIONS OF THE STATIST FRAME

All frames distort, necessarily. The act of calling some aspects of a complex reality into clearer, sharper focus will inevitably blur or steer attention away from other aspects. The question is not the accuracy of the frame but rather its usefulness. I find the state-centered frame sketched above to be particularly unhelpful for understanding global environmental problems, for at least three reasons. First, it miscasts injustice, framing it as a problem to be resolved between countries. Second, it hides what I take to be the most important tasks of the transition to sustainability: reasserting democratic control of unsustainable global production systems and creating space for sustainable lifestyles and livelihoods in the face of corrosive global economic change. Third, it blurs our understanding of power by making it easier to avoid confronting what power is and who holds it.

Miscasting the Problem of Global Injustice

One problem with viewing the world as a collection of autonomous, personified states is that it strongly colors our thinking about global justice. In my experience, it is not particularly difficult for students of global environmental politics to shed simplistic metaphors about earth as a spaceship or lifeboat in which all humanity shares one ecological future. Most students either understand through experience, or else come to realize fairly quickly, that not all of us are equally responsible for the planet's ecological ills and that not all of us can or should be held equally responsible for building a more sustainable world economy. At this point, justice becomes a central question in the classroom. We begin to pay close attention to the fundamental fairness of current practices and various proposals for change. We do so in part for ethical reasons and in part because theory and experience teach that perceptions of fairness are an important condition for durable international cooperation.[7] Most of us do not wish to support proposals that are unfair; nor do we expect durable, broadly based international coalitions to form around them.

But what is fair among countries? Consider Brazil. The World Bank (1999: 190, Table 1) describes Brazil as an upper-middle-income developing country, with a per-capita income that ranks it forty-seventh among the world's nations. The United Nations Development Program (1998: 128) tells us that it ranks only sixty-second in its "human development" index, due to lower indicators for life expectancy and education than for income. These and other authoritative sources tell us that Brazil has the world's eighth largest gross national product and is the world's twenty-second largest emitter of carbon dioxide from industrial sources. Descriptions such as these carry with them a powerfully distorting idea that I refer to as the myth of the average citizen. We begin to see Brazil as a place where people live for 66.6 years, earn $4,720 a year, produce 2.3 children, and annually emit 1.39 metric tons of carbon dioxide, and we compare this place to other places with average figures that differ from these.

The myth of the average citizen is translated into the practical rights and responsibilities of governments in international relations on a daily basis. Despite the fabulous wealth of some Brazilians, Brazil is allowed to borrow from multilateral development institutions such as the World Bank, a privilege denied to richer countries. And despite the grinding poverty of a much larger group of Brazilians, Brazil is not eligible for highly concessionary funds through the Bank's International Development Association (IDA), a privilege reserved for the poorest of the poor among nations. As with rights, so with responsibilities: In international environmental bargaining, Brazil is typically expected to pay more of the price for a sustainable global future than a country such as Ethiopia but less than a country such as the United States. We take it as an article of faith, or perhaps of hope, that seeking justice for the statistical averages that countries represent will enhance justice for their citizens.

The problem with such thinking is that it masks the always large and often enormous disparities *within* countries, rooted in income disparities, class rigidities, regional variation, or inequalities based on race, gender, or ethnicity. There may not be a single Brazilian who lives the life of that mythic average individual. Indeed, a longstanding joke in Brazil is that the country's name should be changed to "Belindia"—Belgium and India—to reflect the stark inequalities of daily Brazilian life. If governments are not instruments of redistributive justice, it is naive to think that changing the distribution *among* them will resolve the question of justice *within* their borders. Such changes may have the desired effect—but they may also worsen existing inequities by reconsolidating elite power. Injustice in this case is not being eliminated by international cooperation but merely shifted to the subnational level, where it is rendered less visible to global society.

Distorting the Nature and Distribution of Power

Our tendency to overaggregate and personify countries also leads us away from a clear understanding of what power is and who has it. We continue to study interstate bargaining as *the* mechanism of global environmental governance. Meanwhile, turbulent, dramatic change in the world economy—including trade liberalization, capital mobility, the communications revolution, and the changing organization of production—are both changing the nature of power in world politics and altering its distribution. Transnational economic actors are better able to resist the reach of national regulation than at any time in recent memory, for several reasons. The greater mobility of transnational capital shifts bargaining power away from the regulatory state. The communications revolution, falling transportation costs, and the rise of post-Fordist "flexible specialization" and "just-in-time" manufacturing systems allows firms to shift rapidly among any of a myriad of globally dispersed subcontractors—making it harder for countries to hold onto their manufacturing base. And the hypercompetitive climate created by these changes can pressure governments to further liberalize conditions for investors, producing a "race to the bottom" of lowered wages and relaxed business regulations.

Recent shocks such as the Mexican peso crisis and the Asian financial crisis have illustrated the shift in power from state to nonstate. In the new global structure of production, even rapidly growing and diversifying economies such as those of the Pacific Rim, Mexico, and Brazil have found themselves dependent on external conditions and decisions they cannot control. Brazil used aggressive measures of neoliberal economic reform to attract an estimated $24 billion in foreign direct investment in 1998—only to see more than $4 billion in capital bleed out of the country in a few days during the January 1999 currency crisis. The American government's initial bailout plan for Mexico during the 1994 peso crisis, announced before the full scope of the problem became apparent, involved a dollar amount equivalent to what was draining out of Mexico every few hours.

Contrast this brave new world with the popular classroom image of geopolitically inspired environmental diplomacy based on national bargaining positions. In our discussions of that fictional world, the conversation often converges on the issue of "state capacity" and how to enhance it, with primary emphasis on its technical and administrative dimensions. Important though these issues are, they beg a more fundamental question: Can *any* government in fact wield that capacity to regulate, through national means, the environmentally impacting activities of the transnational chains of production that pass through its borders?

To be sure, governments are not entirely powerless in this new economic terrain, and claims that they are should probably be dismissed as so much "globaloney." The deepening of economic globalization is not a fact of life or inevitability of history but rather the result of specific state policy choices, such as aggressive trade liberalization and the relaxation of controls on short-term movements of capital. Presumably, the governments that let the genie out of the bottle could at last try to stuff it back in if the right coalition of social forces came to power. But seeing the process in this light means asking not only which states hold relative power in interstate bargaining but also what aspects of *structural* power in the world economy inhibit such a reassertion of social control.

Ironically, even as we tend to overstate the power of states as unified, intentional agents, we also run the risk of ignoring the various forms of power exerted by real states in the real world. Consider the exercise of state power to create a protected area for the preservation of biodiversity. What exactly does state power mean in this context? Are we talking about the power of a legitimate, accountable institution to extract popular participation? Or do we mean the power of the jackboot, the barbed wire, and the armed forest guards? Do we mean coercive power, the legal and administrative power to institutionalize certain forms of property rights, or the power to say authoritatively what is good and true? Even as we recognize the structural dimensions of economic power and the shift of power from state to nonstate actors, we need to retain a careful analysis of the many forms of state power that exist in varying combinations in the real world of real states.

Hiding Potential Solutions

The cartoon of autonomous, personified countries also obscures what I take to be perhaps the greatest challenge of global environmental politics: to salvage what we can of the communities and livelihoods that may be foundations for more sustainable ways of living. This challenge, made infinitely more difficult by destabilizing processes of globalization, is rendered less visible through the traditional interstate lens.

Some of the most powerful metaphors that have guided our thinking about environmental problems and social ecology contribute to the reification of states when we teach global environmental politics. Consider Garrett Hardin's (1968) classic notion of the tragedy of the commons, in which individual herders seeking economic gain produce a collective tragedy by crowding too many cows into a limited common grazing area.

The problems with this model are well known (and for more on this, see Peter Taylor's chapter in this volume). It is a gross distortion of the actual historical experience of the English commons—a durable form of community resource management, and one that was done in not by the calculations of individual herders but rather by the industrial revolution, privatization, and the enclosure of public spaces (e.g., Cox 1985). It also ignores the now abundant evidence of real and potential "triumphs of the commons" grounded in collective rule making and communal management.[8]

In the study of international relations, it becomes a dangerously simple matter to substitute personified, autonomous nation-states for the highly stylized, free floating individuals in Hardin's model and to replace the grazing commons with supranational systems such as the oceans and atmosphere. As in the original example, the conclusion will be that the failure to manage these commons is simply the highly predictable failure of collective action in the face of inherently selfish states-as-individual-agents. The menu of solutions to this problem is limited, as Hardin originally suggested, to some form of authoritative enclosure of the commons, either through privatization and the internalization of market incentives or the iron fist of the regulatory state. It becomes harder for us to see the problem as being rooted in a lack of community, flaws in the design of institutions, or a concentration of power in the hands of those who would plunder and despoil nature—and harder as well to see the obvious, if difficult, responses to these problems.

Another potent metaphor that blurs a critically important source of solutions is the North–South imagery that pervades international environmental politics. It is a short leap of faith from the myth of the average citizen to a world of two kinds of states—the poverty-stricken, eager-for-development countries of a highly stylized global South and the affluent, industrialized, democratic countries of an equally stylized global North. If this were the world we lived in, then the primary challenge would be, as it is often said to be, to deal with the pollution of affluence of the over-consuming North and the pollution of poverty of the marginalized South.

This bipolar view is not completely wrong; it would be a serious mistake to lose sight of the extremes of wealth and poverty, power and powerlessness, voice and voicelessness that mark the contemporary international system. Redressing these inequalities will have to be part of any blueprint for sustainability. But what of the billions who live, work, and consume in ways that fit neither the extremes of overconsumption or poverty-induced ecological marginalization? As with the community-based practices of commons governance so inconvenient to Hardin's model, they simply disappear from the analysis. Global environmental governance becomes a matter of the rich transferring technology and financing (despite their woefully unsustainable technological and financial practices) and of the poor assimilating these transfers—while somehow negating the aspirations of the poor for the consumption levels of the rich that will inevitably accompany such transfers.

What goes unnoticed in this frame is the great ecological crisis of contemporary world politics—the destruction of communities and livelihoods that make it possible to lead lives rich in rewarding social relations, meaningful work, and enjoyable leisure activities, while remaining relatively low in material throughput, energy use, and environmental degradation. Billions of people on this planet still live such lives—some in the so-called North, others in the so-called South, and most in ways that do not register in stark North–South imagery. But as I have argued elsewhere (Conca 2002; Conca 2000), the twin effects of globalization are to imperil such lifestyles from above and below—drawing many of them up into the ranks of the overconsumers, while propelling many others downward into the ranks of the downsized, the outsourced, and the forgotten. Rather than building on our substantial existing stock of time-tested social germ plasm for sustainability, we conjure a world in which the solution is to come from the same gadgeteers and financial wizards who have brought us to where we are today.

CONCLUSION: TOWARD A POSTSOVEREIGN VISION OF THE WORLD OF STATES

Several elements of what I take to be a more useful approach have already been suggested. The point is not to avoid looking at states or to ignore state power but, rather, to look at states more carefully, disaggregating the forms of power they wield and mapping more carefully the reach and limitations of that power. How can we attain this more nuanced vision of states and use it to inform our studies? One useful approach is to have students read about real states in a real historical context. I have found that a text such as Donald Worster's *Rivers of Empire* helps my students to understand what state institutions are, where they come from, and the range of ways in which they typically assert authority. In his account of the construction of a "hydraulic society" in the American West, Worster captures the dimension of structural power. He shows that the social and ecological transformation of the Western landscape came about not simply from the individual actions of freely choosing agents but rather through the forceful workings of the state and the market as institutions deeply embedded in American society. At the same time, however, the state in Worster's account is not an abstract, aggregate thing but rather a collection of real, historical institutions: the Army Corps of Engineers, the Bureau of Reclamation, the U.S. Congress, the Western governors.

A second approach is to deliberately step outside the global commons issues where governments bargain while nongovernmental organizations (NGOs) and multinationals circle the waters. Obviously, it is important to study processes of bargaining and negotiation around issues such as ozone layer depletion, the oceans, biodiversity, and climate change. But at the same time, we should be contrasting these state-based bargaining processes with jarringly different kinds of global problems. Why is there no global regime for a localized cumulative problem such as soil erosion? Are various watershed-scale schemes of managing river basins, which have proliferated in recent years, adding up to a different sort of environmental regime, based on the nonstate or substate diffusion of norms, ideas, or management techniques? Why does virtually every country in the world have a network of protected areas, and why have they converged on similar means and ends of conservation, despite the absence of any effective international accords to make it so? States participate in these increasingly institutionalized practices, but in ways that differ from the central problem dynamic of interstate diplomacy that we have constructed in the classroom.

Third, we need to vary the types of states we study. Our attention is drawn, inevitably, to high-profile states such as the United States, China, Japan, or Brazil—either because of their contributions to global problems, their influence in crafting or resisting international responses, or the stark evidence they offer of the consequences of environmental change. This means, in practice, creating a world in the classroom populated by the G-7, a few big less-developed countries, and failed states populated by the poorest of the poor. In an earlier analysis of the changing character of state sovereignty, I argued that we would also profit from focusing on states that are "strong enough to potentially resist significant international pressure, but also weak enough that there are serious doubts about their capacity to respond to the tasks being assigned to them or embraced by them." This means, in practice, bringing to the center of our analysis countries such as the more advanced industrial countries of the global South, the newly emergent polities of Central Europe, and peripheral states of the OECD such as Ireland, Portugal, Greece, or Australia.[9] These midrange cases are likely to yield the truest test of systemwide changes in state power, authority, or sovereignty. They are also likely to be the best place to find actually existing practices that manage to evade the twin perils of a pollution of affluence and a pollution of poverty.

In the pop anthem "Imagine," John Lennon (1971) implored us to imagine that countries do not exist. Such imagining, said Lennon, is not hard to do, if we put our minds to it. Imagining of just this sort has reinvigorated international studies, moving us from a narrow understanding of interstate relations to an infinitely richer vision of world politics. But in the classroom, such imagining can still be quite hard to do, and requires the careful, nurturing attention of both instructors and students.

QUESTIONS FOR REFLECTION AND DISCUSSION

1. "The state" emerges in everyday conversation more than one might first realize: "separation of church and state," "the state vs. (fill in the defendant's name)," and "state-sanctioned executions" are familiar phrases. In these usages, the state is something more than "government" yet something less than "society." What do we mean exactly when we talk about "the state"?

2. Professor Conca argues that introductory courses in international relations and world politics confer a narrow and not altogether use-

ful understanding of the state. Many of you have taken the kinds of introductory courses to which he refers. From your experience, has Conca accurately characterized the impact of these courses upon students' ability to think imaginatively about the state?

3. Conca attacks cartoonish images of the state that, from his experience, infect the classroom. But isn't there value in simplification, especially at the level of undergraduate teaching and learning? One person's cartoonish depiction may be another's useful classroom simplification. What do you say to the argument that the reification of the state, driven by all the forces described in this chapter, is actually rather useful and productive if you're trying to teach students the basics of global politics?

4. This chapter, in part, asks us to hold in suspicion the tragedy of the commons model so familiar to students of environmental problems and international politics. Why? And in ways that anticipate arguments broached by Peter Taylor in chapter 6 of this volume, Conca notes that the English commons was "a durable form of community resource management, and one that was done in not by the calculations of individual herders but rather by the industrial revolution, privatization, and the enclosure of public spaces." Why might this distinction between individual calculation and larger social forces be important? And what are its implications for our study of global environmental ills and our imagining of responses to these ills?

5. In what additional ways does "the myth of the average citizen" miscast the problem of social justice and impede our ability to imagine global policies that might enhance justice and thus foster environmental sustainability?

6. Conca speaks of "structural power" and "the structural dimensions of economic power." Both terms point to what, exactly? What is meant when the words *power* and *structure* are paired, and what connection does this pairing have to prevailing images of the state?

7. "The great ecological crisis of contemporary world politics" is, for Professor Conca, the squeezing of a middle stratum of sustainable consumers who live in "rich" or "poor" countries alike. What would be some defining characteristics of these consumers—how, in other words, would you know them when you see them? What forces are at work, would you guess, that move people from sustainable ways of living and into more destructive consumption and production practices? And how, ultimately, do cartoonish depictions of the state limit our capacity to recognize both the value and extent of this stratum and the forces working to erode it?

8. What other cartoonish images inadvertently enjoy reinforcement in the global environmental politics classroom and limit our capacity to make sense of and act productively upon the world?

NOTES

1. See for example Roskin and Berry (1999: 3) or Papp (1997: 1).

2. On the social construction of the state, see Biersteker and Weber (1996).

3. See for example Biersteker and Weber (1996), Finnemore (1996), and Strange (1996).

4. For example, Keck and Sikkink (1998), Lipschutz (with Mayer, 1996), Risse-Kappen (1995), Rosenau (1990), and Wapner (1996a).

5. See Der Derian and Shapiro (1989), Inglehart (1990), Lapid and Kratochwil (1996), Shapiro and Alker (1996), and Tickner (1992).

6. See for example Kuehls (1996), Litfin (1997), Princen and Finger (1994), and Immerfall (1996).

7. On the role of fairness in international cooperation, see Rowlands (1991).

8. See Ostrom (1990) or Feeny, Berkes, McCay, and Acheson (1990).

9. Conca (1995).

6

❂

Nonstandard Lessons from the "Tragedy of the Commons"

Peter Taylor

In the previous chapter, Ken Conca alerted us to the pitfalls of becoming captured by the conceptual frameworks we employ. Though Conca's gaze focused on the state, his glancing blow to the "tragedy of the commons," an organizing frame that fixes responsibility for an array of social irrationalities on the individual calculations of rational actors, surely struck some of you as provocative—this because Hardin's idea of the "tragedy of the commons," though sometimes critiqued for its claim that groups of individuals are incapable of self-organizing, remains an influential framework for environmental policymakers and activists alike. Many intermediate treatments of environmental policymaking embrace the tragedy as an organizing framework; and introductory textbooks, especially in environmental science, often present the tragedy as a fact of life. Like "the state," the "tragedy of the commons" retains a strong grip on our thinking—yet, if accepted acritically, this popular concept (and assumptions we more generally make about the utility and neutrality of simple models) can make it difficult to imagine how to devise workable systems of global environmental governance without a supranational and technocratic world government unafraid to coerce.

Peter Taylor, a professor in the Critical and Creative Thinking Program at the University of Massachusetts, Boston, is an environmental and science educator who illuminates established ideas from new angles. He helps his students understand hidden assumptions, especially where they concern people's agency—their ability to influence the practice of environmental research and politics. His contribution to this volume begins with a report on his classroom simulation of the tragedy. His observations of students' responses to the simulation lead him to highlight the shortcomings of "the tragedy" and also to comment on how people use simple models to address ecological and social complexity. In a second section he describes extensions appropriate for more advanced undergraduate and graduate classes. In the final section, he spells out his vision of critical thinking and the productive role for ambiguity. If you'd like to know in advance where Taylor is taking you, and why, turn this chapter on its head and read the final section first. If you just let the ideas emerge as the chapter unfolds, though, your experience will more closely approximate the one he intends for his students.—M.M.

G arrett Hardin's (1968) idea of the tragedy of the commons (the "tragedy") is widely invoked in discussions of conservation and natural resource management. In a hypothetical common pasture, each herder in the community follows the same logic: "I will receive the benefit in the short run from increasing my herd by one animal; everyone will share any eventual cost of diminished pasture per animal; therefore I will add another animal to my herd." Overstocking and pasture degradation thus become inevitable. The same model has been applied to explain the degradation of a range of environmental and social resources, from the atmosphere to library books (Berkes et al. 1989).

RESPONDING TO A SIMULATION OF THE TRAGEDY OF THE COMMONS

Like many teachers of environmental politics, I use a classroom simulation to introduce students to the tragedy.[1] I ask students to act as herders who are each given the same amount of cash and number of cattle. Each year, they have an opportunity to buy cows to add to their herd, and they receive income from the sale of milk and excess calves. I sum up everyone's purchases and calculate the income per cow everyone earns during the year from milk and calves. In the formula I use for this calculation, the income declines once the combined herd on the common pasture exceeds some threshold and the pasture becomes overgrazed. I inform the herders of the per cow income and they do the arithmetic to update their tally of their own individual herd size and cash. The only other stipulation is that on my own I make no more rules. Herders have to decide whether they want additional rules and how to get them implemented in their community.[2]

Before reading further, ask yourself what purchasing strategy you would use if participating in this simulation and what rules you would try to get implemented. Try this even if you are familiar with the idea of the tragedy. To encourage you to stop for a few minutes and complete this task, let me break the text here with a photo of actual herders who use a common rangeland in the West African country of Mali.

Young Herders in Mali. Photo by Matthew Turner.

OK reader-herders—what did you come up with? Would you promote private ownership of the land so that individual herders factor the full costs into their decisions? Would your remedy be external government control to "restrain people who find it irrational to restrain themselves" (McCay 1992: 189)? These were Hardin's solutions. He claimed that unless resources are privatized or there is government coercion, individual self-interest leads inevitably to overexploitation and resource degradation. In contrast to Hardin, some of you might have proposed taking turns to use the pasture, with the length of each herder's stint determined by someone appointed by the community to monitor the pasture. To this, you might have added sanctions against "overstinting" to be enforced by the community as a whole or their authorized representatives. Such a strategy is in line with a growing body of research that has been examining the management of actual nonprivatized common resources. This literature now documents many cases in which people, communicating and working together in communities, successfully maintain local institutions for managing a resource held in common (e.g., Berkes et al. 1989; Ostrom 1990).

I simulate the tragedy in my courses to alert my students to this literature and to the general weaknesses of Hardin's model. However, in ways described in this chapter, my students and I also work through two nonstandard lessons from the simulation: we explore and discuss fundamental shortcomings of the tragedy model, and we more generally examine how people use models to analyze ecological and social complexity.

These two nonstandard lessons point to a set of skills necessary for participating critically and creatively in debates about environmental, social, and scientific change.

Four Conventional Levels

Recall my stipulation that my student-herders have to work out for themselves whether they want additional rules and how to get them implemented in their community. As the simulation progresses, students begin to express objections, and some attempt to mobilize fellow herders into adding or changing the rules. Usually the responses do not gel in time to prevent dire overgrazing and the herders' annual income drops almost to zero. I then call time out to review what has happened. First, we observe the group's combined income is much less than it was at an earlier point in the simulation. Moreover, the initial equality among herders has given way to large disparities in wealth—the group has differentiated. I ask students to keep these observations in mind as we continue the simulation and negotiate what to do. In the lively discussions that ensue, certain voices count more than others. Herders who have the largest herds and greatest wealth can use their resources to exert disproportionate influence not only on what propositions are accepted but also on the procedures for making decisions. Students who had purchased few or no cattle—usually because they did not want to contribute to overgrazing—are poor and less influential.

The changes my students seek during the simulation fall typically across four levels. As you read, notice where your own response to the simulation fits. My students:

1. Want more realism or detail in the rules—to allow cattle to die, purchase prices to vary, herders to trade among themselves, income to vary with season, and so on. They seek such changes even though they do not prevent overgrazing.
2. Communicate about their actions, plans, and norms (e.g., "greedy herders should be shunned").
3. Allow exchanges with the outside world. For example, the simulation assumes that cattle can be bought from some unspecified place and that milk and calves can be sold. Cattle themselves, then, could be sold in this outside market. Some students even propose to leave the game to become agriculturalists, traders, or urban workers.
4. Get involved in conflicts and negotiation among unequal parties, that is, in the politics of collective governance. Common proposals include halving every herd, setting a common upper limit on all herds, taxing large herds, and privatizing pasture. Instituting any

proposal, however, turns out to be more difficult. The poor, conservationist-minded herders see the halving proposal as unfair to them, while the wealthy herders tend to use their muscle to resist proposals that level the playing field. If land is privatized, for example, the wealthy want it to be subdivided in proportion to current unequal herd sizes. Many students, when faced with the stratification of wealth and influence, want to begin again from the conditions of equality, which I disallow. After all, a state of equality exists nowhere in the known world. Some students then invoke an outside government (as in level 3) with power to impose such changes over the objections of the wealthy herders. Some of the wealthy herders are confident they can get the government to do their bidding.

Through their responses, my students communicate with each other, make exchanges with the outside world, and negotiate conflict and cooperation among unequal parties. Broadly speaking, these are the coping responses highlighted by post-Hardin research on actual common resources. The class simulation could stop there and focus on the lessons of this research.[3] My students and I push on, however, in order to explore the meaning attached to simple models, such as the tragedy, and to model making in the practice of science.

Two Nonstandard Alternatives

At first glance, the progression of students' responses (from 1 through 4) matches the standard interpretation for how we use models: start simple and improve by incorporating more factors. In this light, the tragedy is an ideal model, one to be built upon. Reality differs from it in details or in more significant ways. One learns about reality by starting with it, then comparing it with observations, adding postulates, and progressively improving it. Activists might see it in an equivalent way: The simple model draws attention to a problem—degradation of resources held in common—and stimulates people to get involved. And through such involvement, they learn more about the complicating details and build experience in implementing policy. Let me, however, contrast this seemingly straightforward progression—from simple to more complex accounts—with two nonstandard alternative views about the way the simple tragedy model shapes people's understanding of environmental politics.

Alternative View 1

This view questions systems: natural units that have clearly defined boundaries and coherent, internally driven dynamics. Examples of what some people think of as systems include lake ecosystems, the earth's climate, national economies, and resources subject to the tragedy. This organizing idea of systems, as applied to environmental problems and ecological complexity, can be usefully challenged and reinterpreted in ways that correspond to the four levels at which students sought change during the class simulation:

1. Instead of viewing a system as composed of individuals who will interact in ways given at the outset, consider the nature of their interactions to be changing and mutable.
2. Examine the rich network of social relationships in which people are embedded, instead of viewing individuals as the basic building blocks. For instance, instead of Hardin's atomized individuals, think about the networks of social support in which people are raised and in which they then operate as adults. These networks make communication—even through people's silence—unavoidable. The withdrawal of social connections within such networks becomes an effective sanction.
3. Consider the permeability of any boundaries that are drawn.
4. Analyze the paths that individuals can pursue, including their responses to developments outside the system, in terms of the interactions among unequal individuals subject to further differentiation as a result of economic, social, and political dynamics.

Notice that student responses in the tragedy simulation underscore the importance of reflecting on levels 3 and 4. My students, perhaps like you or yours, tend to maintain the distinction between inside and outside, in that they assume the existence of some outside governing power to which they can appeal to implement policies against overgrazing. What happens, however, to the government policies they propose? Conservationist measures and votes of equal weight tend to be resisted by wealthy herders. The wealthy may accept moves to privatize the commons but usually not until land allocation is proportional to current herd sizes, which gives the wealthy more land. In other words, potential outside governance is refracted through internal features—especially inequality—of the herding system. Attention to inequality and dynamics that cross boundaries can lead to a rather different perspective on the reasons underlying the degradation of the commons and what can be done about it. This lesson comes through even more strongly after students promoting external governance as a solution are prevented from returning to the pregame equality.[4]

Some readers might accept that environmental change involves unequal and changing political dynamics but still want to maintain the standard interpretation of the use of models in science and politics. They might construe the steps from one level to the next (1 > 2 > 3 > 4), through which the system of equivalent units is broken open to expose more complex dynamics, as an instance of the process in which the simple model is progressively improved upon. Read that way, simple models remain a valuable, perhaps even necessary first step for scientific inquiry or for formulating policy or action proposals. This is where the second alternative to standard interpretations comes into play, one that does not allow the use of simple models to be so simply rationalized.

Alternative View 2

Instead of thinking about models as representing aspects of the world— sometimes approximately, sometimes more faithfully—we can consider them as devices for rhetorical effect. Rhetoric refers to ways that an audience is influenced by the framing of a case as much as by its substance.[5] To expose the rhetorical effects of science means not to accept literally what scientists say they are doing, namely, proposing simple models as first approximations to reality, but instead to consider how these models themselves frame issues and channel thinking. The rhetorical effects of the tragedy, and of the post-Hardin research that challenges it, include the following:

- *Simpling:* Sometimes sweeping claims are first made for the general applicability of some simple model, but then postulates are successively added to address the discrepancy between the model and observations. This can be interpreted as "simpling":

  > Like sampling, "simpling" is a technique for reducing the complexity of reality to manageable size. Unlike sampling, simpling does not keep in view the relation between its own scope and the scope of the reality with which it deals. . . . *It then secures a sense of progress by progressively readmitting what it has first denied.* "Simpling" . . . is unfortunately easily confused with genuine simplification by valid generalization. (Hymes 1974: 18; emphasis added)[6]

- *Reinforcing foundational assumptions:* In Hardin's presentation of the tragedy, as in most of neoclassical economics, selfishness is seen as a fundamental characteristic of humans, and this determines the dynamics of the system. The tragedy then becomes a result of the "immutable logic of self-interest" (Picardi and Seifert 1976). The belief that the ideal dynamics of the simple model are fundamental or foundational tends to be reinforced by the process of tinkering with the model to produce numerous variants for different situations (see simpling above). Moreover, the idea that self-interest is human nature is reflected in the very name "tragedy," which classically was something bad that happens to mortals despite their best intentions; it took the gods to prevent it. Ironically, many of Hardin's opponents reinforce this view of human nature when they argue that use of non-privately held resources can be governed satisfactorily, provided appropriate social sanctions or regulations are in place to counteract individual selfishness (Berkes et al. 1989).

- *Privileging the powerful:* The categories and relations in the model of the tragedy of the commons can be seen as favoring certain political positions and processes. In the actual world, privatization often cements the current claims of unequal individuals. To speak of common resources in terms of the tragedy, *which imagines interactions among equal individuals,* is to distract attention from the special interests of those with greater claims. The tragedy model thus makes it easier for powerful interests to get their way, a result evident in the concessions made in the early 1990s to secure the United States' ratification of the Law of the Sea. The concessions ensured that existing seabed claims of U.S. corporations could not be reallocated to the world community (Broad 1994).

- *Rendering the special typical:* When illustrating problems of managing resources held in common, critics of Hardin's model tend to focus on special situations, such as those in which the resource and its users are somewhat autonomous from the influence of the government, markets, or industries (Ostrom 1990). With the accumulation of studies of such situations, however, they no longer appear special but are employed to support more general claims. Inquiry that seeks, instead, to define how the situations arise, as special cases of more general processes, goes to the back burner.

Let me summarize the contrasts between standard interpretations and the two alternatives. Conventional strategies in science give priority—in method, theoretical development, and aesthetics—to simple principles that are held to lie behind complex appearances. But new thinking can be opened up when we consider the complexity lying behind models that merely appear simple. Hardin and others analyze environmental resources as simple, coherent systems, but we can ask how the analysis would differ if these resource systems were viewed as changing and mutable, infused with richly complex social relationships, and characterized by permeable boundaries and social inequality. Analyses that skirt these issues represent themselves as accounts of reality, but we can ask whether special circumstances have been selected for study, we should examine the rhetorical effect of the analysis, and we should be particularly sensitive to worldviews and political positions the models favor.

FROM SIMULATION TO RESEARCH

The two alternatives open up lines of inquiry not well addressed by the post-Hardin research mentioned earlier. Although institutions of collective governance are emphasized in that research, less attention is given to the significance of inequality, permeable boundaries, and the processes whereby institutions of collective governance arise and evolve. Interpretation of ways that the social context shapes research and debates about common resources is also underdeveloped (but see Peters 1987 and Agrawal 1998). I believe that the two nonstandard alternatives are important to explore with students who intend to undertake socioenvironmental research. Thus, when I lead seminars with advanced undergraduates or graduate students in disciplines such as geography, anthropology, and development sociology, I follow the simulation class with further discussion of commons research.[7] Let me review the kinds of material I introduce that amplify the contrasts and lessons that emerge from the simulation.

Pastoralism Embedded in Intersecting Processes

Although Hardin illustrated his thesis with a scenario of herding on a common pasture, his example was purely hypothetical—no actual or historical cases were given. However, over the last twenty-five years, the ecology and economics of nomadic pastoralists have been intensively studied. (Nomadic pastoralists are herders who live in semiarid climates—where rainfall is variable, unpredictable, and spatially patchy—and who spend at least part of their year roaming in search of patches of watered pasture. See Galaty and Johnson's 1990 volume.) This research began with an environmental determinist outlook. Range degradation and desertification were attributed to pastoralists allowing grazing beyond the environment's supposed carrying capacity. Simple models at that time reduced nomadic pastoralism to a plant-herbivore system, or an instance of the tragedy of the commons (Taylor and García Barrios 1995). Policy embodied that picture: for a decade in the 1970s and early 1980s, the goal of development projects was to produce fundamental changes in pastoral practices, through, for example, privatization of pasture, stock reduction, and large-scale ranching schemes. These projects generally failed; the increased research effort that came with the international attention led belatedly to the perspective that herders respond skillfully and sensitively to their variable and uncertain semiarid environments, provided that herders can remain mobile, maintain species diversity in their herds, and apply their local ethnosciences of range management (McCabe and Ellis 1987; Horowitz and Little 1987).

An alternative picture of the sources of environmental degradation focuses not on the deficiencies or selfishness of individual pastoralists but rather on ongoing transformations of the economies and ecologies of nomadic pastoralist groups. This picture highlights historical forces—taxation, establishment of military control, imposition of borders, and other aspects of colonial and postcolonial administration—and more contemporary processes, such as severe droughts, extension of agricultural areas, privatization of access to resources, regulation of conflict over resources, sedentarization, development projects sponsored by national governments and international agencies, and the changing economic conditions and terms of trade accompanying "structural adjustment" (Taylor and García Barrios 1995).[8]

Some pastoralist societies have been rapidly restructuring with their boundaries becoming permeable. Wealthy pastoralists break their reciprocal relations with agriculturalists to become cultivators themselves; agriculturalists become absentee herd owners; and the poorer peasants and herders become their hired laborers. Squeezed for time to take their herds out on the range, these herder-laborers allow their livestock to overgraze areas close to their settlements, not—in contrast to Hardin's picture—out on the common grazed rangeland (Little 1988).

Simple models, like Hardin's tragedy of the commons, imply clearly defined boundaries and coherent dynamics based on interactions within a consistently operating system. The emerging picture of nomadic pastoralism challenges these assumptions and instead emphasizes that:

- Prevailing structures and behaviors are mutable and changing. Nomadic pastoralism has, for example, been combined with and constrained by agricultural activities in recent years (recall aspect 1 of alternative view 1).
- Conceptual and material boundaries are permeable. Pastoralists are new agriculturalists; herders are also selling their labor; climatic forces interact with economic forces to produce resource degradation. Likewise, levels and scale of analysis are not so easily separable; local, national, and international processes all enter the dynamics of the pastoral situation (recall aspects 2, 3, and 4).
- Broad policy initiatives and the analytic generalizations upon which they rest are difficult to justify. For example, there may be widespread degradation of common property resources; however, if such degradation is understood to be the result of a complex and unequal politics rooted in local conditions, rather than the inevitable result of some fundamental, apolitical dynamic, then general policy recommendations are not warranted (Peters 1987; Berkes et al. 1989; McCay and Jentoft 1998) (recall aspects 2 and 4).

The idea of *intersecting processes* summarizes this whole picture. That is, social and environmental change can be analyzed as something produced by the intersection of economic, social, and ecological processes operating at different scales. These processes transgress boundaries and restructure internal dynamics, thus ensuring that socioenvironmental situations do not have clearly defined boundaries and are not simply governed by coherent, internally driven dynamics (Taylor and García Barrios 1995).

An intersecting processes picture raises interesting questions about pastoralism viewed as a system. Suppose, say, socioenvironmental researchers found pastoralist societies isolated from external social currents. These bounded systems could be viewed not as the natural situation of pastoralism but as special cases. The researchers might then examine how these societies closed themselves off, possibly in response to pressures to become involved with agriculture and incorporated into wider currents (Wolf 1957; Wolf 1982: 385–91; Smith 1984). Similarly, if researchers found a situation in which social stratification was lacking, they might ask how the socioenvironmental dynamics had leveled previous inequalities.

If we go further and apply rhetorical analysis (alternative view 2) as well, we might look into who chooses to study and document these societies. For example, human ecologists and biological anthropologists whose interests centered on the adaptation of human societies to their environment established their research project in a remote area of Kenya (Little et al. 1990)—far from the turbulence and intersecting processes of many other districts in Kenya (Little 1988). Their choices make well-defined pastoral systems a special case, not an ideal type from which other cases depart.

How the Tragedy Becomes Accepted as Common(s) Knowledge

The questions raised about the tragedy thesis—conceptually, empirically, and as applied in policy—might constitute sufficient grounds for giving that simple model no more attention. Indeed, some socioenvironmental scientists have left it behind by conducting detailed, regionally specific empirical studies, in which the particular historical contexts are given greater weight (Turner 1993; Peet and Watts 1996). Instead of simply turning our backs on Hardin's model, though, we should seek reasons for its persistent appeal. (Responding to the tragedy in this way follows from my earlier discussion about how models work rhetorically to secure support.) If we can interpret the tragedy's appeal in relation to the social context in which knowledge becomes established and applied, additional ways to challenge the continued use of the model should emerge.

Consider the idea that pastoralists living in more or less isolated systems are special cases, which invites us to examine either the history by which they became closed off from the wider world or the sociology of the scientific field that chose to focus on them. The tragedy, which assumes a system of equivalent users of a common resource, can no longer be viewed simply as a first approximation to a more complex theory of common, nonprivatized resources, nor even a crude first approximation. Indeed it may serve as a *diversion* from developing such a theory. This possibility invites us to examine whether certain politics are built into the categories and relations in the model. That is, we can try to interpret science as socially shaped not only in its sources of funding, the day-to-day practices of scientists, or its applications but even in the heart of its conceptual formulations. The following broad brush illustration should help to make such an interpretation plausible.

The assumption of equal, undifferentiated individuals is central to the tragedy. With this assumption, the model's dynamics permit only a limited range of options. Hardin explicitly advocates two: privatization of the resource and "mutually agreed coercion." Mutually agreed coercion raises the specter of communism and fascism—recall that Hardin first wrote about the commons in the 1960s—and has not been widely invoked in discussions of the commons. The other three options that the model allows are also readily discounted: Individuals can leave the system, but this cannot be a solution for every case; individuals can all abandon their desire to accumulate in favor of conservation, but this is never presented as very likely; individuals can drive the system to the inevitable degradation awaiting all nonprivatized resources. In short, of the five options, privatization is clearly the privileged one. This message stands, even when the actual record of development efforts casts doubt on the effectiveness of that policy. More generally, negotiations and contestations among groups with different interests, wealth, and power—the messy stuff of most politics—are kept out of the picture. The tragedy thus naturalizes the liberalized economics of structural adjustment and obscures the politics through which structural adjustment is imposed and implemented in poor, indebted countries.

This strategy of appearing to bypass politics, one common to environmental politics, invites interpretation. The strategy brings two positions to center stage: the enlightened guide, who can instruct us how we—an undifferentiated *we*—must change to avoid the impending crisis; and the technocrat, whose analysis shows all of us the scientifically justified or most efficient measures, to which it would be in our best interest to submit.[9] Moralistic views of social action are particularly comfortable for those who imagine themselves as the guides or educators; technocratic views befit planners or policy advisers. These roles do not require long-term and necessarily partisan engagement in specific situations. They especially suit natural scientists who can employ their status and skills without retooling in political economic analysis.

This rhetorical exclusion of politics has a broader appeal to people in affluent countries. In those countries, atomized consumers find it difficult to build institutions that would ensure that private, corporate, or military property holders bear the full environmental costs of their activities. Concerned consumer-citizens have reason then to be anxious about their capacity to unite and organize with the goal of influencing corporate and military decision making. In this light, the attention given to irrationality of nonprivatized resources in poor countries can be interpreted ironically, as a displacement from unspoken issues closer to home (Haraway 1989)—issues other than what the tragic commons is *literally* about.

Turning the Tables on Oneself

An extra layer of complexity in rhetorical interpretation arises if we consider the simplifications I have been making here. My interpretations of the tragedy as rhetoric—naturalizing structural adjustment, bypassing the politics of inequality, and displacing concerns close at hand to some distant, different people—are, of course, overgeneralizations. Instead of accepting my interpretations, it would be best to view them as another example of a rhetorical strategy to frame our view of the world. In this light, my claims serve to reinforce the idea that the tragedy can be interpreted, that is, it does not have to be taken literally as a scientific account of the commons.

My critique of systems thinking in alternative view 1 raises additional questions about my interpretations of rhetoric and framing. They would seem to suggest that the social status, politics, and social location of scientists determine their preferences for some kinds of social action and politics over others and that this in turn can influence their scientific analyses—my argument that the tragedy of the commons view persists because it reinforces a moral and technocratic view common to many scientific experts is a case in point. Nevertheless, interpreters of science would do well to be skeptical of such direct determinations and instead attend to the particular details of researchers' different situations and how researchers draw upon multiple resources to make their science. More specific interpretations would illuminate the ways that actual peoples' actions and the views of social action or politics they favor are built into, facilitated by, and co-constructed with their accounts of the real world (Taylor 1995).

This chapter has not, however, teased out the complexity of any particular situation in which research is or was undertaken.[10] So I admit some rhetorical excess in baldly connecting analyses that imagine everyone as equal on the commons with a kind of moralistic and technocratic politics that exalts the expert or moral guide. Nevertheless, let me affirm the value of teaching such interpretations, for they remind us that theories such as the tragedy—and policies based upon those theories—should not be assumed to stand or fall on their empirical merits as accounts of reality. And they suggest that science has effects on society other than through revealing the nature of the world.

To acknowledge these political, rhetorical dimensions of science is, however, to open up a further challenge. Suppose the work of certain scientists is tied up with simpling, reinforcing foundational assumptions, and so on. This means that the scientists will probably not change the way they make science about complex situations simply because other scientists or interpreters of science raise objections to systems views. They might not change even if my alternative view 1 draws their attention to accounts that are more faithful to the complexity of socioenvironmental situations. The challenge then—one that corresponds to a tension between writing and reading critical chapters like this one, and actively engaging the world—is for critical scientists and commentators on science not only to interpret but also to get involved in mobilizing different resources to reshape how research is undertaken.

TEACHING CRITICAL THINKING ABOUT ENVIRONMENT, SCIENCE, AND SOCIETY

Student engagement is key to my approach to teaching. Personally, I favor the two nonstandard alternatives described above, but I do not dictate those positions. Instead, I use activities, such as the extended tragedy simulation, so that students participate in discovering such alternatives themselves. When I summarize what transpired in the terms described in this chapter, I hope to provide themes for their ongoing questioning in more advanced classes or in other contexts.

This chapter cannot, of course, replicate the full experience of interactions in a class simulation or seminar discussions. As an attempt to compensate, let me articulate my overall pedagogical approach to teaching critical thinking about environment, science, and society. This is directed more at teachers of environmental politics than students, but students should not stop reading—what follows will help you better appreciate the path this chapter has described.

In a sense subscribed to by all teachers, critical thinking means that students are bright and engaged, ask questions, and think about the course materials until they understand well-established knowledge and competing approaches. This becomes more significant when students develop their own processes of active inquiry that they can employ in new situations beyond the bounds of our particular classes, indeed, beyond their time as students. My sense of critical thinking is, however, more specific; it depends on inquiry being informed by a strong sense of how things could be otherwise. I want students to see that they understand things better when they have placed established facts, theories, and practices *in tension with alternatives*.[11] Critical thinking at this level should not depend on students rejecting conventional accounts, but they do have to move through uncertainty. Their knowledge is, at least for a time, destabilized; what has been established cannot be taken for granted. Students can no longer expect that if they just wait long enough the teacher will provide complete and tidy conclusions; instead, they have to take a great deal of responsibility for their own learning. Anxieties inevitably arise for students when they have to respond to new situations knowing that the teacher will not act as the final arbiter of their success. A high level of critical thinking is possible when students explore such anxieties and gain the confidence to face uncertainty and ambiguity (Taylor 2001).

My research and teaching connects environmental studies and studies of science and technology in their social context. Over the last decade, I have had the opportunity to focus my teaching on critical thinking. Unlike many others teaching environmental studies, I have not felt the pressure to cover all the facts, issues, or established analyses that students must know. The challenges are somewhat different. An emphasis on critical thinking implies, even in large classes, an individualized model of teacher-student interaction, and students' corresponding raised expectations are difficult to fulfill. Their responses are sometimes emotionally intense, especially in the case of science students, which makes sense when we recall that their success in science has depended on learning what others already have discovered and systematized. This has forced me to—in much the same spirit that I expect my students to take more responsibility for their learning—experiment, take risks, and through experience build up a set of tools that work for me. In recent years, I have made more time to learn from others about writing through the curriculum, designing opportunities for cooperative, experiential, and project-based learning, and fostering students' different learning preferences.

A final question left open by this chapter concerns the productive role of ambiguity for critical thinking. I mentioned that anxieties inevitably arise for students when they have to respond to new situations, knowing that the teacher will not act as the final arbiter of their success. I claimed, moreover, that a high level of critical thinking is possible when students explore such anxieties and gain the confidence to face uncertainty and ambiguity. Yet, because a certain level of confidence is needed to deal with ambiguity, I also realize the importance of presenting some propositions in which students can be confident. A sense of ambiguity is generated when during the class simulation I disallow students' appeals to me to make or clarify rules and thus withdraw from the role they expect of a teacher. I rein in the ambiguity, however, when I follow the simulation with a presentation of the classification of the four levels in their responses, draw out the lessons, and summarize them in terms of two alternatives.

A similar tension is present overall in this chapter. Its relevance was not supposed to be limited to science and policy about the commons. In environmental politics courses and in socioenvironmental research, I think it is important to examine ways that simple models frame our thinking, giving priority to simple principles about individuals over differentiated and complex social dynamics, and favoring powerful interests over others. But I have not demonstrated that nonstandard lessons apply beyond the case of the commons. I can only hope that readers—students and teachers alike—have been stimulated to experiment, take risks, and through experience weave my approach into their set of tools for working in other areas of science and environmental politics. I suspect that, if I had presented a fully developed analysis of a particular concrete case, readers interested in some other area of the world, the environment, or politics would have skipped the chapter. Yet I know that reading such a case would have made some readers more confident about whether and how to employ the nonstandard alternatives this chapter has introduced. I have to admit that a tension between opening up questions and establishing confidence in answers continues to run through my work (Taylor 2002). So, before reading further, ask yourself what changes you would seek in order to foster critical thinking about environmental politics.[12]

QUESTIONS FOR REFLECTION
AND DISCUSSION

1. This chapter assumes that "tragedy of the commons" thinking is common to college courses in environmental studies and global environmental politics. Has this been your experience, as a teacher or as a student? If so, why do you think this is so? And, if not, why has your experience been rather different from what appears to be the norm?

2. Some invoke the "tragedy of the commons" to refer generally to the degradation of resources held in common due to any number of possible reasons. Others, like Taylor, use the term more narrowly to refer to a conceptual model that attributes this degradation to the selfish behavior of equal, noncommunicating individuals. What are

the consequences of these contrasting interpretations of Hardin's work?

3. When Taylor simulates the tragedy in his classroom, "the responses," he says, "usually do not gel in time to prevent dire overgrazing." Doesn't his own experience with students show that the tragedy is real and that much of his critique of Hardin's model is ill founded?

4. The idea of equal, undifferentiated actors is central to the idea of the tragedy of the commons. Perhaps a major message to take from Taylor's chapter, then, is how easy it has become when exploring environmental politics to assume the existence of broad equality and invoke the undifferentiated "we" when talking about the cause and cure of environmental ills. (This despite Conca's claim in the prior chapter that his students quickly come to understand the importance of inequality to any analysis of global environmental politics.) In their discussion of the 1992 Earth Summit in Brazil, Pratap Chatterjee and Matthias Finger (1994) suggest that the ubiquitous use of "we" ("we are responsible for environmental problems," "we must pull together to solve them," "if we weren't all so selfish and short-sighted, we wouldn't be in this environmental mess") is the result of careful political rhetoric and concept shaping by actors who benefit from the spreading around of blame and responsibility. Why, when it comes to talking about environmental problems, is it so easy to fall into this "we" trap? How, do you think, would Taylor answer this question?

5. Simple models, says Taylor, can be more political then they first appear: simpling, reinforcing foundational assumptions, privileging the powerful, and rendering the special typical are four ways in which they can subjectively elevate some interests over others. Think about other simple models common to the college classroom—the model of the perfectly competitive free market, for example, or that of pluralist politics in which the ability of groups to organize and defend their interests is thought to drive policy, or the "billiard ball" model of independent sovereign states described in the last chapter. In what ways does Taylor's analysis apply to these simple models of social organization?

6. Why might it be that the scientific community has been so slow to grasp the complexities and dynamics (the "nonsystemness," in other words) of actual life on grazing lands held in common?

7. Imagine yourself in an introductory course in which the professor has just presented the tragedy of the commons as an indelible truth of human social organization. What two or three questions would

you politely raise to spur a heightened degree of skepticism on his part, and on the part of your fellow students?

8. Critical thinking is becoming a buzz word these days: everyone uses it and often means something different in the process. By describing his classroom work with the tragedy and the importance he places on presenting alternatives in tension with one another, Taylor seeks to bring some concreteness to the term. How does his view of critical thinking compare to your own or to others that you have encountered?

NOTES

1. See, for example, Holle and Knell 1996, or Mitchell 1997—each offers a tragedy of the commons simulation. Classroom activities that illustrate Hardin's conclusions also are described in Bybee 1984, Meadows and van der Waals n.d., and Wheeler 1995. See also the "Report on Course Exercises" at the main Web page of the Project on Teaching Global Environmental Politics, webpub.alleg.edu/employee/m/maniate/GepEd/geped.html.

2. For simplicity of making calculations while running the class, I set the threshold at a total herd size of 100 cows. Below this threshold, the income per cow per year is $100 and above it the income is $200 minus total herd size, that is, a drop of $1 for each additional cow. I do not inform herders of the threshold or the formula used to calculate the income; they make their own sense of the trend. If the class has N members, I set the initial number of cows per person at about 80/N. I set this figure as the maximum number of cows a herder can purchase in any one yearly cycle and, multiplied by $100, set this as the initial cash per person. That is, if N = 20, herders begin with 4 cows and $400 each. The buying price per cow I set at $100. Herders indicate purchases on pieces of paper. I add these up as I collect them and then update the total herd size and income per cow on the board. Herders then update their accounts and decide on the next year's purchases.

3. The standard post-Hardin lesson is that agents communicating and working together in communities can overcome their short-term self-interest and maintain local institutions for managing a resource held in common. Successful institutions are operated by those directly concerned with the resource and are "externally accepted," that is, the government, markets, or industries tolerate or even support the community of users' jurisdiction over the resource (Berkes et al. 1989; Ostrom 1990). I intend to extend the simulation in the direction of these post-Hardin lessons. After arriving at the situation of unequal assets and overstocking, my idea would be not to continue negotiations as a whole class but to break up into groups of three—each including a well-off, a poor, and an in-between person. I would give each group a different scenario (e.g., nomadic pastoralists, Western U.S. cattle graziers, New England fishing people) and ask them to attempt to come up with a mutually acceptable arrangement in their particular situation. After a while, I would ask them to respond to a little devil who whis-

pered in their ear: "Add another cow to your herd or pull in another fish—you'll get all the benefit and any cost will be shared by all." (I suspect that the responses will be more qualified and contingent than Hardin implies.) The simulation would end with reports back to the whole class on (1) the group's negotiations and outcomes and (2) different individuals' responses to the little devil.

4. The four aspects of alternative view 1 could also be used to open up questions about simple models of systems other than the tragedy. For example, in more general complex situations, in biology as well as in society, instead of viewing the properties of units as fundamental, they could be viewed as contingent on the units' embeddedness in their context.

5. See Dabelko and Matthew's chapter 7 in this volume for more on the political significance of framing.

6. Hymes, a sociolinguist, invented the term to describe the way Chomskyan linguistics gradually reconsidered the meaning of expressions after having first stripped the idea of language down to its underlying "generative" grammar. The term is, however, apt in this context as well.

7. Analogous conceptual tensions are worth exploring in ecology proper, conservation biology, and studies of science and technology in their social context (Taylor 2002).

8. Structural adjustment refers to the effects of conditions attached by international lending agencies on loans granted to poor countries, often to cover interest from previous loans, that require measures such as reduction in government spending on domestic services and infrastructure, devaluation of currency to make exports cheaper and imports more expensive, openness to foreign investment, and elimination of programs to stimulate or favor domestically owned businesses. Green (1995) provides an accessible overview of the neoliberal economic theory underlying structural adjustment.

9. These positions are dominant in environmental discourse more generally; see Taylor and García Barrios (1995).

10. My expository choices invite interpretation using the very framework I have presented. See Taylor (1995; 2002) for extended and more reflexive accounts of the social construction of models.

11. The image I often use is of a spring, with a standard view and an alternative at its two ends. When the spring is stretched it pulls back; when compressed it pushes out. That is, the standard view cannot be considered without taking the alternative into consideration, and vice versa. Nor can the two of them be collapsed into one concept. I also use the term "critical heuristic." By heuristic I mean a proposition that stimulates, orients, or guides our inquiries, yet breaks down when applied too widely. Critical heuristics are ones that place established facts, theories, and practices in tension with alternatives. For example: "There will be a qualitative change in the analysis of causes and the implications of the analysis if an emphasis on short-term interest is replaced by a focus on institutions of collective governance." The alternatives in this chapter can be rephrased in this way as critical heuristics.

12. In this chapter I have reworked Taylor (1998) so as to explore its implications for teaching critical thinking. I acknowledge the comments of Yaakov Garb, Michael Maniates, the Changing Life working group, and an anonymous reviewer.

7

❂

The Last Pocket of Resistance
Environment and Security
in the Classroom

Geoffrey Dabelko and Richard Matthew

Dabelko and Matthew, one a policy analyst in Washington, D.C., the other a university professor in California, argue that our teaching and learning about global environmental problems suffer from the absence of careful focus on "environmental security." Their chapter raises some tough questions. Why, for instance, do instructors systematically downplay ideas of environmental security in their classrooms? How might the study of environmental security open doors to new insight into global struggle to resolve environmental ills? To what degree do crosscutting currents in the environmental security literature offer untapped opportunities for interesting student projects and insightful classroom discussion? And what do we ultimately gain—as professors looking to make our classes hum and as students struggling to understand the field and prepare ourselves for careers—from integrating environmental security into the lexicon of the environmental studies classroom?

One's initial reaction to this chapter might understandably be "oh no, not another topic that I need to cram into my teaching (or study) of global environmental issues." It would be a mistake, though, to let first reactions prevail. There are good reasons to believe that environmental security will become a key organizing concept in the study of global environmental politics—though just how the term will be finally defined, and who will win and who will lose as a result, remains to be seen. By pushing us to think hard about both the politics of language and the evolution of defining concepts, Dabelko and Matthew lay the groundwork for active classroom discussion and debate about what we mean by security, how the conceptual categories that govern the classroom can constrain or expand our ability to shape the future, and ultimately what's at stake.—M.M.

Since the end of the Cold War, the national security implications of environmental change have received considerable scholarly attention and have contributed significantly to the framing of policy, especially in the United States. Yet these same implications have been largely ignored in college courses that explore the cause and cure of global environmental ills. This is unfortunate and almost certainly unwise, for today's college students may well discover that some of the greatest threats to their long-term well-being—to their security, in other words—emanate from the negative, often unanticipated consequences of environmental change.[1] The time has come to incorporate, with both care and zeal, a security perspective into the study of global environmental problems.

Some may argue that the college curriculum in environmental studies is already too crowded and diverse and that college courses in global environmental politics struggle in particular to cover too much material too quickly.[2] Why increase the burden by adding a security perspective to the mix? This is a good question, one deserving of careful consideration by students and instructors alike. In making our case for a security perspective, we thus seek to provoke and inspire discussion among students, and between students and their instructor, about exactly why and how this perspective might deserve a place at their classroom table. We think it exceedingly important (for reasons that will soon become apparent) that college students and their instructors begin talking about what we mean by environmental security and how the term can best be employed in scholarly and policy debate. If such conversation remains muted in the classroom, it will continue to flounder in the body politic, to potentially great cost to us all.

To ensure that all our readers share a basic familiarity with our field, we begin by explaining how environmental factors have always been relevant to human security, despite the fact that security specialists generally refused to acknowledge this relevance through much of the twentieth century. We then highlight misperceptions about the linkages between environment and security—and we point out several reasons instructors and their students would profit from more fully exploring these connections. To demonstrate the fluidity of the concept of environmental security and to underscore the current struggle taking shape to define and apply the concept, we then turn to a review of the literature of the field and its critics. We end with a survey of emerging policy implications of environmental security, an explanation for why we believe citizens must come to understand these implications, and a discussion of teaching and research resources. Our aim throughout is to lay the groundwork for in-class discussion of why we teach and study what we do, and what risks we run by living with the commonly accepted set of current curricular choices.

SECURITY AND ENVIRONMENT?

Human history over the past 100,000 years is the story of a constant struggle to survive and flourish in the face of diverse and unrelenting environmental challenges. Climate change, natural disasters, epidemic disease, food shortages, and resource scarcities (not to mention large predators) have taken a heavy toll on the human species. But these challenges also have inspired humans to adapt to new circumstances and develop language skills, complex societies, and a vast array of technologies designed to reduce nature-based insecurities.

As human society progressed and as technological innovation appeared to bring nature under control, people focused less on threats from the environment and more on the threats they posed to one another. When the study of security was institutionalized in our system of higher education half a century ago, human technological mastery over the forces of nature seemed so assured that the environment was not considered sufficiently threatening to be the subject of serious research and teaching.

This exclusion was powerfully reinforced by an unusual set of circumstances in the middle of the twentieth century. Two world wars, the invention of weapons of mass destruction, and the rivalry of two ideologically opposed superpowers convinced the vast majority of observers that the principle security threat facing humankind was the possibility of nuclear Armageddon. The public seemed to agree. From "duck and cover" drills and personal fallout shelters of the 1950s and 1960s, to the spate of nuclear annihilation movies in the 1970s and 1980s ("Mad Max" comes particularly to mind), to the preoccupation with a "star wars" type of missile defense in the 1980s and again today, nuclear threats to common security have largely monopolized our imagining of the terrible.

Against these horrifying images of nuclear apocalypse, environmentalism has struggled to bring attention to scientific research that suggested that growing pollution and looming resource scarcities also represented important—and very imminent—threats to human welfare and security. But from 1962, with the publication of *Silent Spring*, to the late 1980s, the mainstream security community resisted expanding its concerns beyond the ever present problem of war. It is true that a small number of international relations scholars argued vigorously for a broadening of security concerns to encompass environmental threats (Sprout and Sprout 1971;

Falk 1971; Brown 1977; Ullman 1983). But their arguments fell, by and large, on deaf ears. To some in the security field, environmentalists were advocates whose claims and goals were not well-supported by scientific evidence. To others, environmental problems were primarily domestic problems, with little relevance to high-priority and high-prestige discussions of superpower rivalry and military planning.

Over the past decade, however, as the connections between environment and security have been acknowledged by a growing number of scholars around the world, policymakers and military officials freed from Cold War mindsets have responded with remarkable enthusiasm. Some observers have even gone so far as to suggest that environmental problems may become the dominant security issues of the next century (Myers 1993; Kaplan 1994). Establishment thinkers and policymakers are finally coming to see that security concerns cannot be delinked from a hard-nosed appraisal of the integrity of environmental systems and processes upon which so much of human well-being depends.

That is the good news. The bad news is that college level inquiry into global environmental ills—organized as it is around themes of sustainable development, environmental justice, environmental law, social movements, and transnational nongovernmental networking—either neglects or ignores any coherent focus on emerging ideas about security.

How can this last pocket of resistance be explained? We believe that the failure of professors to include environment and security in their courses, and of students to request it, might be rooted in misperceptions and personal judgments about the concept. In the words of one professor, the "whole debate leaves me cold." This unreceptive attitude might be due to a sense that security is a misguided, counterproductive, and even dangerous lens for studying environmental problems. The concept, after all, does suggest a conservative, status quo orientation. It evokes a picture of great powers using military assets to steal resources from the developing world or coerce poor countries into shouldering the burden of costly environmental rescue strategies. It conjures up images of secrecy and distrust, of intransigent national interests and resource wars, and—above all, perhaps—of the endless conflict between rich and poor.

Misperceptions about the research and policy agenda of the environmental security camp also drive a certain classroom wariness. A prominent intellectual thrust of the environment and security field focuses on the links between environmental scarcity and violent conflict; how, for example, might the scarcity of water in the Middle East inflame existing conflict or to what extent might deforestation and soil erosion in sub-Saharan Africa lead to war? Many professors and their students could be easily forgiven for assuming that this very influential strain of the environmental security field is, in fact, the entire field, and decide that it is too narrow a take on the politics of environmental degradation. As important as the scarcity/conflict thesis is, however, it is in fact only a small part of a rich and varied discourse that has a long history, an interdisciplinary character, and a growing portfolio of insights, controversies, and prescriptions. Much more is going on in the field than may initially meet the (mind's) eye.

This second issue of misperception, of misappreciation of the rich potential of the field, can be easily addressed by summarizing the environment and security literature, which we do shortly. The first set of objections ("the whole debate leaves me cold") is trickier terrain. Who are we, after all, to say to professors and students what it is they should be most interested in studying? We believe, however, that regardless of one's normative preferences, there are compelling political, practical, and educational reasons for including environmental security in the global environmental politics curricula. These include:

- Philosophical Value: Study of environmental security inevitably raises important philosophical and definitional questions, such as "what is security?" and "what does it mean to be environmentally secure?" These kinds of questions would seem to stand at the center of inquiry into global environmental struggles. Why not make them explicit?
- Rhetorical Value: The concept of environment and security has a very clear rhetorical or strategic aspect: relating the environment and security attracts public and policy attention. Former Secretary of State Warren Christopher, for example, used it in his famous 1996 speech outlining a new environmental thrust in U.S. foreign policy. The rhetorical aspects of world politics, however, do not always receive much classroom attention. The environmental security perspective offers an excellent opportunity to consider the politics of language, especially as it relates to building global norms around environmental issues.
- Policy Analysis Value: Looking at global environmental struggles from an environmental-security perspective offers special insight into current policymaking processes, highlighting important features such as the role of nongovernmental organizations, the impact of science and scientists, and the complex interactions among domestic and foreign agendas, constituencies, and resources. For example, the U.S. military has used the concept of environmental security as a basis for dialogue with countries such as China, India, and Russia; for cooperating with other government agencies including the EPA and the Department of Energy; and even for improving its image in

the eyes of environmental groups harshly critical of the ecological impacts of military activities.

- Predictive Value: Much research suggests that the causal linkages among environmental scarcity, population growth, and conflict are significant and likely to become more so, especially in developing countries in parts of Africa, the Middle East, and the Asia-Pacific. By grappling with these causal elements in the classroom, we can become better versed in understanding the present and, perhaps, anticipating the future.

- Grab Value: The concept of environment and security resonates positively with an idea that is very familiar to the current generation of students: humankind now has the capacity to cause unprecedented environmental destruction. Through our often reckless and extravagant behavior, we might have put the future of our planet and ourselves in danger.

- Opportunity Value: The environmental security lens provides a nice view into a host of research problems, such as those posed by undertaking interdisciplinary studies, bringing nature back into social science discussions, understanding conflict and instability, and making compelling arguments about cause and effect. Happily (from the perspective of an ambitious student), research on environment and security is still in an early phase of development. Opportunity abounds for students looking to undertake original scholarship.

- Comparative Value: Finally, linking environment and security has been essentially a Western effort. But rather than simply accept the Western paradigm, researchers and practitioners in the non-Western world have begun to explore this issue, with results that are remarkably different and that provide the basis for interesting discussions of how extensive the grounds for cooperation on an environmental agenda are between North and South (Naqvi 1996).

Which of these seven elements are most compelling? Which might best frame and inspire classroom discussion about the utility of the environmental security perspective? Which, put plainly, are most important? We have our preferences, to be sure. But rather than lay them out on the basis of our expertise, we'd rather that students and instructors of environmental politics—through careful conversation with one another—arrive at their own conclusions. In the process, we hope, the student can become teacher, the teacher the student, and all can begin to see the opportunities missed when we neglect to bring the environmental security perspective to bear on global environmental challenges.

THREE APPROACHES

Of course, coming to grips with the opportunities inherent in closer study of environment-security relationships presumes a deeper familiarity with the field than we have yet provided. In service of demonstrating the nuanced nature of the field (in order to undermine any lingering assumptions that environmental security is only about drawing connections between environmental degradation and conflict), allow us to delve rather deeply into three overlapping approaches to understanding the field and evaluating its usefulness to students and instructors of global environmental politics. We believe that an appreciation of these three approaches—which we label the chronological, the advocacy vs. analysis, and the competing perspectives—will facilitate the kind of informed classroom discussion that we believe to be so important. And we think that they begin to shed light on just why it is that issues of environmental security need to find their way into regular classroom discourse.

There is another reason for wading with us through this literature review that will be relevant to some but, we acknowledge, not all students: reviewing the myriad ways scholars have come to think about environmental security illuminates how varied academic disciplines and ways of knowing can come together to generate new insight with policy relevance. Unpacking the concept of environmental security, in other words, shines light on the multiple processes of interdisciplinary problem analysis. Since many students come to courses on global environmental politics with an interest in learning how interdisciplinary academic work is done (perhaps with hopes of one day joining the fray), we find further virtue in allowing environmental security to stake a claim to some portion of the environmental studies classroom.

The literature on environmental security is extensive and includes much scholarship that one might judge to be rigorous and innovative (though we confess that the literature is also marred by repetitiveness and sensationalism). Analyzing these perspectives reveals how scholars and students alike seek to understand the complicated arena of global environmental politics. It also provides a necessary context for critiques of the security perspective, which we describe in a following section. Most importantly, though, a brief review of the literature provides us with the raw material we need to struggle with the questions central to this chapter: how, and why, might we better integrate environmental security into our understanding of global environmental politics?

Chronological Approach

It is altogether reasonable and rather natural to think of current work on environment and security as the latest contribution to a literature that extends back into antiquity, one that ponders the relationship between human conflict and cooperation on the one hand and environmental factors on the other.

For instance, recent work by paleoanthropologists and environmental historians suggests that conflict and cooperation might have been driven largely by climate change and resource scarcity since the dawn of the human species some one to two million years ago (Fagan 1990; Ponting 1991; Diamond 1997). One need not venture into a new discipline, however, to convey a sense of the rich historical context that undergirds contemporary theory and practice. Within the canon of international relations theory, Thucydides' *Peloponnesian War* can be read as a comparative analysis of the foreign policies of an aggressive sea power (Athens) versus a defensive land power (Sparta). This theme is discussed in early modernity by Jean-Jacques Rousseau in his *Discourse on the Origins of Inequality* and other writings and becomes a focus of much geopolitical research on power, security, and geography in the nineteenth and early-twentieth centuries (Mackinder 1944). Throughout history, the state of the environment has affected human security—directly through disasters and other impacts and indirectly by conferring advantages and disadvantages on groups of people.

Unfortunately, after World War II, suggestions that political power (and, perhaps, social superiority) were somehow rooted in environmental conditions reminded scholars too much of a just-vanquished fascist/Nazi ideology. As the field of international relations became institutionalized and began its remarkable ascendancy in the postwar period, investigations of links between environment and political power and conflict were marginalized. But as scientific evidence of human-generated environmental change has mounted, the importance of examining how these changes affect the power and security of people around the world has become clear. It is time, one might say, to recover a fundamental theme of international relations—environment, power, and security—that was neglected for decades after World War II.

The field as a whole has gradually come to this realization. Concern about the various implications of human-generated environmental change began to emerge in the late nineteenth century, resurfaced in the interwar years, and assumed its contemporary personality in the 1960s. In the 1970s, it began to infiltrate the margins of international relations. In the 1980s, this concern moved towards the center of social science thinking, especially in the areas of international organization and international political economy. Finally, in the 1990s and now the 2000s, worries about global environmental stability and change have begun to influence the very character of security studies.

It is helpful to think of this recent infiltration (which, recall, has yet to consistently crack the classroom) as unfolding in three distinct waves (see Levy 1995). The initial wave simply argued that global environmental change ought to be thought of as an issue of national security (see, for example, Brown 1977 and Ullman 1983; later instances of this view are found in Mathews 1989 and Myers 1989). The second wave of scholarly work explored the dynamic connections between environmental change and violent conflict (Lipschutz 1989; Gleick 1991; Homer-Dixon 1994; 1999; Baechler 1999). Finally, the current wave, which we are now riding, is refining earlier work (e.g., Wolf 1998; Gleditsch 1998; Diehl and Gleditsch 2001). It is going beyond previous contributions to examine the actual policy process of integrating environmental concerns into national security agendas (Dabelko and Simmons 1997; Matthew 1996; VanDeveer and Dabelko 1999), and develop a more robust concept of human security in the twenty-first century (Myers 1993; UNDP 1994; Lonergan 1999). It is characterized by the presence of a distinctive Southern perspective (Naqvi 1996).

This third wave has yet to crest. In the years ahead, we expect a new generation of researchers to venture into the field, often cooperating with their Southern counterparts, to undertake fine-grained case studies that will further elucidate the complex causal network that links ecological and social systems in ways that render individuals and groups vulnerable and insecure. The college students of today, now struggling with the multiple dimensions of environmental politics, will be among these scholars, and they will be doing some of the most important work the social sciences will have to offer.

To recap, then, the chronological approach offers three essential insights:

- The relationships among conflict, security, and the natural environment have been an important feature of human history, recognized and discussed since antiquity. For political reasons, however, these relationships received little attention in the decades following World War II.
- Recovering this tradition is important, especially given the sheer magnitude of human generated environmental change. Processes of environment interaction have been a focus of scholarship for over a century but have become a permanent feature of the global agenda only in the past thirty years.
- The environmental security literature has matured rapidly through three waves. Much of it is accessible to the beginner, and all together it offers a provocative springboard for classroom discussion, debate, and research.

The chronological approach also reveals the extent to which competing interpretations of history lie at the root of much present day controversy. Some analysts look at the past and see a story of great human accomplishment in the face of unbelievable obstacles. Others look at the same evidence and note that along the way, many people—the poor, women, children, or ethnic minorities—have suffered tremendously and been denied many of the gains associated with progress. Looking ahead, the first group sees the human species continuing to make its way toward higher levels of material comfort, while the second group wonders who will bear the brunt of growing scarcity and pollution even if technological solutions are found for many of our current problems.

Advocacy versus Analysis Approach

A second way of parsing the literature is to view it as a debate between advocates who seek to advance an environmental political agenda by raising awareness and mobilizing support (Mathews 1989; Kaplan 1994; Connelly and Kennedy 1994) and analysts who labor to describe, explain, and predict interesting and important phenomena as objectively as possible (Lipschutz 1989; Westing 1989; Homer-Dixon 1994; 1999; Homer-Dixon and Blitt 1998; Wolf 1998; Gleditsch 1997; 1998; Kahl 1998; Deudney and Matthew 1999; Baechler 1999).

For example, some writers make strong claims about the effects of environmental scarcity in the developing world in the hopes of influencing the quality and quantity of development aid flowing from the rich world to the poor. Others draw upon the same information but are far more cautious, perhaps overly so, in describing the effects of environmental scarcity and prescribing particular policy responses. Comparing these two approaches raises interesting questions about environmental studies, social science, and contemporary politics.

It has long been axiomatic that democracies require informed citizens if they are to flourish as political forms of government. But as a review of the literature on environmental security makes clear, information does not flow freely from researchers into the public realm. Researchers have their own values and preferences that influence the kinds of questions they ask and the way in which they interpret data. Even the most objective pieces are biased and subjective, influenced as they are by the mores of the discipline and the demands of professional credibility. As research work moves out of the journal or laboratory, it is often misrepresented and thus reaches the public in a form marked by distortion and incompleteness. Sometimes this trend is due to the simplifying processes of mass media. Other times, special interests choose to represent scholarly work in ways sympathetic to their causes. Whether through human error or political calculation, it is clear that information cannot always be trusted, especially in a field such as the environment that is characterized by high stakes, competing values, and much scientific uncertainty.

It would be a mistake to assume that one camp is automatically superior to another. Some of the best advocacy work has served to sharpen our analytic focus, and some of the best analytic writings have provided a foundation for effective advocacy. Perhaps what the student of global environmental politics should most take from this way of framing the environmental security literature is simply this: a tension between advocacy and analysis runs throughout the literatures on global environmental studies, and it is this tension that makes so much of the literature interesting to so many. As we seek to make sense of the global politics of environmental degradation, we would be remiss if we did not search for and struggle to understand how this tension plays out in the definition of issues, and of their ultimate resolution.

Competing Perspectives Approach

Yet another way to cleave the literature and organize our conversation about environment and security is to draw upon three perspectives that run through much of the political science debate about environment and politics. These perspectives are the ecologic, the humanist, and the statist—and together they offer a set of useful categories for thinking not only about environmental security but about other aspects of global environmental problems and politics.

The Ecologic Perspective: The Security of Nature

Ecologists working within this framework (e.g., Sessions 1995) challenge thinking that centers on humans and seek to view *Homo sapiens* as one of millions of species that, together with inanimate material, make up nature. Their work has much to say to scholars and activists of global environmental policymaking.[3] Humankind, they argue, is an especially destructive species that must be diverted from the brutal and damaging trajectory of its history. By following nature in the sense intended by classical natural law thinkers such as Zeno and Chrysippus (that is, by adapting ourselves to natural patterns, rhythms, and thresholds), we will not only cease those activities that are destroying our own life support system, but we may also recover some of the rich purpose of life that has been lost in our consumer society such as spirituality, artistic expression, and morality.

The Humanist Perspective: Individual and Community Security

Humanists, in contrast, are unapologetically focused on the welfare of people (e.g., Myers 1993; UNDP 1994; Lonergan 1999). They tend to see a close relationship between the productive technologies that have exploited and degraded nature and the economic, political, and cultural practices that have degraded and exploited large segments of humanity. Awareness of environmental change gives us an opportunity—and a motivation—to rethink our relationship with nature and other humans. Humanists, following the example of human rights arguments, advise us to begin with the individual or group and their material and moral needs and use this as a basis for criticizing current practices and designing new ones. Humanists fear a world in which we save the environment at the expense of the earth's poor and powerless. For them, we must harmonize nature and civilization and seize this opportunity to correct unjust imbalances that appear in all of our relationships.

The Statist Perspective: Conventional National Security

Statists are motivated to consider the implications of environmental change within the framework of the national interests of states and national security (e.g., Deudney 1990; Homer-Dixon 1994; 1999; Matthew 1997; Dabelko and VanDeveer 1998.) How do states protect access to environmental goods beyond their borders? How do states protect their environments from harmful external forces? What should states do when faced with scarcity-based humanitarian disasters? How does the environment fit into the traditional understanding of threat and vulnerability? In short, in an age of transnational environmental degradation, how do we secure the health and welfare of our citizens, protect our territory and its resources, and ensure that we will have the raw materials we need to continue to develop economically? Within the state-based framework, much research has focused on the causal links between scarcity and conflict (Homer-Dixon 1999). Other issues include making military practices less environmentally harmful (Butts 1994; 1999; Matthew 1998), using defense tools to support environmental policy through data gathering and treaty monitoring (Butts 1999) and promoting interstate cooperation through military-to-military contact programs designed around environmental themes (Butts 1999).

On balance, the ecological "nature first" perspective has a number of strong supporters but resides at the margins of scholarly and practitioner discussions explicitly focused on the links between environment and security. By placing individual or group well-being at the center of human or ultimate security, humanists offer a compelling case for using environmental, demographic, and health considerations as an alternative to state-based visions of security. Filtering the environmental problematique through the traditional statist security paradigm remains the most common approach of those advocates and analysts concerned with scarcity and conflict and the role of the military and intelligence community.

What does this final categorization tell us that the chronological and advocacy vs. analyst approaches do not? Perhaps that, void of context, environmental change has no meaning. Placing environmental change in context is not an easy task, however, because there are no rules that determine how one selects and shapes context. Throughout the world, values, needs, fears, and aspirations differ, as do perceptions of time and space. Degrees of vulnerability, perceived threat, and capacity to cope with surprise and adversity also vary. Consequently, people are bound to frame environmental issues in different ways. Anyone wishing to work in this area must find ways to be sympathetic to other perspectives and be able to build bridges across them.

BEING CRITICAL

While support for the environment and security perspective has grown rapidly, the field is not without its critics. Some (e.g., Lipschutz 1989; Deudney 1990; Levy 1995) challenge the claim that environmental degradation contributes to conflict and hence can be a threat to national security. They point to the lack of empirical evidence for a prominent role for environmental variables in conflict between states. In response to these criticisms, the proponents of this linkage acknowledge that most evidence points to an indirect effect on conflict within states. Despite this modification of the general claim, some critics continue to question the ability to separate and rank environmental contributions from the mix of political, social, and economic factors that are related to violent conflict (Gleditsch 1997; 1998).

Many of these same critics also challenge the research designs of the prominent case studies that purport to show strong connections between environmental degradation and social instability and conflict. In what has become the best-known critique, Levy (1995) questions case selection techniques that identify only cases where environmental scarcity and high levels of conflict were both evident and exclude cases in which environmental degradation was evident but conflict was not. And, as quantitative techniques developed in the mid-to-late 1990s, additional criticisms have surfaced. Questions concerning the poor quality of environmental data raise doubts about the ability of quantitative methods to capture environmental contributions in a complex causal chain.

A final category of value critiques shifts attention from the environment and conflict thesis to the broader environment and security pairing. Such critiques focus on the political slogan rather than the analytical tool perception of the environmental security subfield (Dokken and Græger 1995). The matching of environmental priorities with security is viewed by some as an unwise tactical alliance to gain resources and policy attention for otherwise neglected environmental concerns. Observers cast doubt on whether the military will really be "greened." They worry that environmental policy could instead become militarized, turning into an area where force is used to influence environmental practices. The conflictual instruments of the military are identified as "mismatched tools" that are inappropriate for fostering the cooperation necessary for transboundary environmental treaties (Deudney 1990; Kakönën 1994; Wæver 1995; Conca 1998; Peluso and Watts 2001). Finger (1991) identifies the military as an agency that creates environmental problems rather than solves them. Dalby (1999) and Conca (1998) raise doubts regarding the utility of a Northern-formulated environmental paradigm that emphasizes security in engaging Southern countries in environmental cooperation. From a more traditional security perspective, observers lament the widening of security definitions to include nonmilitary threats, thereby undermining the clarity of doctrine and preparedness of military force (Walt 1991). The more time the military spends fighting fires, in reality and in metaphor, the less time it prepares for its primary war-fighting missions.

While these diverse critiques pose a formidable challenge to the field, one should be careful not to throw the baby out with the bathwater. Using a security lens to understand the dynamics of environmental politics still has much to offer, and scholars are at work refining research strategies and participating in policy debates. Beyond the ivory tower of academe, many policy institutions and think tanks are taking seriously and putting into political play varied elements of the literature we have just reviewed. This work and struggle in the policy arena make tangible the theoretical struggles just described. They provide, too, a place for students to investigate the ongoing evolution of environmental security policies and programs.

A NEW SECURITY AGENDA?

Over the past decade a number of governments and international organizations have focused on connections between environment and security linkages, adopting official positions and establishing policies and programs aimed at addressing the challenges posed by those links. The policy manifestations in environmental security vary widely by country, government, department, and geographic location, and frequently capture a striking shift in official policy.

For instance, when the Soviet Premier Mikhail Gorbachev called for ecological security programs in the United Nations in the late 1980s, the United States government was reticent to embrace the term. But in the 1990s, the United States emerged as a leading consumer of environmental security ideas. Not surprisingly, different agencies and departments within the U.S. government frame environment and security linkages in very different fashions, often in accordance with their particular policy toolboxes. This diversity of environmental security conceptions illuminates bureaucratic interests at play in the policy struggles to shape and control a newly emerging security agenda. For instance:

- The U.S. military focuses on the environment and conflict thesis and environmental impacts of the military (Matthew 1996; Dabelko and Simmons 1997; Chen 1997). Created in 1992, the Department of Defense Office of Environmental Security applied its approximately $5 billion annual budget to greening military activities, cleaning up the environment around military bases, and investigating environmental contributions to instability in areas where political leaders may ask the U.S. military to intervene.
- The U.S. intelligence community is using work on environment and conflict to help in its predictions of where conflict is likely to occur. It also pursues more proactive efforts to use intelligence equipment for environmental purposes. In 1994, Vice President Al Gore asked the U.S. intelligence community to investigate environmental contributions to "state failure," leading to the ongoing effort of the State Failure Task Force. The Central Intelligence Agency established an Environmental Center to investigate environmental flash points (Chen 1997). A group of scientists received security clearances to use secret spy satellites to study the environment (referred to as MEDEA) (Richelson 1998).
- The Environmental Protection Agency (EPA) focuses on communism's toxic legacy in the former Soviet Union and its impact on human health (EPA 1999). In cooperation with the Department of Defense and the Department of Energy, the EPA is helping the Baltic countries of Lithuania, Latvia, and Estonia clean up and convert former military bases into safe civilian facilities.
- The Department of Energy, and in particular the nation's national laboratories, worked throughout the Cold War on techniques and equipment to monitor weapons systems and verify arms control treaties. DOE officials now seek to apply lessons from this experience to environmental treaty monitoring (Allenby et al. 1998).

- The U.S. Agency for International Development (USAID) pursues a broad human security agenda through development aid similar to the human security blueprint outlined by the United Nations Development Program (1994). USAID provides aid designed to improve human well-being that is in part justified on the basis of the perceived links among declining environmental conditions, growing populations, and social instability (Atwood 1995).
- The Department of State, often considered the lead agency on issues of environmental diplomacy, fights to exert diplomatic leadership, with miniscule budgets in comparison to the other departments (Matthew 1996). Former Secretary of State Warren Christopher established an "environmental hubs" program in selected U.S. embassies abroad to promote reporting on local and regional environmental conditions and their impact on wider regional politics (Christopher 1997).
- Outside the United States, a number of interesting environment and security initiatives have taken place. While these are far too numerous to list, they include several NATO Advanced Research Workshops bringing together scholars and practitioners from NATO and former Soviet bloc countries; workshops in South Asia under the auspices of the South Asian NGO Summit; a state of the art study funded by the OECD's Development Assistance Committee; and work undertaken throughout the developing world by the International Union for the Conservation of Nature.

One cannot help but be struck by the different policy interpretations of environmental security. These differences repeat the scholarly struggle to settle on an accepted definition of environmental security or even a hierarchy of priorities. The multiplicity of voices and interpretations grows when one looks outside the United States to compare environmental security policy across countries and regions. Wide differences persist across security and environment agendas in developed and developing countries (Saad 1991; Naqvi 1996; Conca 1998; Dalby 1999; Barnett 2001). Differing historical roles of traditional security institutions (such as military and intelligence services) within given countries also account for alternative priority rankings on environmental security agendas.

If the term means different things to different people, can it be a meaningful part of efforts to facilitate global forms of lasting environmental governance? We think it can, for three reasons. First, the disputes over meaning suggest that people are concerned about the concept. For some it is the most compelling idea of our age; for others it is misguided, alarmist, perhaps dangerous. As with other environmental terms such as "sustainable development" and "environmental justice," debate is important, especially in a democracy, because it is through debate that we express our values, fears, and aspirations; listen to those of others; and replace or adjust our beliefs—or gain support for them.

Second, the concept is politically and intellectually valuable insofar as it brings previously excluded perspectives into environmental discourse. Military and intelligence agencies, for example, now meet with both their foreign counterparts and environmental groups to discuss this issue. These, we believe, are dialogues that can prove instrumental in moving environmental policy forward. Third, it is clear from research carried out to date that some forms of environmental stress make some groups more vulnerable and insecure than they would otherwise be, by contributing to violent conflict as well as to deprivation and disease. This is an important, albeit preliminary, finding, and it merits further consideration.

Hence, while advocates of environmental security as an organizing concept have failed to provide a comprehensive blueprint for policy action, it is this diverse constellation of values, perspectives, and policy possibilities that makes teaching and researching this evolving topic stimulating, frustrating, and challenging—and critically important. Happily, a host of newly published research and online reference materials makes struggling with these intellectual challenges much easier than even a few years ago.[4] Regarding the question of the environment's role in contributing to violent conflict, Thomas Homer-Dixon has published a single-authored capstone volume to his ten-year joint research effort and an edited volume with cases from his University of Toronto–based research projects (1999; Homer-Dixon and Blitt 1998). Combined with recent efforts from Günther Baechler (1999) of the Swiss Environmental Conflicts Project (ENCOP) and from Nils Petter Gleditsch and colleagues from the International Peace Research Institute in Oslo (1997; 1998; Diehl and Gleditsch 2001), professors and students have access to a rich set of environment and conflict cases from which to choose.[5] The case study is not the sole research method that has been applied to test the environment and conflict thesis. A special issue of *The Journal of Peace Research* (Diehl 1998) and Phase I and II results of the U.S. State Failure Task Force (Esty et al. 1995; Esty et al. 1998) represent the most prominent quantitative research to date.

Edited volumes by Deudney and Matthew (1999), Carius and Lietzmann (1999), Suliman (1999), and Lowi and Shaw (2000) provide broader discussions of environment and security linkages that include but are not limited to the environment and conflict thesis. For those looking for a brief introduction to the subfield, an excerpted collection of articles such as the one found in the anthology *Green Planet Blues* (Conca and Dabelko 1998) provides a shorter set of readings by many of the primary contributors.

Other reference resources are available as more explicit attempts to bridge the scholarly and practitioner realms. The Woodrow Wilson International Center's *Environmental Change and Security Project Report* is one such example.[6] This annual reference report provides feature length journal articles on a broad range of environment and security topics. Its updates include short descriptions on nongovernmental organization, scholarly, and U.S. governmental activities in the area. Official statements by senior U.S. and United Nations leadership combine with extensive Internet and bibliography sections to provide students and faculty with a jumping off point for conducting research. The policy manifestations of environment and security linkages have become especially prominent these past five years or so, making the topic a ripe area for original and ongoing research.

A PLACE AT THE (CLASSROOM) TABLE: ENVIRONMENTAL SECURITY WITHIN GLOBAL ENVIRONMENTAL POLITICS

As an organizing concept in the field, environmental security has become many things to many people using different tools to achieve different goals. Thus, those who would bring the same critiques leveled at "sustainable development" (e.g., Lélé 1991) to bear on environmental security wouldn't, perhaps, be that far off the mark. Yet the fact remains that these terms and the sometimes inchoate concepts that underlie them are becoming ground zero for important struggles over how pressing global problems are framed and attacked. And in politics, as Sarewitz and Pielke (2000) remind us, "everything depends on how an issue is framed: the terms of debate, the allocation of power and resources, the potential courses of action."

In ways that still escape the attention of the classroom, critical struggles over the framing of global environmental threats has coalesced around environmental security. Students and instructors of global environmental politics would be wise to take notice, for there is much to learn. The definitional and institutional conflicts among actors as diverse as the Worldwatch Institute, the Pentagon, the Nordic peace research community, and the United Nations Development Program present remarkably sharp contrasts for revealing the highly political and contested nature of global environmental politics. Environmental security also provides a useful tool for critically interrogating the widespread faith in rational scientific or techno-managerial solutions to the environmental problematique, which is especially pronounced in this area that has attracted so much bureaucratic interest and support. Ironically, while the academic debate surrounding environmental security is increasingly philosophical as well as empirical and analytical, policymakers exhibit a remarkable capacity to lift a few ideas from academic debates and press these into service—often to reinforce well-established paradigms and protect budgets, while creating the impression of innovation. Yet behind the academic disagreements, the bureaucratic mindsets, and the political maneuvering, many people are persuaded by the concept for a simple reason: it speaks directly to the magnitude and urgency of our global environmental challenges.

The stakes, consequently, are not trivial. It matters which understandings of environmental security predominate and are adopted in policies and programs and which are rejected. Given the increased policy attention and funding devoted to environmental security (in the Unites States at least), the struggle over which version of environmental security will win out carries tangible and significant implications for the environment. It will influence, for instance, which actors with what special interests have legitimate and enduring influence on the formulation of environmental policy.

One extreme possibility is that mainstream ideas about national security are "greened," making human and ecosystem well-being central objectives to be secured. At the other extreme is the possibility that the environment is militarized—that military tools and raw power become the principal means of dealing with environmental threats and approaching environmental negotiations (Kakönen 1994). Between the two extremes rest concerns about environmentally induced conflict, the toxic legacy of the Cold War, and the intelligence community's monitoring of environmental treaties, to name a few. There is no lack of real-world problems that have both an environmental and security component, and we have reason to believe that policies will increasingly be influenced and guided by an environmental security perspective.

Environmental security is no fad (Dabelko and Simmons 1997; VanDeveer and Dabelko 1999)—it is here to stay.[7] Even if one opposes linking environment and security for the reasons outlined by the critics, this alone argues for one's continued examination of the environment and security subfield and engagement in the unfolding politics of problem framing. But there is also another reason for taking notice. At a time when college students are increasingly disaffected from conventional politics (e.g., Halstead 1999) and exploring, in tentative ways, alternative paths for making a political difference (e.g., Featherstone 2000), the evolving discourse of environmental security offers both hope and guidance. It shows how ideas and the terms we employ to describe them matter, and that the struggle to define and put into action these terms and ideas is up for grabs. It demonstrates too that real-world policy flows from the struggle over ideas; and thus, policy can be shaped as well. Most important, perhaps, it suggests that our encounter with a multiplicity of ideas and perspectives in the classroom is not busy work—we are not sequestered away in some ivory tower while the "real world out there" goes about its business. Our classroom debates and confusions mirror those in the policy realm. The more seriously we engage these debates now, as students and instructors, the better suited we will be for the important struggles to come.

As we continue our search for ways of translating our expanding knowledge of the world into real power that can make a difference, we'd do well to uncover mechanisms for integrating an environmental security perspective in our investigation of global environmental politics.

QUESTIONS FOR REFLECTION
AND DISCUSSION

1. This chapter was written before the tragic terrorist attack on the World Trade Center. In what ways do these events and those that have followed either underscore or undermine Dabelko and Matthew's arguments and recommendations?
2. What do we mean when we speak of security: national security, regional security, or even personal security? Does the concept imply, for you, a "conservative, status quo" orientation? And, in your view, do environmental threats to human well-being appear to be extensive or powerful enough to threaten or erode our security?
3. Are the ways that we think about security, and about environment, sufficiently similar or complementary to suggest that the pairing of terms might be beneficial—both conceptually and politically? Or are we just producing another fuzzy buzzword that hurts more than it helps?
4. Of the seven reasons for studying the connections between environment and security (philosophical value, rhetorical value, policy analysis value, predictive value, grab value, opportunity value, and comparative value), which are most compelling? What additional information or insight—or answers to specific questions you have about this chapter—could change your ranking of these seven reasons?
5. Language, as George Orwell once observed, is political. The words we use to describe reality and how words come to be defined in the popular consciousness inevitably benefit some interests over others. How might the pairing of environment and security affect the struggle for influence and power over the resolution of environmental

ills? Are environmental groups, for instance, helped or hurt by the reconceptualization of environmental deterioration into a security problem? Are military and intelligence interests likewise harmed or bolstered by the application of their resources to the remedying of environmental problems? And how, do you think, could the joining of these terms foster public appreciation of environmental problems and the politics of their resolution?

6. It is curious that the United States rejected environmental security as an organizing concept in the 1980s, only to play the role in the 1990s and 2000s as a leading proponent of the term. What hypotheses could one generate (drawing in part from the authors' three approaches to understanding the field) to explain this turnaround by the United States? And what, in terms of environmental protection, might we expect to result from the emerging importance of the environmental security perspective in U.S. policymaking affairs?

7. Staying true to the themes of this volume, Dabelko and Matthew express concern about the sense of powerlessness that pervades today's political culture. They seem to suggest that piece by piece policymaking around themes of environmental security offers real hope for progressive change. What more about the policies and policymaking process would you need to know to share their optimism? And what relatively easy ways could you, your students, or your fellow classmates go about gathering this information?

8. The bottom line for our authors is not a complicated one: (1) environmental security, though still ill-defined, is emerging as an organizing concept for global environmental policy; (2) it is important for educated citizens to be involved in debates over what we mean by the term and how it becomes implemented; and (3) colleges and universities, especially those that offer programs or courses in environmental studies, are falling down on the job of creating these educated and potentially involved citizens. We all lose. Do the reasons our authors suggest for why higher education has neglected environmental security ring true? What alternative explanations present themselves? As instructors, how do we respond to Dabelko and Matthew's critique of the curricular choices we have made, and how might we share this response with our students? And, as students, what do we see as the most important goals of our education? Would deeper study of environmental security (meaning less time to study some other topic) advance these goals?

9. When all is said and done, how do you respond to this overarching question raised by the authors: "how, and why, might we better integrate environmental security into our understanding of global environmental politics?"

NOTES

1. On this issue of unexpected environmental decline, and "environmental surprise" in general, see Chris Bright's "Anticipating Environmental 'Surprise'" (2000). Bright usefully describes how first-, second-, and third-order effects on environmental quality arising from human perturbation creates a high-stakes arena characterized by uncertainty and possible peril.

2. On the dangers of "multidisciplinary illiteracy" in environmental studies programs, see Soulé and Press (1998). For a rebuttal to Soulé and Press, see Maniates and Whissel (2000).

3. A range of biocentric thought is available in a selection of writings edited by Lori Gruen and Dale Jamieson (1994). Key works include Devall (1991), Leopold (1949), and Nash (1989). For a powerful critique, see Luc Ferry's thoughtful and provocative analysis of deep ecology *The New Ecological Order* (1998). The ethical problems posed by deep ecology are neatly presented by Clare Palmer (1998). Several scientists have weighed into this debate with wit and elegance—notably Rupert Sheldrake (1991) and Fritjof Capra (1996).

4. For example, see the environmental security syllabus composed by Simon Dalby of the Department of Geography, Carleton University, at webpub.alleg. edu/employee/m/mmaniate/GepEd/geped.html

5. For environment and security bibliographies, visit the University of Toronto site at utl2.library.utoronto.ca/www.pcs/eps.htm. or the Environmental Change and Security Project at www.wilsoncenter.org/ecsp. For more on case studies and ongoing research programs, also visit the Global Environmental Change and Human Security site at steve.geog.uvic.ca/GECHS/ index.html and the Environmental Conflicts Project site at www.fsk.ethz.ch.

6. The *ECSP Reports* are available online at www.wilsoncenter.org/ecsp. Because the Woodrow Wilson Center prints only a limited number of reports and distributes them free of charge, the Environmental Change and Security Project Web site is designed to enable students to download sections or entire issues of the reports.

7. See the updates sections of the Woodrow Wilson Center's *Environmental Change and Security Project Report*.

8

✸

Civic Virtue and Classroom Toil in a Greenhouse World

Michael Maniates

E fficiency is often a virtue—but too much of it in the global environmental politics classroom can accelerate an erosion of civic virtue that
lies at the heart of the climate change crisis. This chapter pleads for a more
deliberative classroom, one where students take stock of their talents as
citizens and assess how focused moments of civic engagement inform
their grasp of concepts like global civil society. Students and their teachers may wish to debate the validity of this chapter's marriage of the climate crisis to the drawdown of social capital. You could focus on the
startling (for me, at least) data on the curricular overload awaiting students of global environmental politics. Or you may wish to engage in
antisimulations and assess for yourself the power of this exercise. Whatever stance your classroom adopts with respect to this chapter, my hope
is that you leave it—and, by extension, the volume as a whole—
"maladjusted" in the way meant by Martin Luther King, Jr.

A CURIOUS GAP

Now is not a happy time for advocates of climate stability, especially in
the United States. American auto fleet fuel efficiency continues to decline,
oil consumption and imports are up, powerful interests are pressing hard
to open the Arctic National Wildlife Refuge to drilling, and the coal industry is aggressively promoting the virtues of "clean coal." The United

States has disavowed the Kyoto Protocol, and the status quo should give us pause. As David Victor of the Council of Foreign Relations notes, "If the U.S. stays on its present track, by 2008–2012 the nation's greenhouse gas emissions will be perhaps 30 percent higher than 1990 levels, a far cry from the 7 percent *cut* required by Kyoto" (Victor 2000). And this may be optimistic.

Oddly, while the U.S government argues for caution and a wait-and-see approach to the climate crisis, everyday Americans strongly support renewable energy technologies, greater energy efficiency, and a proactive response to the specter of a greenhouse world. A recent Harris Poll[1] notes that 89 percent of Americans know about global warming, while 85 percent consider the possibility of climate change to be a very serious (46 percent) or somewhat serious (39 percent) problem. The poll indicates that 54 percent believe that we need to act immediately and 46 percent confess to worrying about climate change "a great deal." A similar survey[2] shows that over half of likely voters strongly favor a significant government increase in the purchase of renewable energy sources as a way of steering the economy away from fossil-fuel dependence, while another 21 percent favor such a policy. Meanwhile, 70 percent strongly support aggressive dissemination of renewable energy technologies, and 49 percent feel strongly that federal programs for energy efficiency and renewable energy should be enacted immediately, before any ratification of a binding climate protocol, even if energy costs might rise as a result.[3] Even in the midst of debate over President Bush's fossil-fuel-friendly energy plan of 2001, where administration officials were characterizing energy efficiency as merely "a personal virtue" and renewable energy as not yet ready for prime time, national polls showed that over 90 percent of the American public would pay a premium for more solar energy in the nation's energy mix (Hamer and Paranzino 2001).

Americans are worried about climate change and about a fossil-fuel-centered energy strategy that would dump growing amounts of carbon dioxide into the atmosphere. But they are not terribly vocal. They do not organize. There is no "million mom march" on Washington, D.C., for reductions in U.S. carbon emissions, no uprising against federal energy policies that favor fossil fuels and would grant tens of billions of dollars in tax breaks to oil and coal interests while shorting energy efficiency and renewables, no unruly student demonstrations on college campuses—this despite polls showing deep public disquiet with business as usual. With respect to climate politics and energy policy, a striking gap prevails between what Americans say they worry about and what they seem ready to fight for.

What's going on? Does this gap exist because climate change is a silent crisis—it is hard to see and sometimes difficult to understand, and thus people fail to mobilize, no matter how high the stakes? Might it be that national surveys overstate public concern and willingness to pay for renewables and efficiency? Or could it be that Americans are spoiled, fat, and happy, believing that climate change is a pressing problem but steering clear of the hard work of making the world right?

Each of these explanations has its advocates. But the chasm between greenhouse convictions and everyday political practice is perhaps best understood within the context of the recent stark decline in civic engagement and public connection to political life, which makes it exceedingly difficult for Americans to imagine what a citizen response to massive environmental threats like global climate change might look like, let alone how they might act *politically* on their concerns about climate stability. In his book *Bowling Alone: The Collapse and Revival of American Community*, political scientist Robert Putnam sketches the dimensions of this decline in all its gruesome detail, from drops in participation in political campaigns and elections, to a steady, almost shocking attrition of membership in local civic groups and social clubs, ranging from bowling leagues and Boy Scouts to the Lion's Club, Rotary, the PTA, and Habitat for Humanity. Everywhere one looks, Americans are too busy, too tired, too cynical, or too distracted to join in collective enterprises with fellow citizens with whom they might not normally interact, enterprises that simultaneously foster and reward the ability to work in common for the common good. The consequence, in political science speak, is a decline in civic virtue, the erosion of civil society, and a massive drawdown of social capital—the degradation of our ability, in other words, to struggle together, and sometimes against one another, to get things done. As the stock of social capital shrinks, the capacity of democratic processes to deliver legitimate and just political outcomes that fire citizens' imaginations and expand their capacity for good judgment comes under siege.[4]

My aim in this chapter is to persuade you, teacher and student both, of the urgent need to confront now, in the classroom, the erosion of social capital and the wearing away of climatic resilience, rather than wait until graduation day when students venture out into some mythical "real world." After all, as I argue below, most courses in global environmental politics[5] happily demolish the prevalent myth that diligent recycling, apolitical ecoconsumption, and well-meaning, well-trained experts will together rescue us from the big ecoproblems like global climate change. Such courses instead promote a vision of global sustainability animated by escalating civic activism, robust community-based deliberation, and increasingly complex networks of global civil society. The texts they employ insist that the key to enduring systems of global environmental governance is resurgent civic virtue—that is, people thinking of themselves again as citizens who pay attention to and participate in public life.

But if even the smallest elements of this vision are to capture the imagination of "Generation Y-ers" who have little direct experience of community deliberation or civic activism, they must be yoked to classroom exercises that impart a taste and feel for the many dimensions of renewed citizen action and global civil society. If courses in global environmental politics are to dodge charges of intellectual hypocrisy and have any lasting impact on college students and the planet they will inherit, they must walk their civic talk.

The latter portion of this chapter introduces one exercise—call it an antisimulation—through which students and instructors might engage and evaluate the trials, tribulations, nuances, and joys of civic engagement. Most of my students who do the antisimulation report a deeper, more meaningful understanding of why we focus on civil society and transnational civic activism when studying global environmental politics. For some, the experience is transformative, a highlight of their college career. Their experience speaks to the subversive nature of courses in global environmental politics, of which students and teachers of the subject should be proud. But it also highlights troubling deficiencies of higher education that can no longer go ignored.

RECYCLE A BOTTLE, SAVE THE WORLD?

Although Americans seem disinclined to join in political battle over climate change policy, do not assume that they are not fighting for the environment and for climate stability in particular. Many are, but not as citizens coming together to change institutional arrangements or challenge power. Instead, they are attacking the problem as individualistic consumers.[6] In their struggle to bridge the gap between their environmental morals and practices, Americans stay busy—but busy doing that which they find familiar and comfortable: consuming their way to a better America and a better world. We (I write as an American, though I believe that these behaviors extend across the Western world) recycle with a vengeance. We agonize over the paper or plastic choice at the checkout counter, knowing somehow that neither is right given larger institutions and social structures. We think aloud with the neighbor over the back fence about whether we should buy the new Honda or Toyota hybrid-engine automobile or wait a few years until the technology matures, when really what we wish for is clean, efficient, effective public transportation of the sort we read about in science fiction novels when we were kids—but which we cannot vote for with our consumer dollars since, for reasons rooted in power and politics, it is not for sale. So we ponder the energy stickers on the ultraefficient appliances at Sears, diligently compost our kitchen waste, buy a few compact-fluorescent light bulbs, perhaps purchase clothing made from organically grown cotton, and hope for the best.

All this would be well and fine if there were good reason to believe that one could save the rainforests by eating (even more) Ben and Jerry's "Rainforest Crunch" ice cream ("buy it and a portion of the proceeds will go to save the rainforests") or having lunch down at the Rainforest Café. "Green consumption" might make sense as a primary engine of social change if there were strong evidence that driving about town in a new fuel-efficient vehicle or buying shade-grown coffee will alter patterns of policy and power that yield frightening atmospheric concentrations of greenhouse gases or drive the deepening impoverishment of cash crop exporting countries.

But there isn't, as students of global environmental politics soon come to realize. As Ken Conca (chapter 5) and Lamont Hempel (chapter 4) remind us, take a course in the field and you quickly learn that critical transboundary environmental problems do not originate from ill-informed or short-sighted consumer choice. They flow instead from a host of transnational political and economic forces that drive explosive economic growth, discount damages to environmental systems, and perpetuate environmentally undermining patterns of overconsumption and underconsumption. These arrangements benefit some (who will defend them!) while hurting others and hence won't be changed by nice talk or conscientious but uncoordinated choice in the supermarket aisle. Altering these patterns of power and reward will take concerted strategic struggle—struggle that can be rewarding in its own right, regardless of the outcome. When institutions and policies are changed as a result, consumers *do* respond, sometimes rapidly, to the availability of new products or the stimulus of changing prices, often with great effect. The phase-out of chlorofluorocarbons (CFCs), though not a full solution to the depletion of stratospheric ozone, is a case in point: political struggle led to policies that created new technological options, and meaningful changes in consumer choice followed.

To be sure, one should purchase environmentally friendly products, plant a tree, and ride a bike—it is the right, responsible thing to do. Yet as one moves through a typical course on global ecopolitics, it becomes harder to believe that consumption choices are the only or even best way to bring our personal power to bear on global environmental ills. Social ecologist Murray Bookchin (1989) surely had this in mind over a decade ago when he noted that:

It is inaccurate and unfair to coerce people into believing that they are *personally* responsible for present-day ecological disasters because they consume too much or proliferate too readily. This *privatization of the environmental crisis*, like the New Age cults that focus on personal problems rather than on social dislocations, has reduced many environmental movements to utter ineffectiveness and threatens to diminish their credibility with the public. If "simple living" and militant recycling are the main solutions to the environmental crisis, the crisis will certainly continue and intensify.[7] (19–23)

Bookchin, and others too (e.g., Hawken 1993 or Smith 1998), are reacting to several interlocking factors driving this "privatization of the environmental crisis." One, certainly, is the technocratic and scientific bias of mainstream environmentalism (e.g., Dowie 1995), which tends to frame the project of "saving the world" as an exercise in choosing the right technologies, buying the right products, and making the correct household consumer choices. For evidence, go no further than Environmental Defense's (one of the largest environmental groups in the United States) 2001–2002 calendar, which urges Americans to "help our planet" (their words) by recycling, buying dolphin-safe tuna, or purchasing a fuel-efficient car. A second factor is the centrality of liberalism to environmental politics, which has the effect of fixing final responsibility for social outcomes on *individual* choices and actions (e.g., Wapner 1996b). And certainly a third reason is the overall decline in civic participation and shared understandings of civic responsibility, documented by Putnam's work mentioned just a few paragraphs back.

At a time of waning faith in public life and civic activism, it is no surprise that students of global environmental problems more easily think of themselves as consumers than as citizens and act on their environmental concerns through their purchasing decisions. The alternative—engaging in some kind of citizen action—is too fuzzy and unfamiliar to be taken seriously and probably a bit threatening too. Yet this is precisely what the study of global environmental politics suggests must happen and, if it will, both students and their professors must move beyond the normal bounds of lecture-dominated, expert-centric classrooms.

PROFESSORIAL PIPE DREAMS?

Consider, for instance, the theory of social change advanced by the currently popular texts on the politics of global ecogovernance. No single textbook for courses in global environmental politics trumps, but three books dominate, and many courses in the field require students to read two and sometimes all three. If you are in a course on global environmental politics, odds are that you have at least one of these textbooks on your shelf. They are Porter, Brown, and Chasek's (2000) *Global Environmental*

Politics, Conca and Dabelko's (1998) *Green Planet Blues*, and Hempel's (1996a) *Environmental Governance*. The first is the most introductory and focuses primarily on the dynamics of transnational systems of cooperation and governance (or "regimes") that have evolved in response to threats to global environmental systems. Conca and Dabelko's book, by contrast, collects almost forty essays organized around seven themes of global environmental politics and governance. And in ways that mirror his contribution to this volume, Hempel's text explores global environmental norms from the perspectives of political economy and political ecology while advancing a "glocal" approach to environmental governance.

Though they differ in many way, these books are most remarkable for their similarities. Each of the three texts argues that we face perilous times—if anything, they suggest, we underestimate the severity of the ecological and political challenges before us. Porter, Brown, and Chasek talk ominously about "global macrotrends," Conca and Dabelko speak of the "global problematique," and Hempel alerts us to three risky global "experiments" (with climate, biodiversity, and democracy) now underway. All treat with suspicion the corporatist view that we can wriggle out of trouble with the right mix of technology, scientific expertise, and accelerated economic growth.

Most important, each book vests ultimate hope for a sustainable future in a reengaged and active citizenry working within vibrant participatory democracies. For Porter, Brown, and Chasek, citizen activism becomes a source of transnational institutional capacity to govern. They ask their readers to acknowledge the increased intensity of environmental activism around the world and to ponder how transnational networks of citizen activism are laying the foundation for global mechanisms of environmental governance. While many chapters in Conca and Dabelko's volume make the same case, some go further[8] to argue that meaningful public participation in shaping what surely will be costly and coercive environment policies is necessary to achieve a "democracy of restraint" vital to effective policymaking. Citizens of industrial democracies will not support policies for sustainability, in other words, unless they are part of the planning process: meaningful public participation generates consent *and* restraint, two ingredients critical to any transition to sustainability. For his part, Hempel pulls both notions together (civic activism as the basis of transnational networks of environmental governance *and* as a mechanism for facilitating democratically imposed changes in lifestyle), especially as he makes the case that

> only by linking community ecological values with democratic design of policies and markets can the goals of [global] environmental governance be real-

ized in a sustainable fashion. While it may be tempting, in the interest of time, to dispense with citizen education and community-based democratic deliberation and somehow construct the kind of enlightened authoritarian government that can act decisively on behalf of environmental protection and restoration, such forms of friendly "eco-fascism," in the name of sustainability, are themselves unsustainable and symptomatic of the instrumental thinking that has led to our present set of biospheric crises. If effectiveness of [global] environmental governance depends in part on political legitimacy, then not even the most eminent and benevolent environmental scientists should be allowed to assume the role of planetary managers. (Hempel 1996a: 8)

Employed by hundreds of college courses with thousands of students annually, these three books highlight a central irony of twenty-first-century global environmental politics: At that moment when natural science understanding of environmental ills is expanding, society's ability to democratically redress global environmental problems hinges not on the competency of technocratic managers or the brilliance of research scientists but on the capacities of a lay citizenry to debate and resolve, within their neighborhoods and communities, knotty issues of sustainability. That the local is the locus and the citizen is the engine of global sustainability must be a jarring insight for undergraduates who, as Nancy Quirk reminds us in chapter 13, come to college with full faith in scientific management, simple truth, and the ability of experts and interest groups operating in conventional theaters of power to chart a course for society. As social analyst and student of college life Paul Loeb (1999) observes, young people of today tend to view politics—both local and national—as dirty, complicated, and sometimes corrupt, something to be avoided or left to "them." Activists are too idealistic, inherently hypocritical, or just plain show-offs and malcontents.

How, then, might undergraduates (perhaps like you?) be reasonably expected to respond to arguments that a transnational mosaic of local, largely uncoordinated, and often spontaneous struggles—global civil society, in other words—is the last, best hope for humane systems of global environmental governance? Our hearts might hope that students react with curiosity and hope, but our heads know better; deep skepticism or, at best, benign tolerance and detachment is a more likely response. Individuals are inherently lazy, many students assert; humanity will come to care enough about the environment to act collectively only when environmental threats loom too large to ignore. Emergent civil society and grassroots action are the final soundings of most courses on global environmental ills, but for many students they surely come off as professorial pipe dreams to be memorized for the final exam.[9]

CURRICULAR OVERLOAD

Complicating matters is the curricular overload that makes it doubly difficult for students to engage critically important ideas of global civil society and locally based forces for sustainability. Undergraduate students of global environmental politics typically negotiate a hefty chunk of natural and social science material and read in eclectic, often unfamiliar literatures. Many instructors (over 30 percent in my study sample; see endnote 5) hold students accountable for one hundred pages of reading *per class meeting* (where classes meet twice or three times a week). A larger portion of professors (approaching 60 percent in the sample) assign at least seventy-five pages per class meeting, and some instructors (about 10 percent) require almost two hundred pages of reading per class. To some, this workload might seem appropriate. Remember, though, that courses in global environmental politics ask students to become knowledgeable in a variety of disciplines and subfields—from international political economy to biogeochemistry, to economic development theory to social movements—that don't easily build upon one another. Readings often are conceptually advanced, even cutting edge, and sometimes require the cultivation of advanced disciplinary vocabularies. Against this backdrop, a typical reading load of 75–100 pages per class meeting begins to look daunting.

Why are professors wedded to such jam-packed courses? Often, only one course in global environmental politics is offered at an institution, obligating the instructor to cover the field in a single shot. Since it is unclear what constitutes "the field," instructors may try to capture all that might reasonably lie within its boundaries. Those who teach the subject, moreover, often do so out of a commitment to build a better world—and this can lead them to pack their courses with every bit of information they believe their students need for the fight ahead. Yet another factor is the diverse disciplinary background of students in the course (as Professor Warshawsky notes in chapter 12), which obliges instructors to lay intellectual groundwork in international relations and environmental science before moving to advanced topics. A final culprit is the empirics of global environmental politics (protocols, international agreements, framework conventions, negotiations in process), which invite close inspection but which can chew up large chunks of class time.

Together, these factors drive curricular overload: too much information crammed into too little time, necessarily taught in the most leanly efficient of ways—through information-packed lectures. Such courses surely teach students a great deal about global environmental politics, but at what cost? By unconsciously underscoring the primacy of expert knowledge and placing students in an environment where passive acceptance of authority tends to yield the greatest rewards (i.e., the highest grade), the highly efficient, tightly ordered, lecture-dominated classroom can inadvertently stunt the development of the democratic sensibilities and citizen skills of students.[10] Imagine a scene where students sit passively, banking knowledge from their professor-expert who is lecturing about how active citizen participation is *the* vital ingredient of evolving forms of global environmental governance. In this way, the rhythms of the overloaded, hyperefficient course in global environmental ills almost naturally contradict the lessons about social change that permeate the field. They aid and abet inherent student skepticism about the ubiquity and personal rewards of grassroots activism and hence do violence to the very reasons we come, professors and students both, to college and university with faith in the power of education to shape a better world. Such courses are strong on content, weak in practice and political outcome, and all too commonplace.

ANTISIMULATIONS FOR A
GREENHOUSE WORLD

This is not to say that most courses in global environmental politics are forced marches through the mud. Many feature creative elements meant to bring course material alive. Some courses, for example, ask students to simulate "the tragedy of the commons" (see chapter 6). Others convene mock Earth Summit meetings, semester-long electronic state-to-state negotiations on environmental protocols, or nongovernment organization (NGO) coordination simulations. More narrowly constructed exercises around whaling and ozone regimes are also in evidence, as are projects requiring students to build Web pages that untangle the details of international environmental protocols and emerging environmental threats. The tried-and-true practice of students undertaking specialized research and presenting the results to their peers lives on as well.

But here is the rub: Though there is much to recommend these exercises, they almost always place students in the role of expert analyst, technocratic manager, or high flying diplomat that privileges state and NGO elites and a transnational technocracy. Grassroots activism, civil society, and local action get lost in these simulations, except as pesky gnats that must, from time to time, be acknowledged, accommodated, or swatted away.

Absent is a breed of simulation that reproduces for students the ambiguities, frustrations, and rewards of citizen struggle over an issue that matters—the very kind of struggle that community members all around the world will experience if Hempel's ideas about the centrality of "community-based democratic deliberation" quoted earlier in this chapter are to bear fruit. Students plunged into an alternative simulation would be able, at semester's end, to evaluate claims about the inherent rewards of active citizenship. They would be capable of testing the argument that small groups of people can make things happen. Most important, they would be forced to confront their own beliefs, often unexamined, about the potency of civic engagement in postindustrial society. More than just an academic exercise, such simulations could lay the foundation for the elusive bridge between the knowledge in our texts and our power in the world.

I call these exercises antisimulations—"anti" because they shun the preplanned, tightly managed, sometimes contrived dimensions of most classroom role playing. These simulations need not be ambitious, contentious, overtly political, or ideologically charged, nor must they focus on environmental topics. They must, however, pitch students into largely unfamiliar waters by involving them in collective work on an issue that matters *to them*, for which both the process and outcome of struggle is initially unclear. Let me share my experience with antisimulations—not because I expect you will find it unusually interesting or praiseworthy, but because it highlights important claims about social change and the power of participation in a greenhouse world.

My first contact with antisimulations was forced upon me many years ago by an unusually persistent group of undergraduates in my seminar on grassroots action and civil society. Inspired by the chronicles of activism they were analyzing, they demanded midway through the semester that they be permitted to "do something active" in lieu of writing yet another research paper. They were especially eager to test the claims from the literature we were reading that local-level political action is fundamentally empowering and emancipatory. After extended discussion, the class decided to push for some sort of alternative civic space on campus, a place where students, faculty, and members of the larger community could meet, in ways both planned and spontaneous. (A new food court had recently swallowed up a popular space that had served this purpose.) Their interest in how the design of public space affects democratic discourse eventually jelled into plans for a campus coffeehouse, which, after months of struggle, planning, recruitment, and self-education by those very same students, opened for business with hoopla and celebration.

"Grounds for Change" is a *student* coffeehouse—it is managed and staffed by students, who are paid in-kind and govern the enterprise. Though it is a remarkable place,[11] what is most striking about it are the lessons my students learned as they struggled to create it. One of my most cherished moments as a college professor came when, speaking for the entire course, one student (who was initially skeptical of the project) confidently asserted that "everyone should work themselves silly to accomplish something they believe in. There clearly is no feeling like it" (Terry 1996). By virtue of butting heads with the college administration and the campus food vendor, not to mention with each other, these young people came to understand that politics is not demeaning; it is not something "they" (i.e., elites) do in Washington, D.C., or at the Earth Summit; it is not necessarily ruthless, and it needn't be mean-spirited. They developed an intuitive feel for the barriers and rewards to community-based deliberation and left the course with concrete experiences against which to judge Jeffersonian claims that citizenship, in the full meaning of the word, makes us more powerful and more human. The experience supplanted my students' easy, simple cynicism about citizen activism and social change with a more mature understanding of the promise and perils of altering institutions and challenging power.

Though the coffeehouse was a once-in-a-lifetime classroom success, it gave me courage to try my hand at less ambitious antisimulations in my course on global environmental politics, which takes climate change as its core case study. After exploring the formal politics of global climate change—The Framework Convention, the dynamics of international negotiation, mechanisms of inter- and intrastate compliance, Kyoto and beyond, and the like—my students and I turn our attention to the centrality of resurgent civil society to new forms of transnational environmental governance. (I follow the lead of the field's three principal texts, previously described.) My students react to this civil-society talk with cautious skepticism and, given their life experience, who can blame them?[12] "People won't become involved," they say. "Individuals can't make a difference." "Civil society is a thing of the past." Or, my favorite, "people will only act when there's a crisis, and by then it will be too late."

Responses like these reveal a common assumption that citizen involvement and political action is personally costly, typically ineffective, largely onerous, and generally rare, occupying the realm of oddballs and malcontents. "Fine," I say. "Let's test your hypotheses about public life." We begin by compiling a list of the dozen or more situations or practices, on campus or in the community, that students find most irritating. In years past, this list has included complaints about inadequate street lighting, insufficient student parking, the banality of the student newspaper, the lack of a student pub on campus, restrictions on access to key campus facilities, neighborhood tensions between students and city residents, inattentiveness to recycling by local businesses, the aesthetic decline of campus in the soggy winter months as students shortcut across the muddy lawn rather than use the sidewalks, the callousness of area landlords, inaccessibility to key areas of the library—and the list goes on.

What students list as "important problems" does not matter, so long as they are complex, rooted in institutional structure and human behavior, and *really matter* to the students. It bears repeating that the issues need not be environmental (this would unproductively limit the field)—the aim is to expand students' understanding of public life, not supplement their burgeoning knowledge of environmental problems. My students form groups (some self-select, others require assistance) and set to work on a plan for how they would attack their problem of choice. "You mean we get credit in this class for figuring out how to raise a little bit of hell?" asked one student a few semesters back. "Exactly," came my reply—so long as any hell raising is focused, thought out, reflective, and puts us in a place to test our hypotheses about public life.

Accomplished antisimulations of civic action, I tell them, will be those that constructively confront prevailing practices, institutions, and ways of thinking. One need not make a huge difference, I say (though one should aim for this); rather, the intensity, intellect, and integrity one brings to the struggle is key. I caution my students against swinging too far to one extreme of apolitical technocratic management or to the other of mindless confrontation and noisy but pointless public protest. The bottom line is that, as students of global environmental politics, they must be well-positioned, six weeks down the line, to evaluate the claim that group struggle can be its own reward and that these rewards are sufficiently energizing to sustain the kinds of grassroots action thought necessary to drive a transition to sustainability.

I confess that sometimes students fail to "get it." One semester, for instance, a group organized a glass recycling project for a neighborhood bar. They sought to educate the pub's patrons about the benefits of recycling, and they periodically carted the collected bottles to the recycling center. Over time, they identified several factors that undermined pub-owner interest in recycling: pubs, under state law, were exempt from existing recycling ordinances; a flat rate for weekly refuse collection discouraged businesses from reducing their waste stream; a general concern about local economic downturn made business owners wary of any new initiatives that might strain their ability to stay afloat. But the students avoided confrontation with these institutional factors and instead did, from their years of schooling, what they knew best—they donned the mantle of expertise and spent most of their time sharing facts with pub owners about "our" social responsibility to behave "ecologically." They met with limited success and, unfortunately, left the experience feeling demoralized and pessimistic about the possibility of any meaningful shift towards sustainability. Their story is a cautionary tale for the student groups that have followed.

Happily, these disappointments do not often occur. Most students quickly grasp the essential elements of the exercise. For instance, one group saw to producing several issues of a three- to four-page underground campus newspaper. They wrote about pressing student issues and saw to the logistics of paste-up, printing, and distribution. The exercise was fraught with ambiguity: the students knew nothing about producing a paper; and they had to negotiate "distribution rights" on campus, debate story ideas among themselves, produce the product, and later respond to charges that their underground paper was unnecessary in light of the "good work" of the official campus paper.

Another group, all women who lived in apartments a few blocks from campus, spent weeks pressuring city hall to improve street lighting near their residence. They did their research, went to meetings, and attracted local media attention. When it appeared that the regional television news station was about to run a story juxtaposing their efforts against the city's apparent recalcitrance, a new streetlight suddenly sprang up. (We drew some interesting parallels in class to Greenpeace's able use of the media.) A third group a few semesters later fought for better crosswalks and a reconfigured pedestrian crossing path across the road that bisects campus. Their efforts yielded a front-page article in the city newspaper. One member of that group was later hired as downtown coordinator by the city, partly due to his group's efforts, and a significant structural ("traffic calming") reconfiguration of the crossing zone is now actively being planned by the college. Yet another group organized a block party in a neighborhood rife with town–gown tension, which set a precedent for subsequent student-resident block parties now coordinated by the college.

These are just a few examples. In every case, students dove into a project they know next to nothing about, puzzled out who the stakeholders were and where the pressure points for change lay, and strategized about how to nudge thinking, policy, and institutions towards their desired outcome. At semester's end, my students write extensively about their antisimulation, focusing on how it has influenced, if at all, their understanding of political struggle and their grasp of the literature on global environmental governance. My students realize that I want critical commentary and self-reflection, not boosterism. Alarmingly, they write with unforced enthusiasm and appreciation. Year in and year out, they describe the antisimulation to be unlike anything else in their educational career and among the most rewarding experiences of their time at college. Many disturbingly speak of a newfound confidence, and almost all demonstrate a deeper appreciation of what scholars and activists mean by civic virtue and why it is important to our shared future. With no prompting, moreover, students commonly argue that antisimulations should be required in more college courses, especially those in environmental science and political science. In the absence of such exercises, they maintain, the easy cynicism of their peers will go unchallenged, to our collective detriment.

The antisimulation's effect on my students pleases me—though note my use of "alarmingly" and "disturbingly" when I describe it. The bright and morally engaged students with whom I work should not find passing moments of collective struggle to be remarkable, exceptional, even life changing. That they do says much about the paucity of citizen capacity among those we consider to be highly educated, and it casts a long shadow over what we define as rigorous and valuable teaching in political science and environmental studies. I can't help but think that those toiling in the classrooms of global environmental affairs would do well to consider how their work unproductively reinforces a state-centric, expert-dominated understanding of politics. If processes of community-based deliberation do in fact lie at the heart of a less statist, less technocratic, more promising global environmental politics, students of the subject must become comfortable with the many facets of democracy in action. That they command such a limited appreciation of collective struggle and deliberation is not surprising. That educators leave unchallenged their pupils' practical political ignorance is more befuddling.

CONCLUSION: ON "MALADJUSTMENT"

In 1958, speaking on the power of nonviolence, Martin Luther King, Jr., declared that

> Modern psychology has a word that is probably used more than any other word. It is the word "maladjusted." Now we all should seek to live a well-adjusted life in order to avoid neurotic and schizophrenic personalities. But there are some things within our social order to which I am proud to be maladjusted and to which I call upon you to be maladjusted. I never intend to adjust myself to mob rule. I never intend to adjust myself to the tragic effects of the methods of physical violence and to tragic militarism. I call upon you to be maladjusted to such things. (Washington 1992: 33)

Because of what they teach, instructors of global environmental politics are inevitably engaged in the maladjustment of their students. By virtue of what they study, students of the field are opening themselves up to a process of maladjustment. How could it be otherwise? The stuff of global environmental politics calls into question core assumptions about how we imagine and manage environmental ills, about how the tension between individuals as consumers and individuals as citizens is best understood. As students and teachers together unravel the many environmental threats of global proportion, it is difficult to imagine how deeply radical questions of personal agency, social change, civic virtue, and personal responsibility could go unasked. Confronting these questions inevitably drives us, teachers and students both, toward what educational analyst Herbert Kohl (1994) calls "creative maladjustment"—the capacity to see social systems from "the outside" and fashion creative responses to their insufficiencies.

Does this make the teaching of global environmental politics subversive? Probably so.[13] But the need for a subversive pedagogy, one that fosters critical capacities of citizenship while creating intellectual space to grapple with the issues of the day, is more pressing than ever in a greenhouse world. The status quo, where people feel deeply about issues like climate change but find it too difficult or mysterious to act as citizens on their concerns, is a dead end. It produces, as political scientist Langdon Winner observes, a futile stalemate that we can ill afford:

> Citizens are strongly encouraged to become involved in improving modern material culture, but only in the market or other highly privatized settings. [As a result,] there is no moral community or public space in which technological issues are topics for deliberation, debate, and shared action.... Under such circumstances it is not surprising to find that people who call for moral deliberation about specific technological choices find themselves isolated and beleaguered, working outside or even in defiance of established channels of power and authority.... The lack of any coherent identity for "public" or of well-organized, legitimate channels for public participation contributes to two distinctive features of contemporary policy debates about technology: (1) futile rituals of expert advice and (2) interminable disagreements about which choices are morally justified. (Winner 1992: 351)

A global environmental politics that leapfrogs such rituals and disagreements will be one that shows itself capable of creating multiple channels of public participation while inspiring an educational process that makes collective deliberation and struggle something more than foreign and feared. These measures, of course, will not be enough: to assume that any resurgence of civic virtue or deepening of global civil society will, by itself, usher in sustainable, humane forms of global governance would be naive.[14] But we cannot get to a transnational system of environmental governance without a resurgent civic culture, where local activism, not green consumption or elite technocratic tinkering, emerges as *the* vehicle for acting out our environmental concerns. The "greening" of the college curriculum, despite a decade of progress, is not yet complete—and the work left to be done must quickly be shouldered by students and instructors alike.

QUESTIONS FOR REFLECTION
AND DISCUSSION

1. "Most people," wrote Saul Alinksy (1969: 94), "are eagerly groping for some medium, some way in which they can bridge the gap between their morals and their practices." Alinsky was an organizer of "peoples' movements," principally in Chicago, and his conclusion about "most people" flows from his work, decades ago, with the urban poor and disempowered. Would you say that his claim about "most people" still holds true today, especially with respect to middle-class Americans concerned about climate change? Does it hold true for those in your seminar or classroom?

2. David Orr writes that "we militantly defend our rights as consumers while letting our rights as citizens wither" (1999: 140). Do you find much support, in your own reading and life experience, for this claim and for the argument of this chapter that Americans respond to global environmental ills more as consumers than as citizens? Where do you find counterexamples? Ultimately, where do you come down on the assertion that a "privatization of responsibility" has colonized American's response to environmental degradation?

3. Civic virtue: It is important, it is arguably on the decline, and it is seemingly critical to the resolution of global environmental ills. Why? How? In what ways?

4. Of the three books discussed in the Professorial Pipe Dreams section, which are most familiar to you? How would you describe, in ways that go beyond this section, the impact of these books on the ability of undergraduates to make sense of environmental ills and actively respond to them?

5. "The local is the locus and the citizen is the engine of global environmental sustainability." How does this claim challenge conventional ways of thinking about the source of and cure for global environmental ills? Is this claim jarring? Do you find it to be empowering, or intimidating, or perhaps something else?

6. This chapter assumes that the work of fostering "citizen education and community-based democratic deliberation" must seem strange and far-fetched to college students with little experience with the joys and challenges of political struggle—and, consequently, students cannot be blamed for checking out or going through the motions when their course begins to zero in on these issues. (I call them "professorial pipe dreams to be memorized for the final exam.") Am I being too hard on the students of today? Or not hard enough?

7. I was genuinely surprised by the results of my reconnaissance of syllabi for courses in global environmental politics. I did not expect such vivid indications of curricular overload. My surprise explains, to some extent, my harsh words for professors who seem insensitive to the consequences of curricular overload for the civic capacities of their students. Am I being too hard on the professors of today who fall into my category of "curricular overloaders"? Or not hard enough? Why?

8. What is "anti" about my antisimulations? Is it really all that important to resist, *in the classroom*, the forces and biases that the antisimulation opposes?

9. I burdened you with my story of antisimulations because, I said, they would highlight important claims about social change and the power of participation in a greenhouse world. What do you take to be these claims? How, if at all, are they important to your study of global environmental ills—and to your role as a teacher or student within higher education?

10. Is the study of global environmental ills unavoidably subversive, in your view? Does your work in the field inevitably lead to your maladjustment? Do others in your seminar or class see it this way? What explains any disagreement on these questions?

NOTES

My thanks to John Whissel and Carlos Shedd for research assistance, to the students in my global environmental politics course for helpful comments on earlier drafts, to Robert Razcka for intellectual support at a critical juncture, and to Richard Cook for his patience with sometimes overenthusiastic citizens in the making.

1. From a national survey of 1,010 American adults conducted by Harris Interactive (parent company of the Harris Poll) between August 10 and August 14, 2000.

2. Commissioned in September 1998 by the American Solar Energy Society and the Sustainable Energy Coalition and conducted by Research/Strategy/Management, Inc., a leading Republican consulting firm. The sample size was 1,003 voting adults.

3. The survey also revealed strong public support for increasing federal subsidies to renewable energy technologies and strong disapproval of subsidies to nuclear power and fossil fuels.

4. See for example Barber (1998), Freie (1998), the National Commission on Civic Renewal (1998), and Sandel (1996).

5. My generalizations about courses in global environmental politics are informed by analysis of over sixty syllabi from courses in the field, drawn from colleges and universities across the nation. Many of these syllabi are posted for

inspection at the Web page of The Project on Teaching Global Environmental Politics, at webpub.alleg.edu/employee/m/mmaniate/GepEd/geped.html.

6. For more on the distinction between consumer and citizen within the context of environmental struggles and processes of consumerism and commodification, see Princen, Maniates, and Conca (2002) and Coleman (1994). Smith (1998) offers a nifty analysis of the forces driving "green consumption" as a primary popular response to environmental degradation.

7. First emphasis in the original; second emphasis added.

8. Especially Ophuls (1974).

9. For instance, the author of a familiar and accessible book that explores global civil society and its importance to emerging forms of global environmental governance once shared with me his disappointment that students in his own global environmental politics course failed to grasp the point of the book. This is not surprising or, in my experience, unusual, despite the fact that case study treatments of "global civil society" (e.g., Rich 1994 or Wapner 1996a) are quite explicit in their description of how those working within or in behalf of environmental NGOs marshal and exercise political power.

10. Dewey (1938) was one of the first to formally advance this argument. Etzioni (1993) and Gatto (1992) offer contemporary versions of the same perspective. Arnstine (1995) extends this argument with his understanding of classroom learning as a set of "acquired dispositions" (such as passivity, a preference for avoiding group work in favor of individual tasking, etc.) antithetical to the social requirements of participatory democracy. For a humanities-based treatment of these ideas, see Randall's (2000) brief but lively "A Guide to Good Teaching: Be Slow and Inefficient."

11. See a small picture of "Grounds for Change" at www.allegheny.edu/tour/U3.html.

12. See Halstead (1999), or Brooks's (2001) assessment of "the organization kid."

13. In ways, in fact, advocated by Postman and Weingartner (1969).

14. As, for example, Falk makes clear in the introduction to *On Humane Governance: Toward a New Global Politics* (1995).

III

EDUCATION EXPANDED
*Paths Are Made
by Walking*

9

❂

Teaching with Theory Plays
The Example of the Ozone Layer in Renewing a Common World

B. Welling Hall

In this most unusual of chapters, B. Welling Hall teaches us about theory plays, the Montreal Protocol, the rewards that come with putting students in the way of novel and rigorous classroom experiences, and the importance of embracing new strategies for making global environmental politics come alive. This piece surely complements any classroom exploration of ozone politics. But Professor Hall's contribution finds its way into this volume more because of its inescapable challenge to all of us—teachers, students, and policymakers—to strain against the bindings of old routines and rise to new levels of creative analysis and problem solving.

It is fashionable to argue that the road to a sustainable society will be paved by creative thinkers and imaginative problem solvers. Professor Hall, in allowing us a glimpse of her accomplished classroom practice, shows us what we might be doing in our own classes should we treat this argument with the respect it deserves.—M.M.

Education is the point at which we decide whether we love the world enough to assume responsibility for it and by the same token save it from that ruin that, except for renewal, except for the coming of the new and young, would be inevitable. And education, too, is where we decide whether we love our children enough not to expel them from our world and leave them to their own devices, nor to strike from their hands the chance of undertaking something new, some-

151

thing unforeseen by us, but to prepare them in advance for the task
of renewing a common world.

—Hannah Arendt (1968: 196)

For millennia, drama has been a significant tool in shaping communities for continuity and renewal, including those of teachers and learn-
ers. Pointing to just a few stars in the galaxy, literary as well as political
theorists can name essays by Aristotle, Plato, Tolstoy, Freire, and Fanon
on the pedagogical implications of dialogue and drama. Indeed, theory
and theater share a common etymological root, *the-*, meaning to gaze at or
to look at in order to understand. Ritual, pageantry, and guerrilla theater,
despite vastly different content, all speak to the presumed power of plays
in motivating participant-observers to insight, commitment, and action.
With this long and varied a pedigree, justifying the use of drama in a
global environmental politics classroom would be akin to justifying the
use of medicine in a clinic.

The most common form of drama in the liberal arts classroom today is
the role play (sometimes known as role playing), often in conjunction
with a case study. The benefits of case studies and role plays are many,
and both my students and I have engaged in some that were tantalizing.
Yet there are occasions, perhaps due to inadequate time for preparation
or insufficient access to primary materials, when both teachers and students can be frustrated by the experience of a role play. Students may feel
that they don't learn enough by exchanging unsupported opinions with
peers who are also novices in the field. Teachers may wonder if content is
subsumed by form (Doty 1996: 20). The name of the generic exercise suggests that *roles* are being replicated or simulated. To use the language of
conflict resolution, far from separating the people from the problem, the
typical role play establishes people as the problem by demonstrating the
ways in which world views are incommensurable. This is especially likely
to be the case when it is easy to portray greed, intransigence, or the plight
of the underdog, and correspondingly difficult to imagine trade-offs and
see through the Gordian knot of a dilemma. Following Arendt, there are
some situations in which assigning or participating in a role play might
leave students to their own devices without providing empowering
vision or background.

The purpose of a theory play is to give students conceptually rich language that transcends roles as well as analytical practice in using these
concepts in dialogue with peers. Couldn't the same result be achieved by
a lecture followed by a small group discussion? Sometimes, certainly, yes.
Most often, however, only a few students speak in discussions and others,

who may understand the material as well or better, remain silent. The combination of lecture and discussion can become active learning but must overcome the inertia of expectation to do so.

In contrast, the theory play literally gets students talking immediately and in doing so opens the door to both wider participation and deeper discussion with students using theories and concepts they already have experience in voicing. Indeed, the most positive experience that my students and I have shared with theory plays is that after speaking with authority in the classroom (although not, in this case, using their own words), students are motivated to investigate the words they have spoken and why. Due to luck, happenstance, or some as yet unknown significant correlation, there always seem to be closet hams or theater hopefuls in my global environmental politics classes. Variety in and of itself has something to be said for it. The variety of having students in effect perform a "lecture" with content shaped by a professor and form shaped by students energizes the class.

The play reproduced here, "Behind the Veil of Ignorance," introduces students of global environmental politics to trade-offs, dilemmas, and potential solutions in protecting the ozone layer by demonstrating the applicability of John Rawls's theory of justice (as interpreted and criticized by Brian Barry in *The Liberal Theory of Justice*). Its genesis involved combining a scenario provided by Barry; political theory concepts such as justice, issue linkage, and public good; juicy quotations from newspaper accounts of the negotiations on the Montreal Protocol; and a sense of humor. Student volunteers then staged the theory play for classmates (who had also read the script), improvising where prudent and concluding with a question and answer session led by the performers.

This experience is reproducible. I have written other theory plays that students have performed and used to engage classmates in discussion of political issues. Other instructors have used these theory plays in their classrooms. The logical next step is for other groups of faculty and students to collaborate in generating their own theory plays in global environmental politics classes. Others will have patterns of collaboration that work most successfully in their settings. What has worked for me and for my students is for the professor to draft the play, pulling together scholarly articles, newspaper reports, and anecdotes and for students to produce the play either in class or in a related setting. Nothing prevents faculty (or students) from identifying a provocative piece of theory or research that contains enough controversy to generate dialogue and asking students themselves to transpose the text from the genre of academic article to drama.

BEHIND THE VEIL OF IGNORANCE

NARRATOR: *(speaking offstage)* Suppose you were a random embryo and you did not know where you would be born. You did not know whether you would be poor or rich, able bodied or not, male or female, intellectually gifted or brain damaged in infancy. "What kind of world would you prefer? One, like the present one, that gives you about a fifty-fifty chance of being born in a country with widespread malnutrition and a high infant mortality rate and about a one in four chance of being born in a rich country, or a world in which the gap between the best and the worst has been reduced?"[1] "What rules would you negotiate in order to achieve a fair distribution of justice? What concerns would motivate your thinking in your temporary position behind this veil of ignorance?"[2]

The scene opens. Undifferentiated actors looking painfully small, if undaunted, are seated at the far side of an enormous round table. The side of the table closest to the audience is empty with unoccupied chairs oriented as if to invite new players to the discussion. Each actor has a pile of papers to which he or she may refer occasionally.

KIM: Can someone remind me what we are trying to decide now?

CHRIS: *(shoving Robin)* Get AWAY from my table.

LEE: Something to do with public goods.

ROBIN: *(throwing Chris's paper on the floor)* It isn't your table. It's everybody's table!

KIM: What do we know about public goods?

ROBIN: Chris is a public BAD.

CHRIS: Am not and you are too!

KIM: *(picking up a piece of paper that fell nearby)* Ah! Here's the definition: "Public goods are characterized by jointness and nonexclusion. This means that consumption by one actor does not diminish the quality or quantify of the benefit available to the other and that there is no way to prevent any actor from receiving benefits."[3]

ROBIN: *(sarcastically)* Oh that really helped a lot. I understand everything now.

CHRIS: Why should you understand everything? You aren't born today!

LEE: No need to be snide, Chris. We're all in this together.

CHRIS: *(gleefully, to Robin)* Lee is a public goody two shoes!

KIM: Will you two act your age!

CHRIS and ROBIN: Am acting my age! Why don't *you* act *your* age!

KIM: We *are* in this all together; this is what this "public goods" stuff is all about. Let's take this ozone depletion thing, for example.

CHRIS: New Zealand, here I come! Get me my sunscreen, mama, baby has sensitive skin!

ROBIN: You don't know where you are going any more than the rest of us do. Right? Why should Chris know if the rest of us don't?

KIM: None of us knows. The point is, according to this public goods thing, it hardly seems to matter. It looks like, eventually, either we all get UV protection from the ozone layer or none of us do.

ROBIN: *(to Chris)* Nah nah nah nah nah!

LEE: Kim, why don't you and I just develop some rules together. These two are so immature! We can work out a good, fair system of international equity just for the two of us.

KIM: No can do. You'll forget all about me after I'm born. And even if you did remember, there's no way to include some people in receiving ozone benefits and exclude others.

ROBIN: *(Robin is looking at Kim and does not see Chris crawling underneath the table.)* You don't know that you'll have any power at all when you are born, Lee! You couldn't keep us out of the game even if Kim wanted to.

(Chris reaches up to the table and pulls all of Robin's papers to the ground.)

Will you STOP it! How are we going to get Chris to stop behaving like this?

KIM: What do you mean "we," Robin?

LEE: OK, OK. Well, let's at least try to construct rational rules of justice by examining relevant perspectives. I'll be the INTERNATIONAL SCIENTIFIC COMMUNITY.

KIM: I'll be INDUSTRY.

ROBIN: I'll represent the GROUP OF 77.

CHRIS: *(crawling back into a chair and sitting as tall as possible)* Typecasting! Unh uh. No way. Why, I think *I'll* be INDUSTRY.

KIM: Lee and I will play the GROUP OF 77.

ROBIN: Well, I guess I'm stuck then with being the INTERNATIONAL SCIENTIFIC COMMUNITY.

At this point, Kim, Lee, Chris, and Robin each produce name placards with their role indicated. When speaking for their role, they prominently display their placard.

INTERNATIONAL SCIENTIFIC COMMUNITY: "There is no longer reasonable doubt that industrial gases containing chlorine (otherwise known as CFCs) are responsible in large measure for a dramatic, large-scale change in the stratosphere."[4] "In fact, if just four developing countries—China, India, Indonesia, and Brazil—increase their domestic consumption of CFCs to the levels allowed by the protocol, CFC production on a worldwide scale would double from the 1986 base level."[5]

KIM: What does that mean?

INTERNATIONAL SCIENTIFIC COMMUNITY: It means that "the rate of ozone layer degradation over the next twenty to one hundred years is going to depend far more on CFC production and use in developing countries than on the degree of reduction the industrialized countries can accomplish."[6]

INDUSTRY: In the industrialized world, we are eliminating the use of CFCs since the scientific evidence proved sufficiently compelling.[7] We are persuaded that the depletion of the ozone layer will result in dramatically higher skin cancer rates and other damage to plants, animals, and ecological systems. Dupont has stopped making Freon. Other producers should be similarly constrained!

LEE: Why?

INDUSTRY: In the absence of international controls, we will be severely hurt if foreign producers can continue to produce, use, and sell CFCs![8]

ROBIN: Who's "we," Chris?

CHRIS: Well, Dupont is a U.S.-based multinational. Americans, I guess.

ROBIN: Nationalist! You'll be up the proverbial creek without a paddle if you aren't born in the U.S.A.!

GROUP OF 77: We don't think that there is any justice in worrying about the profits of multinational corporations when 90 percent of the 1.3 billion Chinese don't have refrigerators. China just built twelve CFC plants in order to provide refrigerators to its population.[9]

CHRIS: And I, personally, would like access to refrigeration. I hear that there are days when Ben and Jerry's *Rainforest Crunch Peace Pop* makes life worth living.

LEE: . . . not to mention the health care benefits!

INTERNATIONAL SCIENTIFIC COMMUNITY: Well, look! Here it says that "a ten year grace period for developing countries would make little difference in long-term ozone depletion."[10] What if we, I mean the INTERNATIONAL SCIENTIFIC COMMUNITY and INDUSTRY, agree to "facilitate access to environmentally safe alternative substances and technology . . . [and] . . . facilitate bilaterally or multilaterally the provision of subsidies, aids, credits . . . to . . . developing countries for the use of alternative technology and for substitute products."[11]

CHRIS: Gee, I don't know. Are there adequate substitutes for CFCs? Won't they be expensive to develop?

GROUP OF 77: "Industrialized countries should provide Third World countries with more expensive substitutes for CFCs free of charge! Don't expect to win concessions from developing countries still suffering from famine and economic hardship. You have no right to tell them what to do or what not to do."[12]

ROBIN: I thought we did! Wasn't the whole basis of this public goods discussion the assumption that we *are* in this all together? The developing countries aren't going to be any better off than the industrialized world if this ozone thing goes haywire.

GROUP OF 77: "There are 1.3 billion Chinese so if the ozone layer breaks down, the one-fifth of the world's population that is Chinese will be hurt and they'll suffer the most."[13]

ROBIN: *(counting on fingers)* That's the second time you've mentioned those 1.3 billion people. I can't even begin to imagine numbers that big.

LEE: Did you know that a woman is giving birth 163 times every second somewhere on earth?

CHRIS: Well, we're just going to have to find her and stop her!

ROBIN: *(groans)* So shouldn't the Chinese (and the Indians, for that matter) be interested in protecting the ozone layer?

GROUP OF 77: *(to INDUSTRY)* "We didn't destroy the ozone layer. You did. I'm saying that you have the capability and the money to restore what you have destroyed. If you think I can go into a middle class home in my country and say, 'Chuck out your fridge because somebody in America destroyed the ozone layer,' then I'm not going to be able to do that."[14]

CHRIS: You don't have to get so personal about it!

INTERNATIONAL SCIENTIFIC COMMUNITY: "Meeting the problems of the 1990s is going to entail increased financial and environmental self-discipline, as well as the transfer of resources and technology to the South."[15]

GROUP OF 77: Self-discipline, my foot! The North has a lousy record of transferring resources to us. "Today, the poor are no more prepared to wait for the promised freedom from hunger and poverty. There will be a social upheaval if they are asked to wait any longer. Lest someone in this conference think of this as charity, I would like to remind them of the excellent principle of 'polluter pays' adopted in the developed world."[16]

INDUSTRY: We are opposed to handouts!

GROUP OF 77: We're not asking for handouts, doofus. We're demanding equity, pure and simple! "Are you prepared to lower your standard of living? You won't drive less miles in your car, but you tell the Third World not to cut down trees. What are you going to do for us? Do you want to rent the trees from us? You know, you can rent them for $1 billion in hard currency, and we won't cut them down. We'll use that money to do the things we need to do. If you don't want to rent them, what is your quid pro quo?"[17]

ROBIN: No need to call names. Besides, you are confusing issues. Global warming and ozone depletion are two separate problems.

KIM: Maybe it looks that way to you, but it seems to us that we've finally got some bargaining leverage here! And besides, if China and India go ahead and produce CFCs, your goose is cooked!

GROUP OF 77: You want to protect the ozone layer? Give us the technology to develop CFC substitutes.

INDUSTRY: But it is in your own best interest to protect the ozone layer!

GROUP OF 77: Pay up and we'll shut up.

INDUSTRY: That's extortion!

LEE: Who's that?

ROBIN: The GROUP OF 77 knows that its interests are better served by protecting the ozone layer than by not protecting it regardless of whether funding is transferred by the North. The GROUP OF 77 is threatening to act against its own interest by producing more CFCs if it doesn't receive technology transfers. And, at the same time, it is promising to refrain from producing CFCs if it receives compensation. That's extortion![18]

KIM: I don't care what you call it. Do you think it will work?

INDUSTRY: (to INTERNATIONAL SCIENTIFIC COMMUNITY) What do you think it will cost us to provide these technology transfers?

INTERNATIONAL SCIENTIFIC COMMUNITY: The cost of finding replacements for the estimated 3,500 applications where CFCs are used could reach $36 billion between now and 2075. In any case, the cost of further deterioration to the ozone layer, especially if China and India proceed with unimpeded CFC production and use, will be much higher. We can guarantee that.

LEE: (to Kim) What will it cost us to carry through on our threat?

KIM: If I'm born in a developing country, I want refrigeration. People don't die of skin cancer in infancy.

GROUP OF 77: Allow us to develop economically, and then we'll talk about environmental protection.

INDUSTRY: (begrudgingly) OK, it's a deal. But if you don't comply with international efforts to reduce CFC production, you'll be subject to trade sanctions. And I believe I speak for the INTERNATIONAL SCIENTIFIC COMMUNITY too?

INTERNATIONAL SCIENTIFIC COMMUNITY: (nods)

GROUP OF 77: OK, but major donors cannot make financing decisions regarding CFC substitution without the approval of the majority of recipient states.

(*GROUP OF 77* and *INDUSTRY shake hands.*)

LEE: (*to Kim*) "We've got a guarantee that if they don't give us the knowledge, we don't have to do it!"[19]

CHRIS: Have we done it? Have we figured this one out? Can we play now?

LEE: I think so. Here it says that "Issue-linkage extortion succeeds when: (a) the cost imposed on the linkee exceeds the cost to the linkee of acceding to the request by *a substantial margin,* and (b) the costs imposed on the linker by executing the threat are low enough so the threat is credible."[20] We just saw that, didn't we?

ROBIN: Well, I saw it, but I don't like it. The whole business makes me feel kinda yucky.

KIM: Yeah, I don't like extortion as a mechanism for trying to regulate public goods. It just seems to go against the grain! Counterintuitive.

ROBIN: Whenever we try to figure out how to achieve justice, somehow or other we end up talking about coercion too.

CHRIS: What a lot of melancholy babies you all are! Knock, knock.

LEE: Well, maybe we've just had to deal with the most difficult problems first. What's next?

ROBIN: Who's there?

CHRIS: Ozone layer.

ROBIN: Ozone layer, who?

KIM: Global population growth and the responsibilities of reproductive freedom.

CHRIS: (*singing to the tune of the Star Spangled Banner*) Oh, zone layer, see!

The collective embryos share an enormous sigh before settling down to their books. The curtain closes, and our narrator (apparently not omniscient) remains audibly silent regarding the incarnate fate of our friends.

QUESTIONS FOR REFLECTION
AND DISCUSSION

1. If you are already familiar with the politics of the degradation of the stratospheric ozone layer, what new light does this theory play shed on the topic? If you are new to the controversy, what questions does the play raise for you?

2. If you were tasked with modifying and extending the play (turning it into, perhaps, a thirty-minute production) what changes would

you make? What existing ideas would you expand upon, and what new themes would you introduce and explore?

3. Does the mix of Rawlsian justice, public goods, First World–Third World conflict, industry and science, and the unborn that sustains this play apply effectively to other global environmental conflicts? Or is the story line of this play largely applicable only to the ozone layer controversy?

4. Like children who aren't happy when different foods on their plate touch, we in higher education take great pains to separate the natural sciences from the social sciences from the humanities. Our pursuit and dissemination of knowledge is highly compartmentalized (just have a look at your college catalogue). Professor Hall's injection of theater into the political science classroom thus borders on the heretical. Would you advocate further integration of the humanities (not just theater, but creative writing, sculpture, the arts) into courses on global environmental ills? Is there reason to expect that such comingling of approaches would help students learn more, and more deeply, and in William Ayers's words, become both more thoughtful and powerful? Or, when all is said and done, do theory plays stake out the limit of innovation in how we might teach and study global environmental politics?

5. Professor Hall's play is grounded in the literature of global environmental degradation; note the chapter's profusion of endnotes. (If you have not yet done so, go to the endnotes now and review them.) To be effective, must theory plays—and other kinds of classroom simulations, such as role playing—be so thoroughly supported? To what minimum standards of scholarship should future theory playwrights be held?

6. Portions of this theory play are humorous. But what is the appropriate role of humor in the study of massive global environmental ills and the patterns of privilege and injustice that make resolution of these ills so difficult to achieve? Is humor a critical component of any effort to empower knowledge? Or is it a dangerous distraction from the serious subject matter we seek to master?

NOTES

1. Barry (1973: 133).
2. Rawls (1971).
3. The discussion of public goods and the debate between developed and developing countries are based on Sell (1994: 24).
4. Michael McElroy (atmospheric scientist), quoted in Dumonski (1989)

5. A research scientist at the World Resources Institute, quoted by Stammer (1989a).

6. Tripp (1988: 742–743).

7. Parsons (1993).

8. Sell (1994: 18).

9. See Stammer (1989c).

10. Haas (1992: 212).

11. Protocol on Substances That Deplete the Ozone Layer, with Annex A. Done at Montreal, September 16, 1987. Entered into forces, January 1, 1989; for the United States, January 1, 1989.

12. Dr. Liu Ming Pi, China's Commissioner for Environmental Protection, quoted in Randal (1989). Also, Stammer (1989b).

13. Zhang Chongxian, spokesman for the Chinese Environmental Protection Agency, quoted in Tyson (1989).

14. India's Environment Minister, Maneka Gandhi, quoted by Stammer (1990).

15. Sell (1994: fn 74).

16. India's Environment Minister Ziuk Rahman Ansari, quoted in Stammer (1989b) and Randal (1989).

17. Kilaparti Ramakrishna, quoted in Stammer (1989d).

18. Oye (1992: 38)

19. Maneka Gandhi, quoted in Frankel (1990).

20. Oye (1992: 38).

10

❂

Water Trade

What Should the World Trade Organization Do?

Thomas Princen and Karl Steyaert

Bulk water transport? The WTO? Getting to "yes"? Multiple stakeholder analysis? A six-hour session on a Saturday?

Yes—and more. Thomas Princen and Karl Steyaert, both from the School of Natural Resources and Environment at the University of Michigan, walk us through a class simulation that Princen has been running for years. What makes this simulation unusual is its brazenness: it hurls students into an issue (bulk water transport) for which there has been little progress in forging international agreement. In asking students to negotiate a resolution to a real issue for which no right resolution has yet to emerge, Princen and Steyaert aim to cultivate within their pupils analytic, negotiation, and risk-taking skills that both complement and advance the study of global environmental governance.

*Though the authors mention it below, it bears highlighting here: this simulation, or one like it of your own devising, can be run by instructors or students, perhaps as a substitute for that required term paper or class project. Read on.
—M.M.*

THE SETTING: IN SEARCH OF TRANSNATIONAL GOVERNANCE

Students of global environmental politics are increasingly recognizing that interstate diplomacy and intergovernmental organization is not the entire or, in some cases, the most important game when it comes to

163

understanding and arresting the degradation of critical global ecosystems. Nongovernmental organizations, networks of transnational activists, and transnational capital all play significant and sometimes critical roles in the unfolding struggle that is occasioned by global environmental threats. This struggle plays out in forums that are sometimes nongovernmental in character—the ISO standard-setting process is one example, the deliberations that produced the Forest Stewardship Council ecolabeling is another—and sometimes governmental or quasi-governmental—the World Trade Organization (WTO) and the Convention on the International Trade in Endangered Species of Fauna and Flora (CITES) are examples. Grasping the political dynamics that shape the interplay between governmental and nongovernmental forces and interests within these forums emerges as an essential task for those interested in global environmental politics.

We offer in this chapter a simulation that aspires to introduce students to the central dynamics of governmental and nongovernmental interactions around a pressing transnational environmental issue. The simulation—Water Trade: What Should the World Trade Organization Do?—highlights the growing need to link local institutions and ecological imperatives with evolving mechanisms of global governance. And it does so in a realistic, yet hypothetical, setting. Bulk water transport, as the simulation materials describe below, is rapidly becoming big business. Technological developments combine with growing water scarcity to create conditions for profitable trade and significant ecological disruption. The ensuing conflicts between those who benefit from water transport and trade and those who shoulder the costs of resulting environmental decline will only be ameliorated by creating forms of transnational governance—forms that, to this point, have failed to emerge from the global trade regime, or any other trade regime, such as that centering on CITES or the International Tropical Timber Organization.

Bulk water transfers, in other words, are happening, and the practice is accelerating. Governing this activity in a way that is fair, efficient, and sustainable calls for systems of governance that transcend nation-state authority and challenge national sovereignty. No such governance systems now sit on the shelf ready-made; they must be developed, and quickly, through a whole series of processes, including protracted negotiations among the many parties involved with or affected by such transfers.

The simulated setting for the negotiation of such governance is an informal gathering of key actors convened by the WTO. The objective of these key actors (who are played by the students in class) is to arrive at a consensus (or near consensus) recommendation to the WTO regarding the tradability of water. Our experience with writing and conducting simulations has taught us that this setting is more workable than trying to simulate an actual WTO deliberation. This is because students get bogged down trying to perform under, yet not really knowing, the formal procedures of the organization, the legal precedents of trade law, and so forth. In the end, students are frustrated; they find the setting just too artificial.

As constructed here, by contrast, the instructor can tell the role players that the simulated situation is not formal, not regulated by arcane procedures and history. The task is only to agree on a recommendation that, although informal, comes from a diverse collection of interested parties and thus can carry significant weight in the hypothetical upcoming formal deliberations. This is credible. Prenegotiations of various sorts occur all the time as lead-ups to formal, highly publicized meetings. And as students of global environmental politics know, prenegotiations can carry enormous weight by their ability to help set the agenda. So while legal precedent and full technical information can be central to real-life prenegotiations (and thus difficult to simulate), in this simulation they are not. At the same time, in real life and here, parties have a strong interest in participating and in reaching an agreed recommendation and thus shaping future, possibly binding negotiations.

Another advantage of this simulated situation is that, at this time (year 2002), no global agreement exists on water tradability and, for that matter, nothing like it is on the international table. This means that students can't simply act out what has already happened. But we can imagine that even if negotiations do commence in real life and even if they lead to an agreement, the process and outcome will remain contentious and unresolved. Thus, we expect this simulation to be ahead of practice for some years to come.

In our experience, the substance and setup of this simulation is appealing to students because they can imagine themselves actually doing something like this, even if they expect to work for a local NGO or a profit-making corporation. It's hard to imagine (as a role or in a future occupation) being a Richard Benedick (the "ozone diplomat"), a Kyoto climate-change negotiator, or a transnational corporate CEO. In addition, we sense that the simulation is appealing because it allows, requires, and rewards imagination and problem solving in a highly realistic setting where the answer is not waiting out there, fully formed, to be plucked.

WHY MULTIPLE STAKEHOLDER ROLES?

In teaching the institutional side of sustainability, a major aim of ours is to show students that policymaking is not just that which occurs among government officials. International is not just between diplomats and local is not just among municipal leaders. In the environmental realm, especially with regard to transboundary and interconnected issues such as persistent toxics, biodiversity, and water, a host of actors invariably and appropriately participate in the complex process of ecosystem management and resource use negotiation. And since the struggles that preoccupy these actors are intimately connected to biophysical conditions, institutional linkages from local to global are often required. Because of its inherently abstract nature, this kind of complexity and diversity—among actors, between interests, across space and even time—becomes difficult for students to grasp, even when they know that doing so is important and potentially interesting and illuminating.

This simulation paves the way for addressing many of these theoretical concerns. We have found that *following* the simulation with readings makes more sense for students because the theoretical notions are grounded.

Although the simulation is written as an instructor-directed exercise, we can imagine a group of students taking it on in lieu of a term paper or group project. One motivation for presenting this simulation in this volume, in fact, is our desire to see more students take on the task of running the simulation in their global environmental politics or international relations course. Our guess is that the level of student engagement and learning would be far higher than the typical paper or project.

ROLE-PLAYING SIMULATIONS:
PLUSES AND MINUSES

In choosing and designing teaching methods, we try to distinguish between the passive and the active. Passive methods such as lecture and undirected reading (passive, that is, for the student) have their role as an efficient means of disseminating information or highlighting key points. But because a major pedagogical objective of ours is to engage students, to create situations where they have to wrestle with tough issues and unfamiliar concepts, we try to lean as much as possible toward the active. One method is role-playing simulations, which enjoy several advantages over lectures and readings.

For instance, we have found that students genuinely enjoy stepping out of their accustomed student role and into a decision-making role, however artificial the situation may prove to be in the classroom setting. What's more, students become intrinsically motivated to do well (see Nancy Quirk's discussion of intrinsic and extrinsic motivation in chapter 13), to really master the material. They pore over readings, and often come to us for clarification and even more information. Thus, if the instructor's primary learning objective is to have students merely accumulate information, the simulation works very well.

Also, because our primary objective in teaching is to have students understand and appreciate the difficulties of real-life decision making in complex situations (we are both at the University of Michigan's School of Natural Resources and work primarily with Master's degree students), we have found that students view issues, and perhaps themselves, rather differently after performing a role. They may have habitually denigrated "politicians," or "big business," only to play such a role and realize how difficult it is to promote one's interests while simultaneously trying to reach an agreement with opponents. They really do get into a role, sometimes getting quite emotional, not all of which can be explained by acting talent.

There are at least two downsides to role playing, however. One is time. To orient students to the task, to set up a room, and then to conduct the negotiations and, not least, to debrief it allowing plenty of opportunity for students to describe their experience and express their frustrations, does indeed take a lot of time. More than once, we have finished a six-hour simulation with a board session highlighting a half-dozen key analytic points and have said to ourselves, gee, I could've covered these points in a half-hour. There are ways to trim the time commitment, for both instructors and students, and there are good reasons to reject the notion that these many hours are somehow lost.

We have found it best to use lab time, that is, a substantial block of time in the afternoon or evening or a full day on a weekend (in our university, Saturday is technically a class day). It really isn't feasible to run the simulation as a series of fifty-minute sessions. Doing so is time consuming, both in classroom set-up and in student warm-up time each day (the best dynamics typically occur toward the end of the hour and thus have to be cut off).

It is also possible to cut out the Preparatory Committee (PrepCom) sessions and just dictate the agenda and procedures to the students. In a sense, this would be realistic at least with respect to formal negotiations where established procedures must be accepted by all negotiators. But an informal setting, and not a few formal ones, typically involve some negotiation over the agenda and rules. This is a crucial aspect to any governance mechanism and should not be dismissed lightly.

Any way you slice it, the simulation takes a large chunk of time, though our experience has convinced us that this time can be justified on pedagogical grounds. When we debrief the simulation, covering procedural, substantive, and negotiating aspects, and ask ourselves how many hours it would take to prepare and deliver lectures that would cover the same ground with such richness, we come to doubt that lecturing would be more efficient. More important, though, we have found that many of the key insights from the material come *from the students*. We can frame the points or tie them to the literature. But, because the students have *experienced* it, because they have wrestled with the constraints of procedures, the uncertainties of information, the manipulations of strategic interaction, we're convinced they *know* the material in a way we could never impart via lecture. Our anecdotal supporting evidence is that when former students contact Princen, they invariably refer to the simulations (never his lectures!). The simulations, they tell him, were not only what they remember but also the most valuable training for the real-life experiences they're currently having (though recall, please, that we work in a professional school).

A final note on time commitment. When we conduct the simulation during a lab or on the weekend, it is an additional time demand on the students—and they know it. But we cannot recall ever hearing a complaint. If anything, during simulations they ask for *more* time, and after the simulation, they recommend allocating *more* time. We don't recall any of our lectures being so received.

The second downside is uncertainty. As with many active approaches (e.g., case discussion or in-class writing), the instructor is largely out of the picture once the simulation begins. What is more, no one in class—instructor or student—knows where the negotiating will go, what positions the players will take, what information or perceptions they will bring to the table, despite efforts the instructor has made to constrain the role assignment. As with all human interactions, people interpret their needs and their environment in very different ways. It can be unnerving, especially if the instructor is accustomed to controlling the content and pace of every class session and the students expect the instructor to be in charge. Yet all this uncertainty, and sometimes chaos, is a lot like aspects of policymaking and life in general. We'd be wise, whatever our real role in courses on global environmental policymaking, to embrace opportunities to inject such uncertainty and chaos into our classroom.

The simulation materials that follow capture the essence of a more detailed (about forty pages) treatment that carefully describes for participating students the varied nuances of the roles they might play. Readers (students and instructors both) interested in reviewing this longer document and discussing, perhaps, how they might run this simulation in one of their courses are invited to drop the lead author a note at his office address.[1]

A Simulation of Water Trade: What Should the World Trade Organization Do?

GENERAL INFORMATION FOR ALL PARTIES

The Setting

The year is 2004.[2] One and a half billion people on Earth lack access to fresh drinking water. As the water crisis intensifies, governments around the world are advocating mass transport of fresh water. Worldwide, the water business of purification, distribution, and recycling is a $500 billion industry.

The Global Water Corporation, a Canadian transnational corporation specializing in water products, has secured permits to ship one billion gallons of water from the Great Lakes Basin to China over the course of the next ten years. Proponents argue that privatization and international trade of water resources is the only efficient way to distribute fresh water. Moreover, such volumes are the proverbial drop in the bucket when it comes to North American water supplies. Opponents claim that selling water on the open market can wreak ecological havoc and does not address the needs of thirsty people.

With environmental and public interest groups in the United States trying to block export of Great Lakes water, the Global Water Corporation has turned to the World Trade Organization (WTO), demanding that the trade organization impose trade sanctions on the United States or Canada or both if these governments prevent the transport of the water.

In the wake of public protests during its ministerial meeting in Seattle in December of 1999, the WTO has been considering ways of changing its decision-making process. To regain public faith the WTO has launched a process of multiple stakeholder public involvement. In this case, it has invited some two dozen stakeholders to consider all evidence on the issue of trade in water and to devise a nonbinding recommendation to WTO member governments.

A recommendation with consensus from all participating stakeholders will carry significant weight in the WTO's upcoming meetings of member nations. Consensus, or near consensus, will also set a strong precedent for future international policy decisions on other environmental and social issues.

The Issues

To craft an effective recommendation, the participants must resolve two major, crosscutting issues in these negotiations:

1. *The tradability of water.* For example, the parties can agree that there should be complete free trade or no trade in water or only limited trade where trade would be explicitly restricted.
2. *The role of the WTO in water trade.* For example, the parties can decide that the WTO should be the primary international decision-making body, or that it should only serve as a court of last resort, or that it should have no role at all.

In deciding these two major issues, the parties will likely have to consider a number of subsidiary issues such as: Who owns water? Who should own it? Should it be privatized? What rights do transnational corporations have to buy water systems? Should water be traded as a commodity in the open market? Is water just like any other resource— petroleum or timber, for example—or is it different? What is the role of government? What laws should be enacted to protect water? How should water be shared between water-rich and water-poor countries? How can ordinary citizens become involved in this process?

The Process

One or more PrepCom meetings will be held to set the agenda for the multiple stakeholder negotiation. Subsequently, two to four Plenary Sessions will be held to decide upon a nonbinding agreement. A facilitator (or two) has been hired by the WTO strictly for the purpose of facilitating the agenda setting and negotiating. Because this process is experimental for the WTO, no other structure will be imposed on the stakeholders.

PrepCom

In the initial PrepCom meeting, the group of stakeholders is charged with first devising the *procedures* to follow in the subsequent negotiations. These procedures can include agreement on questions such as seating, speaking order, time limits, drafting, recording, voting (e.g., issue by issue; consensus on all questions; or simple majority [more than 50 percent] for some questions). Second, the group is charged with setting an *agenda* of negotiating items. The topic is broad, so the group will probably have to narrow it before beginning.

Draft Statement—Assignment 1

After the PrepCom agenda-setting discussions, each individual composes a draft statement, one to two pages in length, double-spaced, to be turned in on the first negotiating session. This should be written as *proposed word-*

ing for the group's eventual recommendation. It should have two components: (1) general principles; and (2) specific actions and mechanisms (what, exactly, the WTO or other actors should do). It should *not* simply be a position statement or a general discussion of the issue, and it should not reveal one's strategy or fallback positions. To draft this, you should think hard about how the talks should proceed to meet your interests. You should think strategically and realistically. For example, if you compose the only draft on a given aspect of the policy, you stand a good chance of getting what you want. Or maybe you can anchor the talks on a controversial issue at one extreme or the another. Or perhaps you can defuse an issue by presenting a fair compromise right off the bat.

Print out your draft statement in large type, double spaced, with wide margins, so it can be easily read by a group of negotiators and easily modified. It can be written as prose (sentences and paragraphs) or, possibly better, as concise bulleted items. Include your personal (real-life) name, your party's name, and the date. You can reference sources to buttress your case. Make enough copies to have one for yourself as well as copies to distribute to the two WTO organizers, the facilitators, and, possibly, to other parties in the negotiation for caucusing. In addition, you might consider putting key phrases from your draft statement on an overhead transparency to share with the entire group.

Plenary Sessions

In the Plenary Sessions, the topics under discussion are the tradability of water across national boundaries and the appropriate role of the WTO in regard to international water trade. There is no limit on the agenda items the parties introduce, but the group's primary objective is to reach agreement on the wording of a recommendation to the WTO. The facilitator's job is to keep the talks focused and moving toward agreement.

Assignment 2

After the first negotiating session, identify likely allies. Exchange draft statements and arrange an out-of-class meeting. During your meeting, attempt to write a joint statement to propose to the entire group. Give a copy to a WTO Organizer (instructor).

The parties will necessarily have to deal with specifics and technical questions, many of which they will not fully understand. Between negotiating sessions, parties can do independent research. In many cases, however, they still will not be able to resolve certain technical questions. The parties should not let this hinder their progress toward agreement. Instead, they should seek creative ways of dealing with such issues much

172 Thomas Princen and Karl Steyaert

as other international negotiators have done in the past (e.g., the Montreal Protocol). The key is to develop a general (but meaningful and useful) framework that all stakeholders can agree to. It should include: (1) a specific decision on the sale of Great Lakes water to China; (2) a set of specific principles and procedures for international water trade policy; and (3) a specific determination of the appropriate role of the WTO regarding this policy.

Interests versus Positions

Negotiating is a difficult process, full of uncertainty and flux. Negotiation experts Roger Fisher and William Ury (1981: 40–42) offer the following advice:

> In negotiating, focus on interests, not positions. . . .
> The basic problem in a negotiation lies not in conflicting positions, but in the conflict between each side's needs, desires, concerns, and fears. Your position is something you have decided on. Your interests are what caused you to so decide. . . .
> The Egyptian-Israeli peace treaty blocked out at Camp David in 1978 demonstrates the usefulness of looking behind positions. Israel had occupied the Egyptian Sinai Peninsula since the Six Day War of 1967. When Egypt and Israel sat down together in 1978 to negotiate a peace, their positions were incompatible. Israel insisted on keeping some of the Sinai. Egypt, on the other hand, insisted that every inch of the Sinai be returned to Egyptian sovereignty. Time and again, people drew maps showing possible boundary lines that would divide the Sinai between Egypt and Israel. Compromising in this way was wholly unacceptable to Egypt. To go back to the situation as it was in 1967 was equally unacceptable to Israel.
> Looking to their interests instead of their positions made it possible to develop a solution. Israel's interest lay in security; they did not want Egyptian tanks poised on their border ready to roll across at any time. Egypt's interest lay in sovereignty; the Sinai had been part of Egypt since the time of the Pharaohs. After centuries of domination by Greeks, Romans, Turks, French, and British, Egypt had only recently regained full sovereignty and was not about to cede territory to another foreign conqueror.
> At Camp David, President Sadat of Egypt and Prime Minister Begin of Israel agreed to a plan that would return the Sinai to complete Egyptian sovereignty and, by demilitarizing large areas, would still assure Israeli security. The Egyptian flag would fly everywhere, but Egyptian tanks would be nowhere near Israel.
> Reconciling interests rather than positions works for two reasons. First, for every interest there usually exist several possible positions that could satisfy it. All too often people simply adopt the most obvious position, as Israel did, for example, in announcing that they intended to keep part of the Sinai.

When you do look behind opposed positions for the motivating interests, you can often find an alternative position that meets not only your interests but theirs as well. In the Sinai, demilitarization was one such alternative.

Reconciling interests rather than compromising between positions also works because behind opposed positions lie many more interests than conflicting ones. . . .

A negotiating position often obscures what you really want, while the object of a negotiation is to satisfy their underlying interests. Explore interests. Avoid having a bottom line.

Nuts and Bolts

The Actors

Facilitator(s)
WTO Organizer(s)
Nations
    U.S. Trade Representative
    U.S. Environmental Protection Agency
    Canadian Ministry of Commerce
    Environment Canada
    United Kingdom
    China
    Israel
    Saudi Arabia
    Mexico
IGOs
    International Joint Commission
    United Nations Environment Program
TNCs
    Suez Lyonnaise des Eaux
    Vivendi
    Global Water Corporation
NGOs
    Great Lakes United
    Greenpeace-International
    Coalition of Conservation Organizations
    Third World Network
    Coalition of Indigenous Peoples
    World Resources Institute

Materials for Each Participating Stakeholder

General Information for All Parties
Confidential Instructions

Readings
Name plate
Name tag

Required Readings: A Representative Sampling

World Trade Organization. 1999. "The World Trade Organization . . . In Brief."
"Why Greens Should Love Trade." 1999. *The Economist.* October 9: 17–18.
Meadows, Donella. 1999. "Why Greens Don't Love the WTO." *The Global Citizen.* November 25.
Egan, Timothy. 1999. "Free Trade Takes on Free Speech." *New York Times.* December 5: 1, 5.
Meadows, Donella. 1999. "The WTO Protesters and the Powers That Be." *The Global Citizen.* December 2.
"The Global Trade in Water." 1999. Blue Gold, a report by the International Forum on Globalization. June 1999: 18–25.
Rizzo, Katherine. 1999. "Great Lakes Officials Worry about Alaska Water Precedent." *Ann Arbor News,* September 21: Sect. B, 3.
Magner, Mike. 2000. "Report: Great Lakes Need More Protection." *Ann Arbor News,* March 16: Sect. C, 8.

Additional Readings

World Trade Organization. 1999. "10 Benefits of the WTO Trading System."
World Trade Organization. 1999. "10 Common Misunderstandings about the WTO."
Public Citizen. 1999. "A Citizen's Guide to the World Trade Organization: Everything You Need to Know to Fight for Fair Trade."
Gleick, Peter H. 1993. "Water and a Sustainable World Population." A summary prepared for the Harrison Program on the Future Global Agenda, "Footsteps to Sustainability." October 28–30, 1993, University of Maryland and the Carnegie Endowment, Washington, D.C.
Green, Colin, John Briscoe, and Bernard Barraqué. 1999. "Who Pays the Piper? Who Calls the Tune?" *The UNESCO Courier.* February 1999: 22–24.

ADDITIONAL GUIDELINES FOR INSTRUCTORS

This simulation is a role-playing, educational exercise intended to immerse students in a multiparty negotiation. The subject is international water trade and the role of the World Trade Organization. As students play the roles of real-life stakeholders, they gain first-hand negotiation skills and grapple with crucial emerging topics of water scarcity and global trade policy.

The simulation contains the twenty-one separate roles listed below (twenty-two if one includes the role of WTO Organizer, the role played by instructors). However, the simulation can run with both larger- and smaller-sized groups. The minimum number of participants required is twelve, including the essential actors marked below with an asterisk. The maximum number of participants is thirty-four, with any of the twelve essential roles (designated below by an asterisk) assigned to two participants.

Facilitator *
U.S. Trade Representative *
U.S. Environmental Protection Agency *
Canadian Ministry of Commerce *
Environment Canada *
United Kingdom
China *
Israel
Saudi Arabia
Mexico
International Joint Commission *
United Nations Environment Program
Suez Lyonnaise des Eaux
Global Water Corporation *
Vivendi *
Great Lakes United *
Greenpeace-International *
Coalition of Conservation Organizations *
Third World Network
Coalition of Indigenous Peoples
World Resources Institute

Distribute readings and roles at least two weeks in advance of the Prep-Com session to give students adequate time to prepare. There is a considerable amount of information to read and assimilate. Also, allow adequate time before and after class simulation sessions for arranging chairs, tables, and overhead.

Total time required in-class, including PrepCom agenda setting, Plenary Sessions, and debriefing, is at least eight hours. A full-day meeting is one option, but it should be preceded by at least one PrepCom meeting to allow students to write assignment 1 (the one to two page draft statement) before negotiations actually begin. If the sessions are spread over a number of class periods, each session should entail at least one full hour.

PrepCom: at least 1 hour
Plenary Sessions: approximately 6 hours
Debriefing: at least 1 hour

Additional Materials to Have on Hand

- Extra copies of roles, readings, name tag, and plate materials
- Overhead transparencies and pens
- Flip chart
- Tape
- Chalk and erasers
- Overhead screen (separate from blackboards)

Room Setup

Arrange seating in such a way that all parties are visible to each other. Set up seating and tables so that students can easily move across and around the room for caucusing. To that end, remove excess tables and chairs and ask students to clear the immediate negotiating area of coats and bags.

Provide an extra large table for facilitators (to spread out materials).

Preparing Your Students

Students should be given ample time (perhaps two to three weeks) to read and digest all distributed materials. But they should read the general instructions first and bring questions regarding the setup and nature of the simulation to class well in advance of commencing negotiations. If students have not had prior exposure to negotiation simulations or their dynamics, instructors should take particular care that students understand the section in the general instructions titled "Interests vs. Positions."

Those students (and instructors) not accustomed to in-class role playing can also be told the following: The success of this simulation *as a learning tool* is highly dependent on each student's willingness to engage fully in the role, to play it as authentically as possible, even if that means saying or doing things that are out of character in real life. The class as a whole must establish a social contract of sorts whereby everyone agrees that whatever one does *in role*, it is only that—role playing—not a reflection of that person's character. To this end (i.e., authentic role playing) it is essential that, once the simulation begins, all discussion, no matter how private it seems, is *in role*.

Experience suggests that if these guidelines are well laid out up front and, occasionally, enforced, students will do remarkable things—*in role*; they will put aside their customary shyness or reserve or politeness and bargain hard, much like real life. The dynamics—and learning—can be fascinating.

The instructor should decide in advance and inform the students whether the students can negotiate out of class. As the simulation is written, students are required (assignment 2) to meet at least once outside of class with potential allies to compare statements and try to come up with a joint statement. But they may want to meet more often, hammer out a tentative agreement, and bring it all to class.

It is helpful to stress that there is no "right answer" in these negotiations. In fact, the topic has been deliberately chosen to be current (even ahead of real-life developments on the Water-WTO issue), provocative, and open-ended. Trade theorists, policy wonks, and environmentalists don't have the answer to this huge and critical question either.

Also, the format as simulated is not entirely contrived. Increasingly, official agencies are employing such techniques to enhance public participation, build legitimacy, and even come up with creative solutions to vexing environmental problems. Maybe of more relevance to professionally bound students engaging in such exchange, negotiating among disparate interests, searching for joint gain solutions, exploring interests rather than pushing positions, caucusing, drafting language, and so forth is very much what they will do in the "real world" of policymaking. This is a safe environment to push oneself to be effective, for one's party and for the larger group of stakeholders.

Regarding the assigning of roles, the instructor can do it mostly randomly although certain key roles (e.g., U.S. Trade Representative, a water corporation, an environmental group like Greenpeace) should be assigned to especially articulate members of the class. The facilitator role is critical. Well before the roles are distributed, it is helpful to explain to students the nature of the facilitating role (in real life), how it is often critical to successful negotiations (for those familiar with the Montreal Protocol negotiations, the work of Mostafa Tolba can be cited), and yet how rarely such facilitators have any training or experience. This simulation offers a relatively low-cost, low-risk setting for one or two students to try out this role. While the role of facilitator is difficult, and sometimes extremely confusing and frustrating, the facilitator will receive some how-to materials on facilitating. Furthermore, during the sessions, the sole task of the WTO Organizer as written in this simulation is to provide backup to the facilitator.

Instructor's Role in the Simulation

A useful class management rule in simulations of this sort is that everyone, that is, *everyone* in the room is *in role*—no exceptions. There is no audience; there are no visitors. If students are going to feel comfortable stepping into a role, especially if they are asked to, in effect, act out of character, they should not have anyone looking over their shoulders, even an instructor. For a simulation to work as a learning tool, both for substance and, here especially, for process, this must be a safe environment. Thus, the instructor's role, as noted, is a representative from the WTO whose sole task is to serve as backup to the facilitator, nothing else. It is often difficult to maintain this role without slipping into teacher mode, managing and guiding and offering advice to students. At the same time, it will likely be necessary to take notes on substantive and process questions that arise in the negotiations as a basis for the debriefing. This can generally be done clandestinely, though.

Should no agreement be forthcoming in the final hour(s) of the negotiation, here is some suggested wording to offer to facilitators:

"The facilitators have consulted with WTO headquarters and have been reminded that agreement is extremely important. Therefore, _____ more minutes have been allotted for the negotiation."

If the negotiation results in a "no agreement," WTO officials and member governments (i.e., trade ministers) will take over this issue on water trade. Please note that the WTO promotes trade. Thus, those who object here to any conditions for water trade will accomplish only one thing: transfer of the issue to pro–free trade, nonecologically minded officials.

Possible means to agreement include:

- Agree that currently some forms of water trade *are* being conducted. What can be expanded or constricted? Consider: temporary use vs. permanent; humanitarian vs. economic; basic needs vs. luxury; bulk vs. bottled vs. embodied in a product (fruit, wood); quantities relative to recharge rate; reduced biomass vs. threatened species.
- Agree on conditional statements. For example: If WTO accepts water trade, it should . . .; If WTO does not oversee water trade, what authority should oversee, govern, regulate, or monitor?

Debriefing

The debriefing is generally most successful if it immediately follows the last session of the simulation and if it begins with reflections from the students. Prompting questions might include: What was most difficult? What surprised you in the process? Who, or what actions, were most effective in getting movement toward agreement? Was it a good outcome? From whose perspective? With respect to what values? To the facilitator: What did facilitating feel like? What worked and what didn't? What would you do differently?

Depending on the purpose of the simulation in the course, the instructor might follow with observations on process, on what worked and what didn't, and on what could have been tried. This can be followed by a discussion of negotiating dynamics—caucusing, drafting, voting, facilitating, threats and bluffs, positions vs. interests, distributive vs. integrative bargains, and competing world views. As for substance, the meaning of trade liberalization with respect to a resource that is so unlike manufactured goods can be explored. The role of WTO and other actors can also be included.

QUESTIONS FOR REFLECTION
AND DISCUSSION

1. Princen and Steyaert speak of "the institutional side of sustainability" and helping students become real-world players in this "institutional side" is what their simulation is all about. What is this institutional side of sustainability—how would you explain it to someone new to the discipline? How does Princen and Steyaert's understanding of it compare to your own? And what would Lamont Hempel, with his notion of "glocalism" (see chapter 4), say about Princen and Steyaert's ideas about institutions and sustainability in the global arena?

2. "We'd be wise," say Princen and Steyaert, "whatever our real role in courses on global environmental policymaking, to embrace opportunities to inject . . . uncertainty and chaos into our classroom." How might you critically evaluate this statement? Is "chaos in the classroom" important enough to cultivating a "wild mind" (chapter 1) or achieving "maladjustment" (chapter 8) to tolerate the discomfort, and even distress, that it will bring to the classroom?

3. Though terribly time consuming, Princen and Steyaert swear by their simulation and improve upon it every year. They do so because they believe it affords students of global environmental politics a glimpse of the work they might realistically pursue after completing their education. What sort of everyday work do Princen and Steyaert envision for such students? What skills, beyond the important but traditional ability to read carefully and communicate clearly, are critical to this work? And how might a college or university student

continue to strengthen his or her command of these skills (beyond, perhaps, engaging in the simulation introduced here)?
4. Consider three exercises described in this volume: the "antisimulation" (chapter 8), "theory plays" (chapter 9), and, now, "simulating water negotiation in the face of uncertainty." How would you rank the importance of these exercises to courses in global environmental politics? Why? What personal assumptions about education and the struggle for sustainability does your ranking reveal?

NOTES

1. Thomas Princen, Associate Professor of Natural Resources and Environmental Policy, School of Natural Resources and Environment, University of Michigan, Ann Arbor, MI 48109–1115.
2. Choose a year in the near future. For simulations run in 2002, we'd choose 2004.

11

❂

The Study of Global Environmental Politics in the Information Age

Matthew Auer

Paula Poundstone's comedy isn't for everyone, and her acerbic quote at the beginning of chapter 1 might prove too strong for some. The virtue of Poundstone's quip, of course, is that it forces us to confront the possibility that knowledge about environmental ills can sap our ability to make sense of and act upon the world. But what about other processes through which information about the biosphere can disempower, especially the problem of too much information, coming at us too quickly? As Professor Auer outlines in this chapter, a fine line separates the "information revolution" (a good thing, full of possibilities) from the "information explosion" (which can overwhelm our ability to understand and act). Making sense of global environmental issues in ways both intellectually and politically empowering means staying on the right side of this line, as he describes below.—M.M.

The expression "Information Age" conjures images of whirring hard drives, crackling power lines, knowledge that's a click away, and an economy powered by 0s and 1s. Information, now as always, is the raw stuff of knowledge and a potential source of power. But as it grows in quantity though not necessarily in quality, and as it is accessed and used in increasingly specialized ways, information may actually foster ignorance and disempower.

If information is a superhighway, then its denizens are not unlike the

181

travelers of ordinary highways: some move forward swiftly, purposefully, and with confidence. Others awkwardly putt-putt along. There are hitch-hikers who can't find a ride and hobos who've stopped trying. There are bad accidents too.

Every homeowner, entrepreneur, and student—including the student of environmental politics—is a potential beneficiary and also a potential chump in the Information Age. Two vignettes from the global environmental politics classroom help illustrate this point.

VIGNETTE 1: THE INFORMATION REVOLUTION MEETS THE TERM PAPER

A depleted, bleary-eyed professor seizes another twenty-page paper from a stack of end-of-semester essays. Already this evening, she has plodded through three papers on global climate change, two on the perils of genetically modified organisms, and one apiece on tropical deforestation and the environmental villainy of the World Trade Organization. She groans upon reading the title for paper number 8. Perhaps "Global Climate Change: Hideous Heat Wave or a Lot of Hot Air?" can wait until tomorrow. The professor gropes for the desk lamp's off-switch as she skims page 1. Turning to page 2, she pauses. Her student has expertly inserted three high-quality color images of the earth dressed in swirls of colorful centigrade temperature. Each image shows sensible heat in the lower atmosphere under different atmospheric carbon scenarios, projected twenty-five, fifty, and one hundred years into the future. Image 3 finds New England and the upper Great Lakes states smeared in pinks and reds. More impressive still, the author carefully explains the methods used to develop the images, the measurement uncertainties built into the projected carbon and temperature scenarios, and the various ways the images have been used by advocates and skeptics of climate change science. Her interest piqued, the professor reads on, feeling energized by her student's masterful presentation and analysis of complex data.

VIGNETTE 2: INFORMATION OVERLOAD AND THE ORAL PRESENTATION

It's midsemester in "POL 215: Seminar on International Environmental Affairs" and small groups of third- and fourth-year college students are making oral presentations on the effectiveness of international environmental regimes. The instructor enjoyed the first half-dozen presentations. Most presenters demonstrated knowledge of relevant theories and concepts and competently used case material to corroborate or refute particular arguments. Some students deftly incorporated statistical analyses or used Powerpoint software to enhance their presentations. Early on, the final presenters of the day gave every indication that they, too, would dazzle with a high tech, informative revue. Within less than a minute, the presenters had displayed more than ten colorful histograms and pie charts as well as a sharp looking JPEG and two slides of densely packed text that melted into one another. By the tenth minute, the audience confronted image number 36. Actually, most students in the class had long since averted their eyes and ears from this particular presentation. Some began their French homework; others indulged thoughts of supper and late evening plans. In the back row, barely stifled yawns gave way to fitful sleep. Though the presenters had practiced their shtick and spoke clearly and with conviction, the presentation fizzled. The few listeners remaining at talk's end felt empty. What, exactly, did that final group present? What was the purpose of all that data and imagery? Why don't I remember anything from that talk? Later that evening, as the professor inspected each group's essays and hard copies of charts and images, he noted that the final group had appropriated virtually all of its graphics, statistics, and even some text for the paper from the World Wide Web. Though the paper's bibliography contained a few Web sites, the paper itself made only superficial references to cited data, and more broadly, the text—as well as the presentation—lacked insight and originality.

These vignettes offer a broad lesson for students and teachers in the Information Age: information is not the answer. It is a means for obtaining the answer, but the essential problem is mastering its use to achieve that end. For the discerning and adroit user, information enables learning, enhances the presentation, informs the audience, and empowers the client. For the unreflective, unskilled user, information retards learning, hijacks the presentation, stupefies the audience, and disempowers the client.

The unhappy truth, as many of this volume's contributors observe, is that information *can* disempower. Freelance writer David Shenk (1997) coined "data smog" to characterize an especially prominent and confounding form of this problem. Too much information can disable rather than enable. Shenk and others offer statistical testimony to the information glut:

- In 1971, the average American was targeted by at least 560 daily advertising messages. Twenty years later, that number had risen sixfold, to 3,000 messages per day.
- Paper consumption per capita in the United States tripled from 1940

to 1980 (from 200 to 600 pounds) and tripled *again* from 1980 to 1990 (to 1,800 pounds) (Shenk 1997: 30).

• According to the cyberspace marketing company Cyveillance, through mid-July 2000, the Internet contained 2.1 billion unique pages, with seven million new pages added daily. And in early 2002, a search on Google.com, a major Internet search engine, would cover over 2.1 billion unique Web pages.[1]

Data smog and information overload are apparent to any student who mistakes an Internet search engine as a good place to begin researching a term paper. Symptoms of "search engine blues" are long lines of belea-guered office hour attendees motivated by the same torment: "I'm drowning in information on topic X! Help!" The problem is not simply too much information; it's information that's scattershot and marginally relevant or worse. As one psychologist frames it, "One hundred percent serendipity equals utter chaos . . . if you're thirsty, it's sensible to stand under a faucet, not the Niagara Falls" (Murray 1998).

Fast and effective remedies for search engine blues and other data smog maladies are at the fingertips of every student and professor. Instructors can perform wonders by reserving one-half of one class period to intro-duce students to powerful and focused information technologies (ITs)—devices that tend to be more precise than generic Internet search engines. The ingredients for this session are one computer, one projector, an ether-net connection, and a chance to pretest the equipment before class. Once class begins, either the instructor or a student can select a relatively nar-rowly defined topic—say, the effects of tropical deforestation on monarch butterfly migration—and conduct key words searches in four or five reli-able news and periodical databases that are available from thousands of university library Web sites.

My intention is not to promote any particular electronic information source. Rather, it is to persuade instructors to perform hands-on demon-strations of their own preferred sources. There is a good chance that stu-dents won't know about them. Students who don't know or who are daunted by the unfamiliar may fall back to the known, the familiar, the easy, and the seductive—namely, random output-generating, undiscrimi-nating, and often maddening Internet search engines.

SMART ASSIGNMENTS FOR
THE INFORMATION AGE

Data- and information-rich homework, essays, quizzes, and exams can generate a false sense of security for both student and teacher. Some students assume that a one-to-one relationship exists between information and wisdom. Meanwhile, too many instructors declare victory when students accurately regurgitate information. In fact, information is a step along the way to wisdom. Finding the way is assisted by introspection, critical thinking, and healthy skepticism. Fact-based assignments tend to be insufficient because they merely demand that students interpret what the data mean. No less important is discerning what data and information *fail to reveal.*

Suppose a student of environmental politics is investigating how income and deforestation rates in different countries are related to one another. Specifically, the homework assignment requires the use of correlation analysis to describe the relationship between deforestation rates in fifteen countries and GNP per capita in those same countries.

The conventional assignment requires the student to compute a correlation coefficient and interpret the results. Often, the genuinely interesting part of the correlation test is contemplated neither by the student nor the assignment's author, namely: What does correlation analysis *fail to elucidate* about the relationship between the two variables?

A prospective answer to the latter question might mention that:

• The correlation analysis says nothing about cause and effect between the two variables but can only suggest either a strong, weak, or no linear relationship between the variables.
• The data mask subregional differences in deforestation rates in the fifteen countries. Deforestation rates are much higher in some parts of some countries, but this trend and the factors correlated with it are not detectable in national level data sets.
• Forests are denuded in different ways in the different countries. Deforestation is driven by different motivations depending on the forest type, economic status of the forest user, and other variables. Deforestation poses different social, economic, and environmental consequences depending on the region and on its human and wildlife inhabitants. By itself, the correlation analysis offers few insights on these matters.
• Per capita GNP is an imperfect measure of private wealth generation. Income inequality and the differential purchasing power of different currencies distort the usefulness of this indicator.

The value of information depends not merely on its quality but on the ability of the interpreter to probe, question, doubt, and ask "what's left out?" Information, particularly in the age of data smog, isn't synonymous with truth. It's a means for closing in on the truth but only after we give data and information a workout.

There are reams of data and information on the Internet, in periodicals, on television screens, and on radio talk shows. Information from these sources sometimes masquerades as unexpurgated truth. Sorting the good from the garbage is an acquired skill and one that can be nurtured in the classroom.

Professor Phil Stevens of Indiana University's School of Public and Environmental Affairs requires his environmental studies students to select an information-rich topic in science, research it on the Web, and, based on concepts and case material learned in class, sort out the Web's offerings of science and pseudoscience. More than an exercise in cross-referencing and fraud detection, this task battles some of the Internet's greatest seductions: instant information, colorful presentation, and misinformation credentialed only by its presence (often fleeting!) in cyberspace. Dr. Stevens's exercise and comparable drills in "cyber truth testing" empower students to take back the information management game—to become more discriminating, more scientific, and better purveyors and users of information for enlightening themselves and others.

HELPFUL WEB SITES

Information is potential power transformable to actual power in the hands of the able user. The Internet, online databases, and myriad other electronic, radio, visual, and paper forms of information are media for great potential enlightenment. The key is unlocking and exploiting the wealth they have to offer.

Just as information overload detracts from teaching and learning global environmental politics, discriminating use of information makes for a rewarding course of study. There are many excellent and user friendly sources of information available to environmental policy experts and experts-in-training. Because the Internet is among the most powerful and fastest growing repositories of information and is a tool for learning, communicating, and creating knowledge, this section profiles seven especially practicable Web sites. These sites not only contain lots of information but also offer interactive exercises, high quality data, and links to the Web pages and information sources of eminent, international, environment-related organizations in the public, private, and not-for-profit sectors. Some of the most helpful Web sites are nothing more than long lists of links to other, environment-related Web sites. Box 11.1 catalogues some

---

**BOX 11.1. WEB LINKS TO ENVIRONMENTAL
TOPICS AND ORGANIZATIONS**

- *The World Wide Web Virtual Library—Sustainable Development*
  www.ulb.ac.be/ceese/meta/sustvl.html
  This is perhaps the single largest compilation of environmental
  links on the Web. It contains alphabetized sublists of links to environmental projects and activities, environmental events, environmental news and discussion groups, and more.
- *Yahoo!'s Directory of Environment and Nature Organizations*
  dir.yahoo.com/society_and_culture/environment_and_nature/
  organizations/
  This Yahoo! page lists Web sites of environmental organizations
  by area of concern, such as environmental justice, recycling, and
  indigenous people.
- *The Environment: A Global Challenge*
  library.thinkquest.org/26026/index.php3
  This site contains short articles on environmental problems, remedies for these problems, and so on. But see, in particular, the site's
  links to environmental organizations and the biographies of environmentalists.
- *The WWW Virtual Library—Environment List O'Lists*
  www.earthsystems.org/virtuallibrary/llists.html
  This is not an especially well-organized list of sites, but nevertheless contains many golden nuggets, including links to environmental organizations and environmental directories in North
  America and beyond.

---

of the best Web pages. Boxes 11.2 and 11.3 list especially informative Web
sites dealing with global and regional environmental affairs.

Web sites mentioned in boxes 11.1, 11.2, and 11.3 are beacons in a vast
(and sometimes unfriendly) sea of environment-related sites on the
Internet. In addition to tapping these preferred sites, instructors and students can avoid search engine blues and other Information Age maladies
by using more focused, more selective information retrieval products.
Among the best are full-text journal and newspaper archives and electronic literature search directories. Box 11.4 points to a few of the most
information-rich and user-friendly information retrieval services, many of
which are accessible from campus-based computers.

BOX 11.2. GLOBAL ENVIRONMENTAL POLITICS WEB RESOURCES

- *Ron Mitchell's Home Pages*
darkwing.uoregon.edu/~rmitchel
This site is a good source for those making initial research forays in international environmental affairs. Mitchell, a professor at the University of Oregon at Eugene, has organized information sources into data; bibliographies; environmental research resources; international environmental links; other international links; and news links for easy searching. His site affords access to the Web sites of several dozen public, private, and nonprofit organizations with international or environmental missions. The site also contains a thoughtful and self-critical assessment of Mitchell's efforts to weave the Internet into his International Environmental Politics course. Among the lessons learned, Mitchell concedes, "I attempted to do too much and some things were bound to fail. I would strongly advise doing three or four main elements and making sure you do those things well, and make them a priority in the class."*

- *Project on Teaching Global Environmental Politics*
webpup.alleg.edu/employee/m/mmaniate/GepEd/geped.html
This site, created and maintained by this volume's editor, contains one of the largest compilations of syllabi for undergraduate and graduate courses in global environmental politics. The site posts dozens of syllabi for undergraduate courses alone, along with course exercises, video resources, and links to other instructors' and relevant organizations' Web sites. More than a Web site, the project is a virtual meeting place for hundreds of instructors, students, and practitioners of environmental politics. There, one finds an invitation to join the Global Environmental Politics Education (GepEd) listserv whose members include scholars, students, government officials, activists, and others.

- *The Consortium for International Earth Science Information Network (CIESIN)'s Environmental Treaties and Resource Indicators (ENTRI)*
sedac.ciesin.org/pidb/index.html
This site contains a wealth of data divided into nine major environmental issues areas (including global climate change; oceans; stratospheric ozone depletion; trade and the environment; and other topics). Within each of these categories, users may query about trends and conditions in more than 150 countries and mul-

tinational settings. So, for example, in the transboundary air pollution issue area, users may request data on twenty different variables from countries and regions around the globe. Within
seconds, users obtain cross-country, comparative data. This data
can be copied and pasted into statistical software for further analysis. There is more to CIESIN's ENTRI than thousands of disparate data cells. ENTRI provides helpful descriptive guides to the
data, suggestions for data analysis, detailed information on data
sources, and is linked to relevant organizational Web sites including CIESIN's own Socioeconomic Data Applications Center—a
powerful database where users can research thousands of environment-related topics.

- *International Institute for Sustainable Development*
  iisd.ca/
  The IISD is a research and advocacy organization that issues policy recommendations on climate change, trade and investment,
  and economic instruments for environmental protection, and its
  site warehouses a huge inventory of research on natural resources
  management. IISD also promotes innovative ways to measure sustainable development trends. Perhaps most remarkable is IISD's
  Business and Sustainable Development resources. Here, one finds
  interactive research tools for companies that are contemplating
  instituting environmental management systems; information
  sources and tips on raising money for environmental capital
  improvements; tools for comparing ordinary companies' environmental performance against the accomplishments of members of
  the Dow Jones Sustainability Group Index; and many other
  "green business" information resources.

- *Network for Change*
  www.envirolink.org
  Network for Change is a community of advocates for sustainable
  development. In addition to its links to environmental organizations, environmental education programs, environmental job
  banks, governmental resources on the environment, and advice
  on household level environmental management, this site posts
  environmental news headlines from around the globe.

- *Political Economy Research Center*
  www.perc.org
  The PERC bills itself as a pioneer of "free market environmentalism." Among its tenets, free market environmentalism proposes
  that private property rights are the best means for promoting

environmental stewardship and that government subsidies often degrade the environment. The site contains provocative opinions on topics such as overhauling the Endangered Species Act (e.g., by eliminating penalties for altering habitat) and making National Parks self-supporting (i.e., eliminating congressional appropriations for National Parks). An excellent tool for promoting lively classroom debates.

- *Resources for the Future*
  www.rff.org
  Resources for the Future is a nonprofit and nonpartisan think tank that conducts research—rooted primarily in economics and other social sciences—on environmental and natural resource issues. RFF posts full-length research reports on a wide range of environmental topics organized within online environmental and natural resources libraries. Especially useful are RFF's concise handbooks on environmental policy analysis tools (e.g., cost–benefit analysis; environmental modeling; regulatory design).

*Incentives played an important role in determining which Internet-related tasks and activities worked and did not work in Dr. Mitchell's class. Students participated actively and spoke favorably about online assignments that were monitored or graded by the professor, including student composition and submission of online discussion questions to the course Web page and student listing of paper prospectuses on the Web. Unmonitored conference areas in the class Web site were shunned by students. Also, given the option of designing an issue-specific Web page or completing the course midterm exam, the vast majority of students selected the latter. Dr. Mitchell speculates that more students would pick the former if extra credit points were exclusively reserved for Web page designers.

Gratifying encounters with these databases and information sources are not guaranteed. Making the most of the resource requires time, patience, and now and then a willingness to click the software's Help menu. It is really no different from the old days of mastering library card catalogs: now, as before, users who learn the basics of information retrieval are rewarded. The greatest rewards remain for those willing to learn the system's idiosyncrasies. But in at least one respect, the challenge for information users is greater today than in the past because the Internet and other electronic information sources charm the user with easy information. Easy is not necessarily helpful.

BOX 11.3. OTHER USEFUL
ENVIRONMENT-RELATED WEB SITES

- The World Resources Institute's Web site www.wri.org is an excellent, one-stop resource for data and analysis on global and regional environmental policy issues. Contains raw data from WRI's *World Resources* series.
- A service of the Fletcher School of Law and Diplomacy (Tufts University), the Multilaterals Project at www.fletcher.tufts.edu/multilaterals.html makes available full-length texts of international environmental conventions and other environmental legal instruments.
- One of India's most distinguished NGOs, The Centre for Science and Environment maintains its Web site at www.cseindia.org. CSE's reports and opinions offer striking counterpoints to mainstream Western governmental and NGO perspectives on environmental protection and sustainable development. CSE's site contains policy reports on climate change, wildlife management, and other environmental issues.
- The Earth Council www.ecouncil.ac.cr/, a Costa Rican–based international NGO, promotes implementation of the 1992 Earth Summit agreements. Besides its links to sustainable development research and advocacy organizations, this site is one of the best Web-based resources on indigenous knowledge of the environment.
- The Cable News Network (CNN) disseminates well-illustrated environmental news at www.cnn.com/NATURE/ and www.cnn.com/TECH.
- Similar to the service provided by the Network for Change, the Environmental News Network at www.enn.com compiles environmental news from national, regional, and international media outlets.

ORDINARY AND EXTRAORDINARY FUNCTIONS
OF INFORMATION TECHNOLOGY IN THE
CLASSROOM

These days, it is not uncommon for university deans and department chairs to set aside money for instructors to integrate the Internet or other electronic information media into their courses. Before taking the cash,

---

BOX 11.4. DATABASES, LITERATURE SEARCH, AND INFORMATION RETRIEVAL RESOURCES

- *Academic Search Premier.* Provides full texts for over 3,460 academic journals covering the social sciences, humanities, general science, multicultural studies, education, and more.
- *ingenfa.* A database of current article information drawn from more than 27,000 academic journals. Contains brief descriptions of more than 13,300,000 articles published since autumn 1988.
- *Lexis-Nexis Academic Universe.* A powerful information and data resource containing news, full-text articles, and data from general new media outlets; legal research including primary source legal texts and academic law reviews; business news; and medical professional literature.
- *Social Sciences Citation Index.* The Index's search engines retrieve articles in the social sciences academic literature by topic, title, and author. It also permits users to track citation histories of particular articles (i.e., to see who is citing whom). The index adds an average of 2,700 new articles and 50,500 new cited references per week.
- *International Political Science Abstracts.* A searchable index of articles dealing with topics in international studies.
- *Public Affairs Information Service.* Indexes materials dealing with political science, governmental affairs, international relations, economics, finance, law, environment, demography, sociology, and business. Contains information from journal articles, books, government documents, pamphlets, and the reports of public and private organizations. More than 1,100 journals and 8,000 monographs are indexed and abstracted each year.

---

instructors should ask themselves—and their students—"What functions will the Internet perform in my course?" Asking and answering this question at the outset prevents information superhighway accidents later on.

Many instructors and students welcome IT in the classroom because it facilitates communication. The Internet and e-mail are valued conduits for information exchange between professors and students. They allow instructors to share syllabi, class notes, grades, electronic periodicals, tabular data, short videos, dynamic graphics, and many other materials with their students, while giving the photocopy machine a break.

Of course, the flow of information between professors and students is two-way. Outside of class and office hours, students reach professors most often by e-mail. Some professors' office telephones feel neglected; e-mail in-boxes chime more often than do phones. Yet most student/professorial e-mail exchanges are, well, ordinary. Review an instructor's e-mail in-box and you'll find students' questions about classroom assignments, apologies for missing class, a friendly greeting with completed homework attached, and so on. E-mail from professors to students are no more remarkable: reminders to double-space the term paper, apologies for rescheduled classes, hello with a map quiz attached, and so forth. Surely, e-mail has expedited and made more efficient these ordinary kinds of communications. But neither instructors nor students can be blamed for craving more *extra*ordinary services from IT in the classroom. Hence, electronic bulletin boards that allow students to extend classroom discussions or to critique one another's written work are means for enriching the course. Properly incentivized listservs and bulletin boards also foster student/student and student/teacher exchange about course concepts and empirical material. As mentioned earlier, students may drive right past these roadside attractions lest they have a compelling reason to pull over. Extra credit points and class participation credit are means to that end.

CONCLUSION

Unfortunately, the search for extraordinary benefits from the wired classroom can leave both instructors and students wishing for the good old days of chalkboards and scratchy overhead transparencies. More than one undergraduate course has been hijacked by otherwise well-intentioned efforts to use IT. One illustration comes from a public policy professor from a Big Ten university who recently required each of his students to develop a policy-oriented Web site. The task consumed almost half of the students' course-related time outside of class and, alas, the final products varied greatly in quality. The students were overwhelmed, but overly ambitious attempts to transform ordinary courses into e-courses can inundate instructors too. Web sites require regular maintenance. For the site to remain useful, site content and links must be continually checked and updated. When bulletin boards and listservs are added to the equation, demands on instructors' time become excessive. Responding to all students' postings on bulletin boards and listservs can be a 20- to 40-hour per week job on its own.

For now and into the foreseeable future, most users of Information Age technologies in the classroom are best served by making calibrated, incremental forays into educational cyberspace. Attempting to do too much with IT may mean the difference between an innovative course of study and a colossal waste of both instructors' and students' time and energy.

The happiest, most satisfied, most richly rewarded users are those who recognize the Internet and other powerful IT tools as *means*. The end remains learning. Environmental politics is hard enough to learn without also having to master the many high-speed turns and lane changes on the information superhighway.

QUESTIONS FOR REFLECTION
AND DISCUSSION

1. Do the two vignettes that begin this chapter speak to your experience as a student or teacher? If you were asked to write a third or fourth vignette for this chapter, what story or stories could you tell? What insights would they offer?
2. Do you sometimes feel lost in data smog? If so, how do you find your way out? In your experience, are particular subfields or topic areas within global environmental politics especially smoggy? Give some examples that build upon Professor Auer's illustrations of the concept.
3. "Fact-based assignments . . . merely demand that students interpret what the data mean. No less important is discerning what data and information *fail to reveal.*" What is your reaction to this statement? What do you think Professor Conca's reaction (see chapter 5) would be, or Professor Taylor's (chapter 6)? Squeezing meaning out of the data before us is difficult enough—now Professor Auer tells us that if we are to be empowered by our study of global environmental politics, we also must figure out what the data are hiding from us. How, in our roles as teachers and students, could we best go about doing this?
4. If we divide the world up into two groups, those who brush their teeth and those who do not, we find that the former group consistently exhibits more tooth decay than the latter. Brushing our teeth, in other words, correlates with tooth decay. If we were to fall into the trap of confusing correlation with causality, what rather silly conclusion would we draw? How would we in fact account for this correlation—what hidden relationship is at work? (Hint: Think about diet.) And what might all this have to do with Professor Auer's overarching concerns about students getting squashed on the information superhighway?

NOTES

Kerry Krutilla shared his extensive list of environment-related Web sites with the author. Ron Mitchell offered rich insight into the promise and pitfalls of instructional use of the Internet. The final section of this chapter bears Dr. Mitchell's imprint, though the author is responsible for any and all errors of fact or omission.

    1. See www.nua.ie/surveys/ and google.com.

12

✹

Confronting the
Multidisciplinary Classroom

Howard Warshawsky

For some readers, the following chapter will be an easy read—it will till familiar ground and repeat, perhaps, already understood arguments and concerns. Others will find this chapter tougher going; the arguments and language may be new and perhaps difficult to digest. Still others, perhaps the majority of you now reading these words, will fall somewhere in between these end points of effortless discovery and gnawing confusion.

But for anyone who has spent time in a college classroom, this isn't news, is it? By virtue of temperament or training or both, we are unequally predisposed toward grasping the complexities and subtleties of any subject. You aren't all supposed to have the same background and talents and training. You're not clones. That, in part, is what makes the classroom an interesting and challenging place. We come together with diverse talents and gifts to combine our strengths to make sense of the world.

Such diversity cuts in less liberating directions, though, and it is this dark side of heterogeneity that Professor Warshawsky wrestles to the ground in this chapter. We all can call up memories of mind-numbing stretches of classroom tedium punctuated by moments of confusion (even terror?) as our instructor reviews in painstaking detail facts and ideas well-familiar to us but new to others, or moves briskly through material that our peers seem to know by heart but that is Greek to us. The more diverse—or, in the words of Professor Warshawsky, the more multidisciplinary—the students in class, the more common these experiences. And the more common these experiences, the more likely it is that students will be intimidated or anesthetized by their studies.

There is good news and bad in all of this. The bad news is that courses in

197

*environmental politics, and global environmental politics in particular, draw an
especially diverse student population and thus are especially vulnerable to the
bored–intimidated dynamic. Students who know too little or too much (relative
to their peers) about the interdisciplinary complexities of the politics of sustainability can thus find themselves marginalized. More bad news: We are not particularly accomplished, as classroom participants, in talking about this problem.*

*The good news, of course, is that we need not accept this dynamic as inevitable.
It can be overcome by strategies and classroom practices of the sort Professor
Warshawsky describes here or by other tactics you may develop through conver-
sation with others in class about the themes and claims of this chapter.—M.M.*

FROM DIVERSITY SPRINGS OPPORTUNITY

For more than three decades, the Higher Education Research Institute,
based at the University of California, Los Angeles, has conducted a
national annual survey of the attitudes and interests of college freshmen.
The survey of the entering 1998 freshmen class revealed that interest in
politics and policymaking is now less than half what it was in 1966 when
the survey was inaugurated. Indeed, interest among freshmen in political
affairs has now reached a record low (26 percent of those polled
expressed a sizable interest). These data reinforce other recent research
that describes Generation X as politically apathetic and cynical, less
informed about political data, less likely to identify with political parties
or to vote, and less likely to take part in democratic citizenship (Mann
1999).

Such student attitudes raise questions about how we learn and teach
about policymaking at the college and university level (if professors
assume an intrinsic interest in politics among their students, both parties
will be disappointed) and how classroom work may encourage democratic participation in general. Students and teachers of environmental
policy often assume, perhaps too optimistically, that students who enroll
in courses on environmental policy are more likely to be politically concerned and active than their cohorts. But even if that assumption proves
valid (though let us not assume that it always does), the student mix in
these classes is especially diverse. Students typically enter into study of
environmental policy from many different places: some are political science or international relations majors; others are biology, chemistry, or
environmental science majors or minors; while still others, taking courses
as electives, bring great interest to the topic but little more. Some, moreover, see these courses as a stepping stone to a career; others enroll out of
a deeply felt commitment to "save the earth."

It may surprise students to learn that instructors of environmental politics and policy find such diversity troublesome—and this is especially the case for any pronounced diversity of disciplinary expertise among students. When students come to our classes with different stores of knowledge, we are forced to present concepts and cover intellectual ground that will unavoidably be new or exciting to some students, boringly familiar or seemingly irrelevant to others, and beyond easy grasp of yet others. An introductory reading or lecture on the policymaking process, for example, might prove deadeningly dull to the political science major. It could pique the interest of a natural science oriented student, however, and loom as alarmingly foreign to someone who has not yet given much thought to policymaking. Later discussion about the natural science aspects of a key environmental problem may delight the political science major while numbing the natural science students and alarming those who think of themselves as natural science disabled. The bottom line: In the traditional classroom where disciplinary diversity reigns, professors who embrace traditional models of classroom instruction (e.g., lectures, reading, and discussion) cannot come close to pleasing all the people all the time.

The disciplinarily diverse classroom takes its toll on students and teachers alike. Students tolerate classroom work that once again plows familiar ground, at a cost to the curiosity and excitement that initially brought them to the course. Instructors teach topics they know fail to inspire a significant minority of their students and may find themselves doing so hurriedly, via lectures that lack passion. Whatever political disaffection and apathy students bring to class is not likely to be challenged and may easily be fueled or amplified by this reteaching of the familiar. No one is to blame, really. Students in environmental policy courses cannot be held accountable for the disciplinary diversity of the class mix. And professors, after all, have been largely trained to guide students who swim in the same specialized pool of knowledge and share one analytic vocabulary. Such commonalities are typical, perhaps, of hierarchical majors such as chemistry or math, where a student cannot proceed onto an upper-level course without having successfully mastered a set of defining concepts and the language common to the discipline. But they are far less the rule in the social sciences, where topical courses (on, say, global environmental problems) are often open to all willing to work and learn.

Diversity of academic interests and preparation, then, together with a reluctance to become engaged in civic discourse and participation, are facts of life in the environmental policy classroom. As teachers and students, we can choose to live with these facts and make do with our lot. Or, we can recognize that the disciplinarily diverse classroom, rather than being something we have to live with, offers opportunities to:

- Model real-world diversity. By focusing attention on the diversity of student interests, knowledge, and experiences, the classroom can become an environment that reflects and elucidates the real-world diversity that students will encounter all their lives. Learning to confront, understand, and adjust to the variety of human skills and goals ought to enable one to make better individual and communal judgments, establish mutually acceptable goals, and enhance the likelihood of their attainment.
- Gain practice in communicating across disciplinary divides. The study of environmental issues is both multidisciplinary and interdisciplinary in nature. Most students and teachers recognize cross-disciplinary study as both appropriate and desirable. Indeed, the multidisciplinary nature of the field is what has attracted many to it. Nonetheless, the resultant classroom diversity we encounter also presents pedagogical problems. How can we best learn and teach about complex topics in ways that will be consistently informative and provocative for all these diverse students? Perhaps the methods we develop to accomplish this may also provide us with skills and insights as to how to accommodate the diversity we encounter in real-world decision making.
- Compare discipline-based perspectives on the importance of a vibrant civil society to the resolution of pressing environmental ills. Students often prefer to enroll in courses that are perceived as having practical applicability relative to their careers or academic credentialing requirements. Can it not also be demonstrated that encouraging participation in civic life has practicality as well? The academic experience can enhance not only the students' personal credentials and individual prospects but by stimulating the involvement of the individual within the wider community can also improve the quality of communal life. Clarifying the interdependence of individual and community well-being ought to be a course and institutional objective.
- Pursue course exercises that draw on disciplinary diversity to foster critical analytical skills and heightened civic sensibility. It is common for colleges and universities to articulate the goal of connecting students' educational experiences to meaningful participation, if not leadership, in community affairs. Increasingly, we define such community engagement in local, regional, national, and global terms. The subject matter of environmental policy courses, which incorporates interactions among all those levels, makes them especially appropriate as mechanisms to establish such connections. Course components that facilitate or simulate student involvement in policy-making at different levels can, therefore, be especially helpful. Exer-

cises that take into account the diversity of student perspectives and skills and utilize them in ways that mirror actual policy and community decision making are, therefore, a means to attainment of a number of educational goals.

SEIZING THE OPPORTUNITY: THE CONSULTANT PROJECT

For several years, I have utilized in my course on environmental public policy a research and writing assignment that, hopefully, develops student presentation and analytical skills, helps identify the complexity and diversity of factors affecting environmental policy, requires the interaction of students with different understandings and perspectives, and relates that interaction and collaboration to real-world experiences. It is an exercise that recognizes the pedagogical dilemmas posed by a disparate student audience while encouraging students to grapple with the larger, later lifelong dilemmas of communicating complex information to diverse societal audiences in ways supportive of rich civic discourse and action. The assignment borrows heavily from an exercise developed at the University of California, Davis, by Geoffrey Wandesforde-Smith, that focused upon issues generated by the 1992 Rio United Nations Conference on Environment and Development (UNCED).

The exercise consists of several stages: client and topic selection; research and draft preparation; submission of the consultant's situation and options report; preparation of a hypothetical actor's response to the consultant recommendations; and class discussion and debriefing of the exercise. Students are expected to consult with the instructor at all stages of the project.

In the project, students are asked to assume that they own and operate an environmental consulting firm, wherein they serve as Director of research. A name and address for the firm are chosen. Each student selects a client that has requested a situation and options report focusing upon a specific environmental issue. Due to the transboundary and intermestic nature of environmental issues and policy, the specific issue could be either domestic or international but must be appropriately limited in focus so as to be amenable to completion within a ten- to twelve-page written report. Depending upon class size, students either work on individual projects, or even better, work in teams wherein there is a mixture of disciplinary backgrounds.

Unlike a traditional analytical research paper, the report is addressed to the client. It is to be professional in all respects, and students are encouraged to think of it as a document that could later serve as a writing sample to be given to prospective employers. Hopefully, this adds a bit of reality to the exercise by equating the clients with actual employers and helping the student to see a connection between personal career interests and academic requirements. In fact, the student is required to submit a fee with the report wherein the costs are itemized and explained so as to better relate the academic analysis and the real costs incurred by researchers and clients.

The selection of the client is a crucial element of the assignment. Students can select either actual or hypothetical clients, but the former are preferred in order to simulate reality as much as possible. Furthermore, clients are generally limited to corporations, citizen's groups, or nongovernmental organizations. This is intended to encourage students to assess the policy process, the role of government within that process, and decision-making dynamics from a nongovernmental perspective. Besides, domestic government agencies and intergovernmental organizations would generally not be prone to hire private consultants to recommend policy options (as distinct from commissioning technical research analyses and reports). However, exceptions to this rule can be made if the students demonstrate a compelling interest and rationale (for example, perhaps the government of a developing nation could request advice on other ways to influence European Union environmental rules or on options for responding to Greenpeace protests).

The client's issue or request must be manageable in regard to both topical scope and access to research materials. Students are encouraged to select issues in which they have a personal interest. This is not only a means to encourage and sustain the research effort but is also a way to stimulate later discussion of the potentially conflicting roles as advocates or objective analysts that students and citizens are likely to undertake. The definition of the client's problem and request should be simple, straightforward, and clearly focused.

Students are required to address particular issues and provide specific information in their final report to the client. The client and its goals must be clearly identified. It must be demonstrated how and why the specific environmental issue affects the client previously, now, and in the future. The client's specific question must be linked to the more general nature, extent, and significance of the environmental topic. Therefore, the impact of the issue on the wider community must be taken into account, and other relevant policy actors and their anticipated responses must be identified. The report must incorporate an overview of prior efforts to address the issue and identify existing institutional arrangements (regimes). The effectiveness of these current rules, structures, and regimes must be evaluated. Finally, based upon the client's goals, several optional courses of action and possible consequences must be provided along with a rationale for the recommended choice.

As an alternative or possibly an adjunct to the use of team-based reports, each student can also be required to submit a response to or critique of the report submitted by some other student (or team). To sustain the value of role playing, the response is written from the perspective of an actor involved in the topical issue being addressed and could take the form of a letter to an editor, a letter to a relevant government agency, or even a letter to the client from the respondents' role character intended to express an alternative point of view or recommendation. This element of the assignment asks students to familiarize themselves with an environmental problem other than the one addressed in their own consultant report, analyze the logic of other students' argumentation, and view policymaking from an additional, albeit simulated, perspective.

Once the reports and responses have been submitted, in-class discussion or debriefing sessions on the client reports are conducted to focus attention on the variety of perspectives and assumptions students, and society generally, bring to bear when considering policy options and the definition of personal and community interest. Making all the reports available to the whole class, perhaps via e-mail or a course Web site, can better inform such discussion, but the fact that each student has already been asked to serve as a respondent or commentator can by itself provoke lively discussion. This can supplement or substitute for the pro and con "taking sides" debates or case study presentations that are common in global environmental policy courses.

ISSUES RAISED, LESSONS LEARNED

How does this project help us together teach and learn? How can it help inform classroom discussion of issues important to the environment, politics, international relations, democratic participation, and governance? How can Generation X and its successors become more civic minded? How can we better promote not just greater awareness of current and future problems but also leadership, in efforts to seek resolution and justice?

In his essay on the virtues of service learning, Thomas Ehrlich identifies four interrelated learning goals that contribute to civic education. *Academic learning* focuses upon descriptions and analyses of societal interactions. *Social learning* entails interpersonal skills needed to function in social, political, and career settings. *Moral learning* depends upon students being able to understand their own beliefs and relating those to the beliefs of others. *Civic learning* involves understanding democratic processes, the diversity present within and among communities, and the need for individual commitment to work collaboratively to resolve community concerns (Ehrlich 1999). In a modest way, the consultant exercise contributes to each of these. It asks students to analyze and participate in community decision making. It encourages engagement and hence provides lessons for citizenship. And as technology and interdependence blur the lines between domestic and foreign policies and challenge the capacity of nations to effectively govern, the need for "global public policy" (Reinicke 1998) and global citizenship increases.

Study of environmental issues provides an ideal means to illustrate the need for greater citizen awareness at local through global levels. The complex interaction of multiple, diverse causal factors that have transboundary impacts and often require transnational regimes to minimize harmful consequences makes meaningful the think globally, act locally cliché. The consultant projects incorporate discussion of all factors involved in determining the costs of behavior and policy, thereby allowing students with diverse backgrounds to work together and share both issue-oriented policymaking approaches as well as pedagogical experiences that illustrate both interdependence and the need for citizen involvement.

This diversity of student interests combined with the wide scope of topical and client choice has been welcomed by students and has probably generated greater enthusiasm for a research and writing project than is normally encountered. The resulting variety of issues selected has been encouraging. For example, students have worked on a request from a New England lobstermen's association in regard to overharvesting of the catch in international waters; a question from an environmental NGO as to how best to help with Amazonian rain forest protection; requests from electric utilities concerning disposal of nuclear wastes and the impact of new power line construction; and a question from a local neighborhood association about cleanup of a toxic waste site. The clients selected have predominately been American, but choice need not be limited to clients of a specific nationality. A broader sampling of clients with a variety of national identities is helpful in introducing discussion of comparative policymaking and of how national identity and culture affect the setting of policy goals and selection of policy options. Students with diverse interests and backgrounds are able to focus on issues that are appealing to them but nonetheless are asked to develop and apply information and analysis in new and insightful ways.

The assignment can be either a solo project undertaken by an individual student or, depending upon class size, students could work in pairs or even larger teams to encourage collaborative learning and an even greater sharing of views and knowledge. Shared assignments can be problematic in implementation, but a collaborative report does allow the pairing of students with diverse interests and also more closely resembles real-world collective decision-making situations. For these purposes, it would be especially fortunate if the classroom's diversity also encompassed a number of non-American or international students. Too often, Americans assume that the attention and priority we give to environmental issues are duplicated elsewhere. The presence of international students may help challenge such preconceptions.

Disparate students who work together to address complex, ambiguous issues and who need to respond to the proposals and perspectives of one another may learn to better cope with the diversity and antagonisms inherent in the real-world policy choices that will confront them throughout their lives. Interaction among a diverse class audience may also encourage individuals to challenge their own preconceptions and to better comprehend the perceptions of others. Whether that leads to mutual understanding and tolerance or discovery of more efficacious means to manipulate one another is problematic. In Chinese literature, art, and philosophy, nature is often depicted as representing the harmony that is attained from diverse and contending forces (the balance of yin and yang). Perhaps study of the environment (i.e., nature) will encourage a more harmonious and less manipulative global policy process.

As students and teachers, we desire objectivity as observers and analysts. While pure objectivity is seldom attained, we aspire to the ideals of the scientific method. Nonetheless, a diverse classroom will include people who perceive objectivity very subjectively. The consultation project asks students to identify the subjective policy goals of relevant actors and to critique the objectivity and logic of the professional consultant reports prepared by their peers. As a consultant, the student assumes roles both as policymaking participant and as objective analyst. This dynamic can help students recognize the subjectivity present in real-world definitions of public interest and proper behavior. Ideally, we can learn to objectively consider the impact of subjective and particularistic motivations.

Will discussion amongst a diverse group, within an academic setting, of diverse sources of information, perspectives, and experiences enable us to better understand environmental issues? Selection of course readings that address the variety of cultural and ideological perspectives that are used to interpret and explain environmental policy (see Dryzek 1997) can better inform this student discussion. In a classroom where students and faculty see themselves as colleagues who are all engaged in teaching and learning, greater objectivity is encouraged. The consultant exercise may enhance a sense of such collaborative learning.

Collaborative learning is also enhanced by the fact that the exercise directs students, with different academic majors and career interests, to integrate information and insights from many academic disciplines and sources. Students who begin the course with knowledge and concern centered upon a limited range of academic subfields are expected to broaden their horizons. Minimally, they should develop greater awareness of the contributions and importance of multidisciplinary thinking. Even better, they may overcome some of the apprehension, suspicion, or even hostility that often characterizes reactions to unfamiliar or different academic disciplines.

Students with primarily scientific and technical orientations and training may become more appreciative and more comfortable with the economic, social, and political factors that affect the development and application of scientific research. Students who are already attuned to the social dynamics and power politics of policymaking may gain better comprehension of the essential role of geography, climate, and biology in informing and establishing parameters for policy debates. Client reports often incorporate cultural sources (art, literature, religion) to describe and explain the dynamics of specific environmental issues. The varied backgrounds of the students can be used to both represent and integrate this multiplicity of factors that affect environmental issues. Students are being asked to take general knowledge and theories from a variety of disciplinary perspectives and apply them to actual problems. Consequently, study of the role of scientists in policy agenda-setting or of how environmental problems relate to goals of social justice can be made relevant to a wider, more diverse audience.

Of course, accommodating diversity and enhancing multidisciplinary understanding cannot be expected to occur automatically. Much time and energy must be expended by both instructor and student to provide active supervision and consultation throughout the exercise. The grade value attached to the assignment can signify the serious commitment needed. And the instructor must be willing to sacrifice some control over course management by providing students with flexibility as to selection of topical content and by ceding some lecture time to group discussion and interaction. This may be perceived as a major sacrifice by some instructors: are we giving up time to provide necessary data and content merely to have more time to pool our collective ignorance within ill-informed discussion? This is a real risk for both students and faculty. A livelier classroom is not inherently better, but a concerted effort by all can lead to better multidisciplinary, integrated comprehension of important issues.

As discussed elsewhere in this volume, global environmental policy courses incorporate abstract and theoretical models and concepts from many academic disciplines. And the complexity of the subject matter necessitates the inclusion of a great deal of factual information. It is understandable why students can be overwhelmed and turned off by course material. Such reactions are accentuated when students enter the course being aware of or interested in only a limited portion of these facts and theories. By focusing theoretical abstractions and an immense database upon their application to a specific policy choice, the consultant exercise makes more relevant the need for multidisciplinary understanding. At the same time, it allows students to practice personal decision making and improve critical thinking skills. They should be better able to observe the interrelationship of natural and social activities and make better choices about policy tactics and goals.

Attention to this interdependence might also be addressed by altering the topical focus of the assignment somewhat. One variant of the consultant project, if the logistics are feasible, would have the student or team focus on environmental issues on campus and in the local community. Recycling, use of campus land as a wildlife refuge, waste site cleanup, among others, could serve as topical issues with the client being the college or local community. This would add a more direct experiential learning component to the course and expose students first hand to the goals and attitudes of real actors whose real interests will be at stake. That dose of reality could be quite instructive. While these topical issues would have a microlevel focus, they could still be related to macrolevel international or "glocal" (Hempel 1996a) issues by utilization of the local problems as examples to illustrate the dynamics of other topics discussed in class and texts. Alternatively, all the consultant reports could be required to focus upon the local impacts of a specific transboundary issue, such as global warming, or event, such as the 1997 Kyoto Conference of Parties on Climate Change.

Similarly, the consultant's need to make specific policy recommendations exemplifies the role of the individual in making choices and engaging in behavior that affects the state of the environment. One is compelled to think about the need for and impact of political participation by both individuals and groups. Students will need to consider not just what has been or is being done, but what should be done by both governmental and nongovernmental actors. This, furthermore, provides a mechanism by which discussion of moral and ethical concerns occurs. Empirical and normative dimensions can be addressed in both the debriefing session and in regard to other course topics. Hopefully, this will be through dialogue, not diatribe.

The exercise then can raise issues concerning the nature of and need for democratic participation in community life. Environmental topics that highlight the microlevel and macrolevel impacts of glocal thinking and behavior are especially apt to provoke discussion of citizenship roles. The connections between political democratization and environmental activism are easily drawn when dealing with issues such as environmental cleanup in pre- and post-Communist era Central and Eastern Europe or the roles and rights of indigenous peoples in rain forests but can also be related to most of the client questions developed by students.

While students need to be able to distinguish between objective analysis and advocacy, the consultant project should also make them aware that the study of policy is itself a political activity. Developing how-to solutions to environmental questions ought to help students to view one another as involved participants and not just passive, neutral observers. Engagement in advocacy can be quite instructive. After all, real-world policymaking includes actors who, both intentionally and unintentionally, do not approach issues from neutral, objective perspectives. By being asked to take a stand, students are asked to examine the consequences of individual and group behavior (i.e., the need for responsible citizenship). They can become not only more knowledgeable participants in democratic processes but may even be encouraged to assume leadership roles.

Students enrolling in global environmental policy courses, especially those with primarily natural science backgrounds, most often lack sophisticated understanding of the dynamics of international relations. Unfortunately, this is a reflection of society as a whole. Perhaps evolving information and communications technologies that facilitate global exchanges at both macrolevels and microlevels will produce better awareness and comprehension of international relations in the future. In the meantime, students in our classes need to learn more about international relations in general and not just environmental policy specifically. Fortunately, lessons learned about global environmentalism can be utilized to illustrate more general international or intermestic trends and concepts. In turn, this process makes clear the need for student and citizen involvement at all levels of community.

How do these student-citizens emerge from the mass of contemporary students who have frequently been described as unmotivated, nonattentive consumers who perceive themselves as buying an education and credentials from teachers whose job it is to deliver the product regardless of whether students work for it (Leo 1996)? Are we to lower standards, raise grades, and entertain? Is the postmodernist student a hopeless case? Probably not! Education ought not to be seen as entertainment, but we ought to seek ways to make learning, for both teachers and students, more interesting and engaging. The consultant project exercise may allow us to take a modest step or two in the right direction.

QUESTIONS FOR REFLECTION
AND DISCUSSION

1. To what extent are you persuaded by the argument that disciplinary diversity in the classroom must be confronted if we are to better learn and teach about the politics of environmental degradation?

2. How persuasive, in turn, is the claim that collaborative learning processes of the sort described here are necessary to challenge the cynicism and passivity that allegedly plagues Generation X?
3. Virginia Professor Mark Edmundson (1997) argues that college life currently functions as "lite entertainment for bored college students" and that we spend far too much time in class waiting to be entertained or working to be entertaining. Would you agree? Don't the in-class exercises of the sort described here risk pushing us further along the road of college as "lite entertainment"?
4. For collaborative learning—and other exercises that might expose students to the intellectual rewards of political analysis and political life—to succeed in the classroom, what skills must students and their teachers command? What obligations to each other must they fulfill? Given our talents and interests, are we up to the task?
5. Time in class, and in college, is finite. If we give over part of a course to some activities similar to the consultant exercise, there is less class time to cover other material, much of which is important in its own right. Tried-and-true approaches to education—lectures, reading, some discussion, and tests and papers—remain the most efficient way of communicating large amounts of information. Is the decline in this efficiency that would occur as a result of moving towards collaborative-based approaches to teaching and learning really worth it?

13

✸

Thinking Globally, Acting Locally

A Service-Learning Approach to Teaching and Learning Global Environmental Politics

Nancy Quirk

Nancy Quirk is not about to bend to the "dynamic of retreat" described in the opening paragraphs of this book. Students, claims Quirk, are tackling tough issues on their campuses and in their communities and are increasingly joining together to foster environmental sustainability and social justice. The rise of service learning—a set of instructional mechanisms and practices that bring the community into the classroom while taking the classroom into the community—is surely one reason for this uptick in student engagement. Professor Quirk argues here that courses in global environmental politics are especially well suited to and advanced by the service-learning approach to undergraduate education—and she provides a range of conceptual arguments and some nifty empirical examples to make her case.

Quirk ends her chapter, and this book, with a quote from Ernest Boyer, past president of the Carnegie Foundation for the Advancement of Teaching: "[C]ampuses," said Boyer, "should be viewed by both students and professors not as isolated islands, but as staging grounds for action." It is an apt final line for this volume, and it underscores Quirk's intention that this chapter be more than a useful primer for integrating service learning into the environmental studies classroom. It is also a call to action and a practical roadmap for students and professors of global environmental politics no longer willing to tolerate the dynamic of retreat.

This chapter can be read, then, for the advice it offers instructors looking to enhance the effectiveness of their courses. Students about to embark on a service-learning experience as part of their environmental studies coursework will also find this chapter valuable. Its usefulness to a more general audience—say, students in a conventional global environmental politics course—at first glance seems less obvious. But don't be fooled. As the discussion questions that close the chapter demonstrate, there is much here to chew on and confront.—M.M.

> Our troubled planet can no longer afford the luxury of pursuits confined to an ivory tower. Scholarship has to prove its worth, not on its own terms, but by service to the nation and the world.
>
> —Oscar Handlin (as quoted in Boyer 1994: A48)

A cross the country and around the world, undergraduates are calling into question reports of growing student apathy by putting their skills and knowledge regarding environmental issues to work in the service of local communities—and beyond. According to Jonathan Collett, an analyst of U.S. student movements, "the student movement for an environmentally sustainable future is large, growing, and well organized" (1996: 310). Students are "thinking globally and acting locally" in a variety of settings and tasks, contributing not only to environmental protection in local and global communities but also to their own education. Consider the following examples:

- At the University of Wisconsin-Madison, students have worked to reduce the use of chemicals in campus laboratories and promote recycling (Lerner 1994: 37).
- Students at Brown University examined the impact of contamination by lead and other pollutants in low-income neighborhoods in Providence, Rhode Island, documenting the extent of health risk to local residents (Enos and Troppe 1996: 173–74).
- An energy management plan for Rochester University in New York was designed by a doctoral student in history. This student worked with other students to audit and inspect energy use on campus, resulting in energy savings of $1.5 million annually (Pierce 1992).
- More recently, students at Allegheny College in northwestern Pennsylvania, inspired by the Rocky Mountain Institute's Community Energy Workbook (Hubbard and Fong 1995), have launched a campus-community program that targets energy-inefficient rental housing (Greely 2000).

- Students from universities around the country travel to Ecuador to help the nongovernmental organization (NGO) People Allied for Nature document the flora and fauna and to help local residents establish alternative sustainable economic activity to support preservation of the cloud forests from encroaching development (Becker 1997).

- Undergraduates across the country have banded together into a "sweatshop movement" that challenges the use of underpaid and poorly treated Third-World labor in the production of textiles (Featherstone 2000). And many are now coming together as part of a "greening the campus" movement to pressure colleges and universities across the United States to divest from the major corporate sources of greenhouse gases (Collett and Karakashian 1996; Mansfield 1998).

When initiatives like these are integrated into academic courses on environmental issues, students are put in the way of rich opportunities to combine service to the community with learning about the complicated dynamics of environmental politics. Such learning projects, which I refer to in this chapter as "service learning," are gaining favor across the disciplinary spectrum, from composition to engineering and history to anthropology, and have in the past decade become part of a larger national effort to involve students in community service as part of their educational experience.[1] At its heart, service learning strives to place community service and classroom learning on equal footing, going beyond volunteerism by utilizing an experiential learning framework that facilitates both community service *and* academic achievement.[2] The key element in service learning is the feedback between course content and the experiences students have in the service context. As Professor Ehrlich, a teacher and analyst of service learning, observes:

> Community service in the context of academic courses and seminars . . . is valuable for two fundamental and interrelated reasons: (1) service as a form of *practical experience enhances learning* in all areas of a university's curriculum; and (2) the experience of community service *reinforces moral and civic values* inherent in serving others. (Ehrlich 1995: 9, emphasis in original)

As an example, a service-learning course in public policy or sociology might focus on issues of poverty, and students could be engaged in service at community homeless shelters. This combination provides an opportunity for students to create an internal understanding of homelessness, while course readings, class discussions, and course assignments can help students widen their understanding of poverty in the larger social and policy context.[3] In the area of global environmental politics, service learning brings students into contact with local environmental commissions, environmental organizations, and similar community efforts to address environmental concerns, while in their coursework students read, discuss, and reflect upon the social, economic, and political aspects of environmental degradation, policy responses, and the relevance of local struggles to the resolution of global environmental ills.

Links developed with the local community, along with in-depth awareness of environmental issues acquired through service activities, are particularly important to students as they assess their own career choices and the contribution they hope to make to society. Environmental considerations will remain high on our agenda and are of concern to persons across the disciplinary spectrum, from politics, education, and science, to business, law, and sociology. The content and methods of service-learning courses in global environmental politics mirror this reality: scientific evidence, sociological insight, economic analysis, and political skills are all necessary to understand community efforts for environmental protection. Interdisciplinary hands-on service-learning courses thus provide students with exceptional opportunities to share insights and skills from various disciplines as they discuss topics and assignments with each other as well as with members of local environmental organizations.

The promise for service learning in courses on global environmental politics goes beyond academic learning, however. It addresses concerns raised by teacher-scholars like Oberlin College's David Orr or Allegheny College's Michael Maniates that environmental education can leave students overwhelmed by the complexity of the issues and feeling unable to "make a difference" by their individual actions. As Maniates suggests in this volume's introduction, courses providing detailed analyses of regional and global environmental ills can inadvertently fuel the fire of a fashionable cynicism about the prospects for meaningful social change. Or worse, as Orr argues, "[t]he study of environmental problems [can represent] an exercise in despair *unless it is regarded as only a preface to the study, design, and implementation of solutions*" (Orr 1992: 94, emphasis added).

When integrated into courses on environmental politics, service learning can transform the classroom experience from a potential exercise in despair to a laboratory for bringing intellectual insight to bear on social problems that matter. For instance, students learn through their service activities how local communities come together to debate, organize, and commit to small-scale or community-wide programs that address local environmental problems. Citywide recycling programs, creation or expansion of bicycle paths, implementation of traffic diversion measures, or local energy conservation and renewable-energy programs are just a few examples of locally based initiatives that students can study or foster. Students come face to face with the benefits and costs of negotiated solutions to shared environmental ills and understand too that resistance to initiatives of sustainable development often flows from real people with genuine concerns (e.g., shopkeepers who might see a drop in business if traffic patterns were changed), not abstract corporations that are easily caricatured and vilified. These experiences help students understand the complexities involved in resolving environmental issues and inspire them to question society's—as well as their own—fundamental values regarding the public goods we collectively pursue. By demystifying processes of local political change and acquainting students with the deep sense of personal satisfaction that comes with pursuing the social good in common, such experiences also foster a broader set of civic sensibilities and habits.

Thinking globally *and* acting locally within courses on global environmental politics isn't common. Most such courses, as other contributions to this volume make clear, ask students to *think* globally and, perhaps, *think* locally, but applied action is curiously absent, despite the contribution that local involvement within a service-learning context can make to help empower students to pursue their own, often passionate, desire to make a difference. It can open the eyes of both teachers and their students to the complex interplay of values, economics, and political stakes involved in environmental politics while providing hands-on experience with devising workable solutions to at least some aspect of the larger problems. It can also bring the abstract world of international environmental negotiations closer to home, on a small, more approachable scale, ensuring that time spent in the classroom will truly make a difference. Why, then, don't we see more service learning within courses on global environmental problems and politics? And how might we best respond, teachers and students both, to this deficiency?

To get at these questions, this chapter places discussion of service learning in the context of larger challenges facing undergraduate education in the twenty-first century. The chapter then outlines pedagogical *whys* and *ways* of utilizing active or experiential learning approaches such as service learning and continues with more specific *how-tos* for constructing a service-learning course to teach global environmental politics. The chapter concludes by raising issues relevant to the greening of undergraduate education.

REINVENTING UNDERGRADUATE EDUCATION

Arguments in support of more widespread use of service learning across disciplines fall within a larger discourse on the nature of education, learning, and the proper role of the university in the early twenty-first century. Boyer's *Scholarship Reconsidered* is but one call for rethinking the role of the academy, to "[re]define scholarship in ways that respond more adequately to the urgent new realities both within the academy and beyond" (1990: 3). Indeed, since the mid-1980s, there have been many calls for reconceptualizing the university so that it might more directly serve the public good.[4] Service learning is a critical element—*the* critical element, some would argue[5]—in this strategy of incremental transformation of higher education. In particular, service learning may be especially relevant to those academic disciplines (like sociology, political science, political economy, and environmental studies) that encourage an appreciation of the importance of power and a willingness to grapple with ethical and moral implications of societal choices. Service learning may be just what the doctor ordered when it comes to making the systematic study of the struggle for influence and power both relevant and real to students accustomed to a contemporary social rhetoric of conflict-free technocratic management of social problems.[6]

This debate on the reform of undergraduate education deserves our attention, regardless of how interested we are in the particulars of service learning, because we are all part of and molded by institutions of higher education. Some, like essayist and educational analyst Charles Anderson, argue that we in higher education "have simply lost track of the overall point of the endeavor."[7] Others, like Ernest Boyer, past president of the Carnegie Foundation for the Advancement of Teaching, are inclined to agree. In 1994, Boyer put forth a proposal for a New American College that would connect the knowledge and skills of the academy to the direct needs of society. This New American College, wrote Boyer, would be

> an institution that celebrates teaching . . . while also taking special pride in its capacity to connect thought to action, theory to practice. The New American College would organize cross-disciplinary institutes around pressing social issues. Undergraduates at the college would participate in field projects, relating ideas to real life. Classrooms and laboratories would be extended to include health clinics, youth centers, schools, and government offices. Faculty members would build partnerships with practitioners who would, in turn, come to campus as lecturers and student advisers. The New American College, as a connected institution, would be committed to improving, in a very intentional way, the human condition. (1994: A48)

Service learning represents one effective vehicle for implementing such visions. In addition, service learning puts into practice widely disseminated principles of effective undergraduate teaching—close student-faculty contact; cooperation and collaboration among students; active learning; time on task; and a respect for diverse talents and ways of learning, among others.[8] In short, the "reinvention of undergraduate education"—and the contribution of service learning to that effort—may constitute nothing less than a "paradigm shift" in how we understand the college classroom (McDaniel 1994).

ACTIVE LEARNING, INTELLECTUAL DEVELOPMENT, AND MOTIVATION

Service learning is *experiential learning*. Experiential learning, in ways and for reasons articulated by educational theorists from John Dewey to David Kolb (1984a; b), challenges conventional understandings of university education. Instructors go from "experts" who stand before a room lecturing, to "facilitators" charged with creating an experience for students. Students shift from passive vessels to be filled with information to individuals who must actively engage course material and make decisions—sometimes difficult ones—about the pace and direction of their education. Most important, perhaps, are the linked issues of control and predictability: rather than neatly ordered by the dates and readings listed on a preplanned syllabus, the experience of both students and teachers in the experiential classroom is less linear, less certain, more episodic. The often unexpected demands and challenges of a service-learning project can come to frame the classroom experience, and while they open up rich opportunity for classroom discussion, debate, and inquiry, they also directly challenge student expectations of an organized syllabus and a teacher's felt need for control in the classroom.

Service learning requires students to participate in their learning and not remain the passive recipient of knowledge from outside experts.[9] Hard as it may be, students and their instructors alike should be aiming for

> a college classroom where students are thought of primarily . . . as individuals to be empowered instead of graded, as responsible associates or colleagues, not as empty pitchers or blank slates, as part of a group that cooperates rather than as individuals who compete, and as intrinsically motivated and talented contributors to a process of education instead of passive receivers of already determined "content" . . . students [should be] . . . considered competent participants in their own educational development. (McDaniel 1994: 28)

Shifting from education as transmission of information to engaged, experiential modes of teaching and learning not only anchors knowledge but also transforms classroom facts to be memorized into usable knowledge to be applied. Linking abstract concepts with reality in this way can address the three pernicious challenges raised by Lee Shulman (1997: 161): "the loss of learning, or *amnesia* ['I forgot it']; the illusion of learning, or *illusory understanding* ['I thought I understood it']; and the uselessness of learning, or *inert ideas* ['I understand it but I can't use it']." Consider the case of a student engaged in volunteer service with an ambulance crew: "[I]n school you learn chemistry and biology and stuff and then forget it as soon as the test is over. Here you've got to remember because somebody's life depends on it" (as quoted in Conrad and Hedin 1991: 74). As educational theorist John Dewey observed, "for knowledge to be usable through recall and application, it has to be acquired in a situation; otherwise it is segregated from experience and is forgotten or not available for transfer to new experiences" (Dewey 1938, as discussed in Giles and Eyler 1994: 79).[10] Cognitive skills are enhanced by active participation in the learning process—and this occurs, it appears, because students more easily see the relevance to their lives of what they are learning and thus naturally link abstract concepts to experiences they've had.[11] Service-learning approaches, in theory at least, offer an opportunity to create "situational niches" within which teachers of global environmental politics can practice their craft and students can truly and deeply learn.

Another common challenge in undergraduate education is students' "dualistic" view of knowledge. For many students, knowledge consists of "facts, correct theories, and right answers" to be memorized and recited, and learning is merely the process of having the instructor reveal the truth rather than "making students perform what to them seem to be senseless tasks" (Kloss 1994: 151–52). Effective undergraduate education attacks this superficial understanding of truth and learning by driving students' intellectual development through a set of critical stages: "multiplicity" in which all knowledge is a matter of opinion, and all opinions are equally valid; "relativism" in which students begin to "weigh evidence and distinguish between weak and strong support" of arguments; and lastly, "commitment" in which students "integrate the relatively objective, removed, and rational procedures of academia with their more empathic and experiential approaches to all other aspects of their lives" (Kloss 1994: 152).[12] These stages exemplify a process of intellectual development in which students move from lower-order cognitive skills such as memorization of facts, to higher-order skills of appraising, critiquing, judging, interpreting, and justifying arguments, written material, and creative works of others (DeZure 1996; Lee 1999).[13]

The use of active learning strategies can help students in this developmental process, challenging them to evaluate evidence and arguments encountered in their service experiences, thus enabling them to construct their own knowledge—"transform[s] empirical evidence into revised and new knowledge structures" (Lee 1999: 4). As students move from stage to stage in their intellectual development—from dualistic knowledge that imagines learning to be little more than the memorization of facts, to multiplicity, then to relativism, and finally to commitment—they will become more confident and capable of "engag[ing] in inquiry, particularly higher-order critical thinking" (DeZure 1996: 3). Service-learning approaches that take students out of the predictable confines of the classroom and plunge them into less predictable real-world settings provide the stimulus necessary for independent judgment and assessment of information and arguments from a wide variety of sources. Many of these nontraditional sources of information in the service-learning context are local activists or agency personnel whose years of experience in the field of environmental politics can help them serve as experts whose knowledge complements, expands, and brings new light to class material. These multiple sources of knowledge may represent for some students a very confusing mélange. Yet, together with other students and the instructor, they can learn from their experiences and from each other how to begin to sift through and to "appraise, critique, and judge" this information.[14]

Studies of cognitive development also emphasize the role of motivation in focusing students on their learning and the importance of utilizing "intrinsic" as opposed to "extrinsic" motivation.[15] The active, engaged, experiential model of service learning builds upon students' *intrinsic* concern regarding environmental issues and offers an opportunity to experience the very direct impact of what individuals and local communities can accomplish. On this point, undergraduate courses in global environmental politics enjoy a natural advantage: students typically come to these courses concerned about environmental degradation, eager to do something about the environmental crisis.

Yet, as previous chapters in this volume emphasize, comprehensive and ambitious courses on global environmental ills can overwhelm students' beginning intrinsic desire to learn in one or more ways: students can feel that experts are attending to these issues and that *only* experts have the knowledge needed to respond to global environmental problems; or that scientific or technical know-how is both necessary and forthcoming, so that the possibility for the actions of individuals, and particularly of students, pales in the face of the highly technocratic nature of needed palliatives. Or students may feel that the problems are so complex and intermingled that any small steps they might consider would prove insignificant at best. As students experience the real-world consequences of individual and local decisions, they return to the global environmental politics classroom with renewed motivation to understand the conceptual frameworks with which environmental politics can be analyzed. Relating concrete experience with formerly abstract concepts contributes to student mastery of course concepts and yields real growth in the self-confidence of undergraduates as they participate in the process of constructing meaning from their experiences (Cone and Harris 1996: 39). Such enlightened self-confidence, supported by a sophisticated understanding of the nuances of global environmental politics, may be the most important outcome we can ask of a college curriculum that purports to help create a sustainable future.

SERVICE-LEARNING IMPLEMENTATION FOR GLOBAL ENVIRONMENTAL POLITICS

In practice, the classroom implementation of service-learning techniques means challenging three comfortable conventions of everyday classroom life: the accepted roles of students, faculty, and community organizations; the nature of course readings and assignments; and the ways in which we think about the tension between academic rigor (e.g., focused attention on texts and comprehensive writing assignments) and community action.

The Players: Faculty, Students, Community

For service learning to get off the ground, faculty must imagine themselves as facilitators that foster a student-as-teacher and teacher-as-student relationship in the classroom.[16] Under this model, notes educational analyst Edward Schwerin, "the teacher does not abrogate responsibility for student learning, but shifts from being expert to being a facilitator who keeps the class moving, provides resources, and chooses appropriate topics to study" (1998: 109). This can prove difficult for faculty who, for much of their professional life, typically have been rewarded and promoted on the basis of their ability to play the expert role. Few if any faculty have received training, encouragement, or rewards for adopting the mantle of facilitator.

Students and faculty actually are in the same boat, though. Students don't have much experience either with classrooms in which the instructor eschews the mantle of expertise and opts instead for a series of ambiguous, somewhat unpredictable learning experiences. It's not surprising, then, that students are sometimes initially opposed to the unfamiliar immersion in active or experiential learning—although in the long run, the service experience proves to be one of the most popular aspects of college courses that adopt this technique (Hudson 1996).[17] Students have to be brought into the process—which requires incorporating these changed roles and expectations into the structure of the course and rethinking actual classroom practices. As Zivi observes, "both teaching and learning must be transformed" (1997: 65).

Though sometimes difficult, these transformations—instructor into facilitator, student into community worker, predictable classroom into experiential laboratory—allow students to more naturally embrace their studies and apply their knowledge in impressive ways. Students, after all, are developing their own expertise on issues and the agencies they are serving. This student expertise in turn fosters an overall higher quality of class discussion, as well as a higher quality in students' written work, as students become "experts on, at least, a portion of the material discussed in class" (Hudson 1996: 88). Allowing students to explore their expertise with others in discussion, or in teaching a unit within the course on their specific area of expertise, further enhances student learning, motivation, and self-esteem.[18]

The process of professor, student, and community organization working together also integrates the expertise of the local community into the university (Ansley and Gaventa 1997). Local leaders, organization members, and nonstudent volunteers become resources capable of enhancing the course for both students and faculty. This inclusion of community expertise can also help undercut the tendency, as Orr describes, "to dismiss or ignore altogether 'nonprofessional knowledge'" (Orr 1994: 101).[19] In order to tap these community resources, faculty must evaluate which local groups will provide opportunities appropriate to achieving course goals and objectives. In my courses, only a small number of organizations are selected for the placements, based on familiarity with the specific sites selected (Minter and Schweingruber 1996) and the applicability of the sites for providing experience that will illuminate course concepts and content (Zivi 1997). Advance discussions with the organizations are used to help not only the instructor but also the organizations determine the specific project or commitment to be undertaken by students for the duration of the semester.

Doing the Service-Learning Course: What's Important?

Effective service-learning courses are not easily or quickly assembled. Experience shows that piggybacking a service-learning module onto a previously designed course ultimately disappoints, usually because insufficient time and course focus is given over to a range of reflective exercises that encourage students to become better observers and analysts of their day-to-day activities at their service site (Zivi 1997). Class meetings therefore must be more open-ended and democratic, which can create unexpected outcomes, such as this described by college instructors Deborah Minter and Heidi Schweingruber:

> [by] giving students the freedom to explore their experiences on their own and *then* move to considering the concepts presented in the readings . . .

[s]tudents developed [conceptual] categories that eventually elicited some of the same concepts we were interested in exploring in class, but in a different form than we had first imagined. The difference in form, rather than proving unworkable, led to richer insights for the class as a whole and for us as teachers. (1996: 100, emphasis in original)

It is therefore critical that instructors offer course readings and a course structure that provide students the time to articulate their experiences, get feedback from the instructor and fellow students, and reflect on their experiences in light of conceptual frameworks presented in readings and lecture material during the course.[20] In a global environmental politics course, students may need help linking the local issues to global environmental concerns. This need makes for a rather different course than the ordinary, a course that is less preoccupied with covering a voluminous amount of material (see Maniates' comments on "curricular overload" in chapter 8) and more focused on drawing shared connections among fewer but more central theoretical claims and insights. In my global environmental politics courses, for instance, I use an analytical framework similar to that presented in Porter, Brown, and Chasek's text *Global Environmental Politics* (2000). The course begins with an introduction to the global environmental "problematique"—or "global macrotrends" as the authors term it—and then focuses in on actors and their (perceived) needs and bargaining positions. Additional readings that illuminate the multiple viewpoints of actors, from nation-states to the local farmer, help students grasp the overlapping and often mutually supportive or contradictory stances of the actors at the negotiating table. Students will experience this diversity as they begin to engage with community actors as part of their service-placement experience; as they move through their community work, classroom discussions shift back and forth between abstract discussions about the roles of actors in environmental politics and concrete analysis of the dynamics between and among local actors with whom they are working.

Students will best understand their experiences if course readings are integrated with activities that encourage student interaction with members of the local organization as well as with other students in the course. As outlined in a prototype syllabus available on the World Wide Web,[21] such activities include keeping a journal, in which students document their experiences and reflections during the course of their interactions with the organization. Questions, contradictions, successes, and ethical debates can be discussed in the informal journal format. These in turn can provide the basis for individual sessions with the instructor, group meetings with other students working with the same organization, and larger class discussions of general interest. Likewise, student interviews of members of the local organization can probe the organization's goals, the kinds of policy recommendations the organization supports or advocates, and the extent to which the organization's efforts have an impact on local, national, and international issues. Class instruction should be provided in assisting students to develop an appropriate interview instrument and in role-playing interview techniques.

Course readings within this context are important and should strive to link theory to practice. Whether they are abstract pieces that lend themselves to discussion and elaboration,[22] or selections from field work in similar contexts, or studies of environmental NGO activity such as those by Princen and Finger (1994), Taylor (1995), and Wapner (1996a), these readings must connect to the experiences students are having in their local community. Readings that illuminate the global implications of local ecological disturbances will also help students link their local experience with larger trends. Utilizing the service placements and students' experiences as a "text" of the course can help instructors incorporate the experiential dimension into their teaching with good results (Cone and Harris 1996: 33; also Zivi 1997).

More general theoretical readings for contemplation might include essays that raise the related issues of community and sovereignty in a manner that would inspire student discussion on the meaning of these concepts in light of the global commons shared by all inhabitants on this planet. Short stories, vignettes, or challenging philosophical pieces could be used to create introspection on our shared—yet often unexamined— definition of community and the extent to which membership in one community impairs belonging to other communities: how does the local community fit in a schematic that includes nations, regional organizations such as the European Union, international organizations such as the UN, and still evolving global institutions? Likewise, a few examples of perforated sovereignty—such as the impact of the internet, drug trade, or arms smuggling—can problematize students' awareness of sovereignty and provoke a more textured argument regarding the meaning and necessity of sovereignty in a world that is rapidly globalizing. Barber's 1992 "Jihad vs. McWorld" essay is the type of provocative piece that might be assigned for this introspective process.

While readings are important, too much reading may well be counterproductive. A central aim of the service-learning course in global environmental politics must be to teach students the skills of linking theory to practice. This takes time and asks of the instructor a willingness to give over significant portions of a course to somewhat free-form discussion and reflection. Conrad and Hedin's study of students in a number of service-learning programs confirms the importance of the reflection activity: "the presence of a reflective seminar was the one program feature that made a clear difference—particularly with respect to intellectual and social dimensions of development" (1991: 747). Giving voice to their experiences and having them validated creates a dynamic by which students construct their own knowledge:[23]

> Reflection encourages critical thinking about the systematic and underlying issues which cause society's problems. . . . Reflection promotes "knowing," which involves the whole of a person—their senses, the intellect, their memories, their emotions, their beliefs, their fears, and their intuition. Knowing is creative. Creativity is simply the ability to see how things from one context fit into another. Knowing is an act that involves conceiving the connection between ourselves and the world in which we live. (Cooper 1996)

Several types of reflective activities are possible, and many of them can be prepared outside of class. Standard but effective examples include journals or logs of student experience. Other reflection activities can make use of small group discussions, oral presentations by students regarding their experiences, or creative activities such as preparing a video documentary, writing a play or short story (see, for example, chapter 9's description of "theory plays"), or creating an art work representing the student's experience in a way that can be shared with others (Cooper 1996).

Research papers also can be employed, if students are asked to apply their on-site experiences to larger theoretical or substantive questions around which the course revolves. Use of a research paper component to investigate the context of the community organization can also be an especially useful option when the service component of a course is optional—the research project can be developed by nonparticipants in the service activity as a complement to the actual service activity of other students in the course (Enos and Troppe 1996). Students and their instructors might be pleasantly surprised by the quality of the papers, as compared to those produced for more conventional courses—veteran service-learning instructor William Hudson (1996: 90) reports that the service experience, "along with empowering students as 'experts' in class discussion, . . . [also] helped them to write better papers and exams, by empowering them to claim ownership of their own words."

Finally, assessment in service-learning courses cannot be based simply on service. Rather, as Hudson properly observes, "students are graded . . . on their reflections on that service and their ability to relate it to the subject matter of the course" (84). Assessment of student work can reflect what McDaniel refers to as "authentic assessment" in which student outcomes are evaluated in a multidimensional manner:

> The concept of authentic assessment suggests that we replace pencil and paper tests . . . with the direct products of student academic work. . . .

Authentic assessment is easily found in the practical arts such as engineering, . . . etc. and in the performing arts. In a chemistry class, identifying chemicals in an "unknown solution" would qualify. (1994: 29–30)

A common and effective assessment mechanism is the "portfolio approach" described by McDaniel. The portfolio would contain products created by the student during his or her placement (news articles, surveys, handbooks, etc.) and would be accompanied by a student-authored analysis of the organization and his or her role in it, together with a broader but carefully crafted discussion of how the service experience, from the student's perspective, usefully illuminated and grounded critical theoretical themes of the course. Karen Zivi (1997) cautions instructors from falling back onto old habits and assessing students largely on their grasp of course readings and performance on exams; doing so will leave untapped an important opportunity for student and instructor learning.

Enduring Tensions

If we study and teach global environmental politics to learn not just about the state of the world, but also about how humans come together to stem further environmental degradation, then service learning has an important contribution to make to the classroom. Moving forward with a service-learning component involves tradeoffs and tensions, however, of which faculty and students must be aware and together negotiate.

The primary set of tensions, which are broadly organizational, are best captured by political scientists Benjamin Barber and Richard Battistoni's (1993a) discussion of the "big questions" that loom large for those who would integrate service learning into the curriculum:

1. Should service be education-based or extracurricular?
2. Should it be mandatory or voluntary?
3. Should it be civic or philanthropic?
4. Should it be for credit or not?
5. Should it be offered as a single course or as a multicourse program?
6. Should the community be a "client" or a "partner in education"?
7. Should students serve in group teams or as individuals?
8. Should the faculty also do community service?
9. Should the pedagogy of service emphasize patriotism and citizenship or critical thinking?
10. Should students participate in the planning process?

Barber and Battistoni's questions don't have firm answers. They're meant to prompt the reader to confront the diversity of service-learning configurations. This diversity (see Barber and Battistoni 1993a; Indiana University Center n.d.; Kupiec 1993) ranges from individual or team assignments in the context of a course, to a class project, in which all students in a course participate in a service project with the same organization for the duration of the course semester, or as a departmental or institutional commitment to provide service over time to the local community. Institutionally, service learning can range from being a requirement for graduation, as proposed recently by the governor of California to the University of California Board of Regents (Ma 1999),[24] to being offered as a fourth credit option, that is, as an add-on to particular courses (Enos and Troppe 1996). This add-on option is particularly attractive in that it allows students, not faculty, to seize the initiative and recruit a faculty member to guide an extra course credit service-learning module that would connect usefully to that faculty member's course. Though service learning clearly is more successful when carefully integrated into existing courses, this extra course credit mechanism does allow less-experienced faculty to become more familiar with service-learning frameworks and options that could be integrated into future courses (Enos and Troppe 1996).

Another set of tensions arise for students already engaged in volunteer activities with campus or off-campus organizations. Robert Bringle and Julie Hatcher observe that in-class service-learning projects can place these students in a "paradoxical" situation of receiving course credit for some, but not all, community work and being asked to reflect deeply on some, but not all, community intervention experiences (1996: 231). They suggest that these already active students could be involved in the planning phase of service-learning initiatives, bringing their expertise to bear on the questions of how these initiatives might best be framed to engage maximum student interest. These students might also be invited to assist in the teaching of service-learning courses.[25] "In the long run," remind Barber and Battistoni, "only those programs that draw students in at the very outset of the planning process and engage them in every step of development will be truly successful" (1993a: 238).

CURRICULAR GREENING:
THE NEXT GENERATION

As colleges and universities—and academic departments and individual instructors working within them—continue to green the curriculum, they would do well to consider David Orr's caution that "we are still educating the young as if there were no planetary emergency" (Orr 1994: 9). Bringing environmental ideas into existing coursework is admirable and necessary and should continue. But this first generation attempt to make the mechanisms of higher education respond to a growing environmental crisis must now be supplemented by second generation educational tactics that advance ideas of the New American College, that place students in the way of enriching experiences, and that reverse the alarming decline in civic capabilities and citizen responsibility.

Now is a particularly auspicious time to link environmental and service-learning courses. It is time, in fact, for courses in global environmental politics, which typically portray environmental problems as less a scarcity of technical expertise than a scarcity of democracy, to "walk their talk." If we come to learn through the study of global environmental ills that citizen passivity is a root cause of environmental degradation, should not these same courses be doing something tangible, even risky, about it? The Teaching Global Environmental Politics Web site provides guidelines and an example of how the components of service learning and teaching global environmental politics can be usefully joined. Together, they reflect Boyer's call for a scholarship of engagement:

> At one level, the scholarship of engagement means connecting the rich resources of the university to our most pressing social, civic, and ethical problems, to our children, . . . to our cities. . . . Campuses should be viewed by both students and professors not as isolated islands, but as staging grounds for action.[26]

QUESTIONS FOR REFLECTION AND DISCUSSION

1. In championing the integration of service learning into the global environmental politics classroom, Professor Quirk would have us believe that the study of global environmental politics is as much a moral enterprise as a scholarly one, as much about value clarification and the honing of civic skills as an analysis of how the distribution of power and privilege drives the global degradation of environmental systems. Do you accept this argument? Would others in your class? At your college or university? Explain and defend your stance.

2. Remember the introductory chapter's discussion of the dynamic of retreat? Is Professor Quirk getting at the same thing when she talks about the study of environmental problems as an "exercise in despair"? To what extent, in your view, can service learning oppose such despair? If you were writing an addendum to this chapter, what other mechanisms, in addition to or instead of service learning,

would you integrate into the study of global environmental politics
to combat this despair?

3. Reflect upon and describe your own experiences with service learning. Were they worthwhile? Did they foster the attributes (e.g., creative problem solving, empathy for others, a more sophisticated
understanding of political dynamics) to which Professor Quirk
alludes? Despite the strong arguments Quirk presents in support of
incorporating service learning into the GEP classroom, what formidable barriers would blunt her agenda? (Think back to chapter 8's
discussion of "curricular overload" or the idea of "stovepipe education" in chapter 4, for example.) What, if anything, can students and
teachers of global environmental politics do, realistically, here and
now, to overcome these barriers?

4. Higher education is the answer, but what was the question? Have
we, in other words, "simply lost track of the overall point" of higher
education, as Charles Anderson suggests early in Professor Quirk's
chapter? What is the point, and what should be the point, of your
teaching or study of global environmental ills?

NOTES

1. An effort boosted by President Bush's National and Community Service Act
of 1990 and President Clinton's National and Community Service Trust Act of
1993 and facilitated by campus organizations like Campus Compact, COOL
(Campus Outreach Opportunity League), and Learn and Serve America. For
examples of service-learning courses and programs, see Battistoni and Hudson
(1997), Gray et al. (1999), Jacoby (1996), Jacoby et al. (1996), Kendall et al. (1990),
Kahne and Westheimer (1996), Kupiec (1993), and Markus, Howard, and King
(1993).

2. Giles, Honnet, and Migliore draw this distinction: "One of the characteristics of service learning that distinguishes it from volunteerism is its balance
between the act of community service by participants and reflection on that act in
order both to provide better service and to enhance the participants' own learning" (as cited in Minter and Schweingruber [1996: 92]). Barber and Battistoni
(1993a) discuss volunteerism vs. civic duty as one of their "ten crucial choices"
regarding instituting a service-learning program. See also Boyte (1991), Kahne
and Westheimer (1996), Lisman (1998), and Zlotkowski (1996) regarding the
larger discussion of "volunteerism" vs. "civic service."

3. Kupiec's syllabus (1993: 161–65) for "Homelessness and Public Policy" is
instructive, as are syllabi for service-learning courses on "The Civic Community,
HIV and Public Policy," and "To Feed the World," among others (see Kupiec
1993). Hudson (1996), Minter and Schweingruber (1996), and Zivi (1997) also provide detailed examples of service-learning exercises for the college classroom.

4. See Bringle, Games, and Malloy (1999); Coye (1997); Delve, Mintz, and Stewart (1990); Jacoby (1996); McDaniel (1994); and Zlotkowski (1996).

5. As R. Eugene Rice argues in "Foreword" (Zlotkowski 1998: xi).

6. As author and scholar Steven Schultz notes, "issues of socioeconomic power and control that may be invisible in the classroom become particularly important when it comes to planning strategy for community action" (1990: 92).

7. As quoted by Coye (1997: 21).

8. See, for example, the "Seven Principles for Good Practice in Undergraduate Education," developed at a Wingspread conference of leaders in higher education and described by Chickering (1989) and Gamson (1991). Experiential methods of teaching and learning (such as service learning) arguably draw out student abilities in areas in which they command "intelligences" not often rewarded in academic settings. On this point see Blythe, White and Gardner (1995).

9. In this way, experiential learning draws upon work ranging from Dewey's *Experience and Education* (as discussed in Giles and Eyler [1994] and in Saltmarsh [1996]), to more recent discussions of learning theory (see Frederick [1989], McKeachie et al. [1994], Svinicki [1991], and Weinstein and Meyer [1991]).

10. Linking knowledge and experience is a guiding principle in current educational reform efforts, as Shulman (1997) and others (Boyer 1994; Coles 1994; Zlotkowski 1996) note.

11. See Bonwell and Sutherland (1996), Cantor (1997), Frederick (1989), Savion and Middendorf (1994), and Weinstein and Meyer (1991).

12. This discussion draws from the "Perry Scheme of Intellectual Development," described in detail by Kloss (1994).

13. Bloom's Taxonomy, in other words. For a detailed outline of "The Six Major Levels of Bloom's Taxonomy of the Cognitive Domain" see the online version of Lee (1999) at www.ntlf.com, or DeZure (1996: 2).

14. Says Kupiec: "As an educational method, service learning provides students with fertile ground on which to test theories acquired in the classroom and to concretize abstract thought. This active, exploratory dimension . . . leads to a deeper grasp of course material. Students develop research, critical thinking and interpersonal skills and come to appreciate the larger social, ethical and environmental implications of knowledge. Agency staff and clients offer expertise and perspectives in addition to those presented in class" (1993: 7).

15. Intrinsic motivation refers to a students' desire to learn for the satisfaction it brings by addressing some curiosity or an issue of great concern. Extrinsic motivation relies on exams and other assignments to motivate students to compete for high grades (Forsyth and McMillan 1991; McDaniel 1994). Service learning seeks to actively involve students in their own learning (Minter and Schweingruber 1996: 92), which can build, and build upon, intrinsic motivation.

16. Saltmarsh (1996: 14) nicely frames this dual role by drawing on Dewey and Friere: "Friere notes that 'through dialogue, the teacher-of-the-students and the students-of-the-teacher cease to exist and a new term emerges: teacher-students with students-teachers' (Freire 1970: 61)." In drawing the similarity between Freire and Dewey's work, Saltmarsh cites Dewey: "In such shared activity the teacher is a learner, and the learner is, without knowing it, a teacher (Dewey 1916: 167)."

17. For discussion of structuring classes that engage students, see Fishel and Segal (1998), Schwerin (1998), Billson and Tiberius (1991), and Tiberius and Billson (1991).

18. As Wagner argues, student "experts" can benefit from being able to "not only take a course in urban society, but [to] *teach* a unit within that course about urban poverty" (Wagner 1990: 51, emphasis added).

19. Respect for local community "expertise" is reminiscent of the need, often cited in discussions of environmental education, to include "indigenous" cultural knowledge along with scientific and technical approaches to environmental problem solving. See Bowers (1999) and Cajete (1999).

20. Kupiec (1993) provides useful examples of syllabi and course assignments.

21. See "The Project on Teaching Global Environmental Politics" at webpub.alleg.edu/employee/m/maniate/GepEd/geped.html.

22. Anthologies such as Barber and Battistoni (1993b) and Albert (1994) offer a diversity of reflective pieces, such as Katherine Mansfield's short story "The Garden Party," as well as William James's "The Moral Equivalent of War," among Barber and Battistoni's selections; and "Why Care about Caring? The Fundamental Nature of Caring" by Nel Noddings and "Landing on the Moon" by Deepak Chopra in Albert's compilation. Ehrlich (1995) mentions using Hawthorne's short story "The Snow Image" in his class on "Altruism, Philanthropy, and Public Service."

23. See Dewey (1938), Lee (1999), Saltmarsh (1996), and Wagner (1990). For further discussion of the importance of reflection activities for students' cognitive development and values clarification, see Hatcher and Bringle 1997.

24. Barber and Battistoni (1993a: 236–37) review the pros and cons of mandatory service requirements.

25. See Bringle and Hatcher (1996: 232–33); also Cone and Harris (1996), and Wagner (1990).

26. Cited by Glassick (1999: 29), who notes that Boyer "finished his later speeches with this commentary."

References

Abbey, Edward. 1983. "One Final Paragraph of Advice: Do Not Burn Yourself Out," in *The Earth Speaks: An Acclimization Journal*, ed. Steve Van Matre and Bill Weiler. Greenville, WV: Institute for Earth Education, p. 57.

Agrawal, Anil. 1998. "Community-in-Conservation: Tracing the Outlines of an Enchanting Concept." New Haven: Yale University Political Science Department.

Albert, Gail, ed. 1994. *Service Learning Reader: Reflections and Perspectives on Service*. Raleigh, NC: National Society for Experiential Education.

Alinksy, Saul. 1969. *Reveille for Radicals*. New York: Vintage Books.

Allenby, Braden, Thomas Gilmartin, and Ronald Lehman II, eds. 1998. *Environmental Threats and National Security: An International Challenge to Science and Technology*. Lawrence Livermore National Laboratory, Center for Global Security Research: Proceedings from the Workshop at Monterey, CA (December).

Ansley, Fran, and John Gaventa. 1997. "Research for Democracy and Democratizing Research." *Change* (January/February): 46–53.

Arendt, Hannah. 1968. *Between Past and Future: Eight Exercises in Political Thought*. New York: Penguin.

Arnstine, Donald. 1995. *Democracy and the Arts of Schooling*. Albany: State University of New York Press.

Atwood, J. Brian. 1995. Remarks to the Conference on New Directions in U.S. Foreign Policy at the University of Maryland, College Park, November 2. Excerpted in "Towards a New Definition of National Security." *Environmental Change and Security Project Report* 2: 85.

Baechler, Günther. 1999. *Violence Through Environmental Discrimination: Causes, Rwanda Arena, and Conflict Model*. Dordrecht, The Netherlands: Kluwer Academic Publishers.

Baldwin, J. 1988. "A Talk to Teachers," in *Multicultural Literacy*, ed. R. Simmonson and S. Walker. St. Paul, MN: Gregwolf Press, pp. 3–12.

Barber, Benjamin. 1992. "Jihad vs. McWorld." *Atlantic Monthly* 269: 53(9).

———. 1998. "Democracy at Risk: American Culture in a Global Culture." *World Policy Journal* 15: 29–41.

Barber, Benjamin, and Richard Battistoni. 1993a. "A Season of Service: Introducing Service Learning into the Liberal Arts Curriculum." *PS: Political Science and Politics* 26: 235–240, 262.

———, eds. 1993b. *Education for Democracy: Citizenship, Community, Service: A Sourcebook for Students and Teachers*. Dubuque, IA: Kendall/Hunt Publishers.

Barnett, Jon. 2001. *The Meaning of Environmental Security: Ecological Politics and Policy in the New Security Era*. London: Zed Books.

Barry, Brian. 1973. *The Liberal Theory of Justice*. Oxford: Clarendon.

231

Battistoni, Richard, and William Hudson, eds. 1997. *Experiencing Citizenship: Concepts and Models for Service-Learning in Political Science*. Washington, DC: American Association for Higher Education.

Becker, Dusty. 1997. Class presentation on People Allied for Nature (PAN) at Indiana University, Bloomington, at www.earthwatch.org/ed/becker/interview.html (accessed August 18, 2001).

Bellah, Robert, Richard Madsen, William Sullivan, Ann Swidler, and Steven Tipton. 1991. *The Good Society*. New York: Random House.

Berkes, F., D. Feeny, B. McCay, and J. Acheson. 1989. "The Benefits of the Commons." *Nature* 340: 91–93.

Biersteker, Thomas, and Cynthia Weber, eds. 1996. *State Sovereignty As Social Construct*. Cambridge, England: Cambridge University Press.

Billson, Janet, and Richard Tiberius. 1991. "Effective Social Arrangements for Teaching and Learning," in *College Teaching: From Theory to Practice*, ed. Robert Menges and Marilla Svinicki. San Francisco: Jossey-Bass Publishers, pp. 87–109.

Blythe, Tina, Noel White, and Howard Gardner. 1995. *Teaching Practical Intelligence: What Research Tells Us*. Cambridge, MA: Harvard Project Zero.

Bonwell, Charles, and Tracey Sutherland. 1996. "The Active Learning Continuum: Choosing Activities to Engage Students in the Classroom," in *Using Active Learning in College Classes: A Range of Options for Faculty*, ed. Tracey Sutherland and Charles Bonwell. San Francisco: Jossey-Bass Publishers, pp. 3–16.

Bookchin, Murray. 1989. "Death of a Small Planet." *The Progressive* (August): 19–23.

Bowers, C. 1999. "Changing the Dominant Cultural Perspective in Education," in *Ecological Education in Action: On Weaving Education, Culture, and the Environment*, ed. Gregory Smith and Dilafruz Williams. Albany: State University of New York Press, pp. 161–178.

Boyer Commission on Educating Undergraduates in the Research University. 1998. *Reinventing Undergraduate Education: A Blueprint for America's Research Universities*. Stony Brook: State University of New York.

Boyer, Ernest. 1990. *Scholarship Reconsidered: Priorities of the Professoriate*. Princeton, NJ: The Carnegie Foundation for the Advancement of Teaching.

———. 1994. "Creating the New American College." *Chronicle of Higher Education* (March 9): Sect. A, 48.

Boyte, Harry. 1991. "Community Service and Civic Education." *Phi Delta Kappan* 72: 765–767.

Bright, Chris. 2000. "Anticipating Environmental 'Surprise,'" in *State of the World 2000*, ed. Lester R. Brown, et al. New York: Norton, pp. 22–38.

Bringle, Robert, and Julie Hatcher. 1996. "Implementing Service Learning in Higher Education." *Journal of Higher Education* 67: 221–239.

Bringle, Robert, Richard Games, and Edward Malloy, eds. 1999. *Colleges and Universities As Citizens*. Boston: Allyn and Bacon.

Broad, W. 1994. "Plan to Carve up Ocean Floor Near Fruition." *New York Times* (March 29): Sect. C, 1.

Brooks, David. 2001. "The Organization Kid." *Atlantic Monthly* 287: 40–54.

Brown, Lester. 1977. *Worldwatch Paper 14: Redefining National Security*. Washington, DC: Worldwatch Institute.

Brown, Lester, et al. 1998. *State of the World*. New York: Norton.

———. 1999. *State of the World 1999*. New York: Norton.

Bull, Hedley. 1977. *The Anarchical Society*. New York: Columbia University Press.

Butts, Kent. 1994. "Why the Military Is Good for the Environment," in *Green Security or Militarized Environment*, ed. Jyrki Kakönën. Aldershot, U.K.: Dartmouth Publishing Company, pp. 83–109.

———. 1999. "The Case for DoD Involvement in Environmental Security," in *Contested Grounds: Security and Conflict in the New Environmental Politics*, ed. Daniel Deudney and Richard Matthew. Albany: State University of New York Press, pp. 109–126.

Bybee, Rodger. 1984. "Human Ecology: A Perspective for Biology Education." Available from the ERIC Document Reproduction Service at edrs.com/ #ED260936.

Byers, Bruce. 1991. "Ecoregions, State Sovereignty and Conflict." *Bulletin of Peace Proposals* 22: 65–76.

Cajete, Gregory. 1999. "Reclaiming Biophilia: Lessons from Indigenous Peoples," in *Ecological Education in Action: On Weaving Education, Culture, and the Environment*, ed. Gregory Smith and Dilafruz Williams. Albany: State University of New York Press, pp. 189–206.

Cantor, Jeffrey. 1997. *Experiential Learning in Higher Education: Linking Classroom and Community*. ASHE-ERIC Report no. 7. Washington, DC: ERIC Clearinghouse on Higher Education.

Capra, Fritjof. 1996. *The Web of Life: A New Synthesis of Mind and Matter*. London: Flamingo.

Carius, Alexander, and Kurt Lietzmann, eds. 1998. *Environment and Security: Challenges for International Politics*. Berlin: Springer.

———. 1999. *Environmental Change and Security: A European Perspective*. Berlin: Springer.

Chatterjee, Pratap, and Matthias Finger. 1994. *The Earth Brokers: Power, Politics and World Development*. London: Routledge.

Chen, Robert. 1997. "Environmental Stress: Concepts and Cases." Paper presented at the Environmental Flashpoints Workshop. Director of Central Intelligence—Environmental Center, Reston, VA, November 12–14.

Chickering, Arthur. 1989. "Appendix: Framework for a Workshop on Good Practice in Undergraduate Education," in *Improving Undergraduate Education in Large Universities*, ed. Carol Pazandak. San Francisco: Jossey-Bass Publishers, pp. 85–88.

Christopher, Warren. 1997. Remarks to Woodrow Wilson International Center for Scholars, January 14 ("The Environment in U.S. Foreign Policy"). Excerpted in *Environmental Change and Security Project Report* 3: 186.

———. 1998. "Diplomacy and the Environment," in *In the Stream of History: Shaping Foreign Policy for a New Era*, ed. Warren Christopher. Stanford: Stanford University Press, pp. 412–424.

Clark, Mary. 1989. *Ariadne's Thread: The Search for New Modes of Thinking*. New York: St. Martin's.

Clark, William. 1989. "Managing Planet Earth." *Scientific American* 261: 47–54.

Coleman, Daniel. 1994. *Ecopolitics: Building a Green Society*. New Brunswick, NJ: Rutgers University Press.

Coles, Robert. 1994. "Putting Head and Heart on the Line." *Chronicle of Higher Education* (October 26): Sect. A, 64.

Collett, Jonathan. 1996. "Reinventing the Classroom: Connected Teaching," in *Greening the College Curriculum: A Guide to Environmental Teaching in the Liberal Arts*, ed. Jonathan Collett and Stephen Karakashian. Washington, DC: Island Press, pp. 309–324.

Collett, Jonathan, and Stephen Karakashian, eds. 1996. *Greening the College Curriculum: A Guide to Environmental Teaching in the Liberal Arts*. Washington, DC: Island Press.

Conca, Ken. 1995. "Rethinking the Ecology-Sovereignty Debate." *Millennium: Journal of International Studies* 23: 701–711.

———. 1998. "The Environment-Security Trap." *Dissent* 45: 40–45.

———. 2000. "Beyond the Statist Frame: Environmentalism in a Global Economy," in *Nature, Production, Power: Towards an Ecological Political Economy*, ed. Fred Gale and R. Michael M'Gonigle. Cheltenham, England: Edward Elgar, pp. 141–155.

———. 2002. "Consumption and Environment in a Global Economy," in *Confronting Consumption*, ed. Thomas Princen, Michael Maniates, and Ken Conca. Cambridge, MA: The MIT Press, pp. 133–154.

Conca, Ken, and Geoffrey Dabelko, eds. 1998. *Green Planet Blues: Environmental Politics from Stockholm to Kyoto*. Boulder, CO: Westview.

Cone, Dick, and Susan Harris. 1996. "Service-Learning Practice: Developing a Theoretical Framework." *Michigan Journal of Community Service Learning* 3: 31–43.

Connelly, Matthew, and Paul Kennedy. 1994. "Must It Be the West Against the Rest?" *Atlantic Monthly* 274: 61–83.

Conrad, Dan, and Diane Hedin. 1991. "School-Based Community Service: What We Know from Research and Theory." *Phi Delta Kappan* 72: 743–749.

Cooper, Mark. 1996. *A Faculty Guide to Reflection*. Florida International University Volunteer Action Center. Miami: Florida International University.

Cox, Susan Jane Buck. 1985. "No Tragedy on the Commons." *Environmental Ethics* 7: 49–61.

Coye, Dale. 1997. "Ernest Boyer and the New American College: Connecting the Disconnects." *Change* 29: 21–29.

Dabelko, Geoffrey, and P. J. Simmons. 1997. "Environment and Security: Core Ideas and U.S. Government Initiatives." *The SAIS Review* 17: 127–146.

Dabelko, Geoffrey, and Stacy VanDeveer. 1998. "European Insecurities: Can't Live with 'Em, Can't Shoot 'Em." *Security Dialogue* 29: 177–190.

Dalby, Simon. 1999. "Threats from the South? Geopolitics, Equity, and Environmental Security," in *Contested Ground: Security and Conflict in the New Environmental Politics*, ed. Daniel Deudney and Richard Matthew. Albany: State University of New York Press, pp. 155–185.

Daly, Herman, and John Cobb. 1994. *For the Common Good: Redirecting the Economy Toward Community, the Environment, and a Sustainable Future*. Boston: Beacon.

Deibert, Ronald. 1996. "Military Monitoring of the Environment." *Environmental Change and Security Project Report* 2: 28–32.

Delve, Cecilia, Suzanne Mintz, and Greig Stewart, eds. 1990. *Community Service As Values Education*. San Francisco: Jossey-Bass Publishers.

Der Derian, James, and Michael J. Shapiro, eds. 1989. *International/Intertextual Relations: Postmodern Readings of World Politics*. Lexington, MA: Lexington Books.

Deudney, Daniel. 1990. "The Case against Linking Environmental Degradation and National Security." *Millennium* 19: 461–476.

Deudney, Daniel, and Richard Matthew, eds. 1999. *Contested Grounds: Security and Conflict in the New Environmental Politics*. Albany: State University of New York Press.

Devall, Bill. 1991. "Deep Ecology and Radical Environmentalism." *Society and Natural Resources* 4: 247–258.

Dewey, John. 1916. *Democracy and Education*, in *The Middle Works of John Dewey*, volume 9, ed. Jo Ann Boydston. Carbondale: Southern Illinois Press, 1976.

Dewey, John. 1938. *Experience and Education*. New York: Collier.

DeZure, Deborah. 1996. "Asking and Answering Questions." *Whys and Ways of Teaching* 7: 1–10.

Diamond, Jared. 1997. *Guns, Germs, and Steel: The Fates of Human Societies*. New York: Norton.

Diehl, Paul, ed. 1998. *Journal of Peace Research* 35.

Diehl, Paul, and Nils Petter Gleditsch, eds. 2001. *Environmental Conflict*. Boulder, CO: Westview.

Dokken, Karin, and Nina Græger. 1995. *Environmental Security: Political Slogan or Analytical Tool?* Oslo: International Peace Research Institute.

Doty, Roxanne Lynn. 1996. *Imperial Encounters: The Politics of Representation in North-South Relations*. Minneapolis: University of Minnesota Press.

Dowie, Mark. 1995. *Losing Ground: American Environmentalism at the Close of the Twentieth Century*. Cambridge, MA: The MIT Press.

Dryzek, John. 1993. "Policy Analysis and Planning: From Science to Argument," in *The*

Argumentative Turn in Policy Analysis and Planning, ed. Frank Fischer and John Forester. Durham, NC: Duke University Press, pp. 213–232.

———. 1997. *The Politics of the Earth: Environmental Discourses.* New York: Oxford University Press.

Dumonski, Dianne. 1989. "Even Stronger Protection Urged for Ozone Layer." *Boston Globe* (March 8): Part I, 6.

Durning, Alan. 1992. *How Much Is Enough? The Consumer Society and the Fate of the Earth.* New York: Norton.

Edmundson, Mark. 1997. "On the Uses of a Liberal Education: As Lite Entertainment for Bored College Students." *Harpers Magazine* 295: 39–49.

Ehrlich, Thomas. 1995. "Taking Service Seriously." *AAHE Bulletin* 47: 8–10.

———. 1999. "Civic Education: Lessons Learned." *PS: Political Science and Politics* XXXII (June). Accessed August 29, 2001; at www.apsanet.org/PS/ june99/ehrlich.cfm.

Enos, Sandra, and Marie Troppe. 1996. "Service-Learning in the Curriculum," in *Service-Learning in Higher Education: Concepts and Practices*, ed. Barbara Jacoby, et al. San Francisco: Jossey-Bass Publishers, pp. 156–181.

Environmental Protection Agency. 1999. "Environmental Security: Strengthening National Security through Environmental Protection." Washington, DC: EPA Office of International Activities.

Esty, Daniel, Jack Goldstone, Ted Robert Gurr, Pamela Surko, and Alan Unger, eds. 1995. *State Failure Task Report.* McLean, VA: Science Applications International Corporation.

Esty, Daniel, Jack Goldstone, Ted Robert Gurr, Barbara Harff, Marc Levy, Geoffrey Dabelko, Pamela Surko, and Alan Unger, eds. 1998. *State Failure Task Report: Phase II Findings.* McLean, VA: Science Applications International Corporation.

Etzioni, Amitai. 1993. *The Spirit of Community.* New York: Simon and Schuster.

Eyler, Janet, and Dwight Giles. 1999. *Where's the Learning in Service Learning?* San Francisco: Jossey-Bass Publishers.

Fagan, Brian. 1990. *The Journey from Eden: The Peopling of Our World.* London: Thames and Hudson.

Falk, Richard. 1971. *This Endangered Planet: Prospects and Proposals for Human Survival.* New York: Random House.

———. 1995. *On Humane Governance: Toward a New Global Politics.* University Park: The Pennsylvania State University Press.

Featherstone, Liza. 2000. "The New Student Movement." *The Nation* 270: 11–15.

Feeny, David, Fikret Berkes, Bonnie McCay, and James Acheson. 1990. "The Tragedy of the Commons: Twenty-two Years Later." *Human Ecology* 18: 1–19.

Ferry, Luc. 1998. *The New Ecological Order.* Trans. Carol Volk. Chicago: University of Chicago Press.

Feshbach, Murray. 1995. *Ecological Disaster: Cleaning up the Hidden Legacy of the Soviet Regime.* New York: Twentieth Century Fund.

Finger, Matthias. 1991. "The Military, the Nation State and the Environment." *The Ecologist* 21: 220–225.

Finnemore, Martha. 1996. *National Interests in International Society.* Ithaca: Cornell University Press.

Fishel, Jeff, and Morley Segal. 1998. "Transformational Teaching: As if Students and Faculty Really Mattered," in *Transformational Politics: Theory, Study, and Practice*, ed. Stephen Woolpert, Christa Slaton, and Edward Schwerin. Albany: State University of New York Press, pp. 155–168.

Fisher, Roger, and William Ury. 1981. *Getting to Yes.* New York: Penguin.

Forsyth, Donelson, and James McMillan. 1991. "Practical Proposals for Motivating Students," in *College Teaching: From Theory to Practice*, ed. Robert Menges and Marilla Svinicki. San Francisco: Jossey-Bass Publishers, pp. 53–63.

Frankel, Glenn. 1990. "Governments Agree on Ozone Fund." *Washington Post* (June 30): Sect. A, 26.

Frederick, Peter. 1989. "Involving Students More Actively in the Classroom," in *The Department Chairperson's Role in Enhancing College Teaching*, ed. Ann Lucas. San Francisco: Jossey-Bass Publishers, pp. 31–40.

Freie, John. 1998. *Counterfeit Community: The Exploitation of Our Longings for Connectedness*. Lanham, MD: Rowman & Littlefield Publishers.

Freire, Paulo. 1970. *Pedagogy of the Oppressed*. New York: Continuum.

Gaines, Ernest J. 1993. *A Lesson before Dying*. New York: Vintage.

Galaty, J., and D. Johnson, eds. 1990. *The World of Pastoralism: Herding Systems in Comparative Perspective*. New York: Guilford.

Gamson, Zelda. 1991. "A Brief History of the Seven Principles for Good Practice in Undergraduate Education," in *Applying the Seven Principles for Good Practice in Undergraduate Education*, ed. Arthur Chickering and Zelda Gamson. San Francisco: Jossey-Bass Publishers, pp. 5–12.

Gatto, John. 1992. *Dumbing Us Down: The Hidden Curriculum of Compulsory Schooling*. Philadelphia: New Society Publishers.

Gelbspan, Ross. 1998. *The Heat Is On*. Reading, MA: Perseus Books.

Giles, Dwight, and Janet Eyler. 1994. "The Theoretical Roots of Service-Learning in John Dewey: Toward a Theory of Service-Learning." *Michigan Journal of Community Service Learning* 1: 77–85.

Glassick, Charles. 1999. "Ernest L. Boyer: Colleges and Universities As Citizens," in *Colleges and Universities As Citizens*, ed. Robert Bringle, Richard Games, and Edward Malloy. Boston: Allyn and Bacon, pp. 17–30.

Gleditsch, Nils Petter, ed. 1997. *Conflict and the Environment*. Dordrecht, The Netherlands: Kluwer.

———. 1998. "Armed Conflict and the Environment: A Critique of the Literature." *Journal of Peace Research* 35: 381–400.

Gleick, Peter. 1991. "Environment and Security: The Clear Connections." *Bulletin of the Atomic Scientists* 47: 16–21.

———. 1993. "Water and Conflict: Fresh Water Resources and International Security." *International Security* 18: 79–112.

Gray, Maryann, et al. 1999. *Combining Service and Learning in Higher Education: Evaluation of the Learn and Serve America, Higher Education Program*. Santa Monica, CA: The Rand Corporation.

Greely, Kathleen. 2000. "Energy Ratings For Rental Units." *Home Energy Magazine* (July/August), pp. 11–12.

Green, Duncan. 1995. "Rival Economic Models," in *Silent Revolution: The Rise of Market Economics in Latin America*, ed. Duncan Green. London: Latin American Bureau, pp. 244–249.

Gruen, Lori, and Dale Jamieson. 1994. *Reflecting on Nature: Readings in Environmental Philosophy*. Oxford: Oxford University Press.

Haas, Peter. 1989. "Do Regimes Matter? Epistemic Communities and Mediterranean Pollution Control." *International Organization* 43: 377–403.

———. 1992. "Banning Chlorofluorocarbons: Epistemic Community Efforts to Protect Stratospheric Ozone." *International Organization* 46: 187–224.

Halstead, Ted. 1999. "A Politics for Generation X." *Atlantic Monthly* 284: 33–42.

Hamer, Glenn, and Michael Paranzino. 2001. "Two of Cheney's Energy 'Fat Cats' Fess Up." *Los Angeles Times* (July 29), at www.latimes.com/news/opinion/commentary/la-000061707jul29.story (accessed August 6, 2001).

Haraway, Donna. 1989. "Teddy Bear Patriarchy: Taxidermy in the Garden of Eden, New York City, 1908–1936," in *Primate Visions: Gender, Race, and Nature in the World of Modern Sciences*, ed. Donna Haraway. New York: Routledge, pp. 26–58

Hardin, Garrett. 1968. "The Tragedy of the Commons." *Science* 162: 1243–1248.

Hatcher, Julie, and Robert Bringle. 1997. "Reflection: Bridging the Gap between Service and Learning." *College Teaching* 45: 153–58.

Hawken, Paul. 1993. *The Ecology of Commerce*. New York: Harper Business.

Hempel, Lamont. 1996a. *Environmental Governance: The Global Challenge*. Washington, DC: Island Press.

———. 1996b. "Roots and Wings: Building Sustainable Communities." White Paper, League of Women Voters Population Coalition (January).

Hirschman, A. O. 1991. *The Rhetoric of Reaction*. Cambridge, MA: Harvard University Press.

Holle, Oliver, and Markus Knell. 1996. "The Tragedy of the Commons Game." Retrieved August 28, 2001 from the World Wide Web at www.wuwien.ac.at/usr/ai/mitloehn/commons/.

Homer-Dixon, Thomas. 1994. "Environmental Scarcities and Violent Conflict: Evidence from Cases." *International Security* 19: 5–40.

———. 1999. *Environment, Scarcity, and Violence*. Princeton, NJ: Princeton University Press.

Homer-Dixon, Thomas, and Jessica Blitt. 1998. *Ecoviolence: Links Among Environment, Population and Security*. Lanham, MD: Rowman & Littlefield Publishers.

Homer-Dixon, Thomas, and Marc Levy. 1995/96. "Correspondence." *International Security* 20: 189–198.

Homer-Dixon, Thomas, and Valerie Percival. 1996. *Environmental Scarcity and Violent Conflict: Briefing Book*. Toronto: University of Toronto Press.

Horowitz, M., and P. Little. 1987. "African Pastoralism and Poverty: Some Implications for Drought and Famine," in *Drought and Hunger in Africa: Denying Famine a Future*, ed. M. Glantz. Cambridge, England: Cambridge University Press, pp. 59–82.

Hubbard, Alice, and Clay Fong. 1995. *Community Energy Workbook: A Guide to Building a Sustainable Economy*. Snowmass, CO: Rocky Mountain Institute.

Hudson, William. 1996. "Combining Community Service and the Study of American Public Policy." *Michigan Journal of Community Service Learning* 3: 82–91.

Hymes, D. 1974. "Traditions and Paradigms," in *Studies in the History of Linguistics: Traditions and Paradigms*, ed. D. Hymes. Bloomington: University of Indiana Press, pp. 1–38.

Immerfall, Stefan, ed. 1996. *Territoriality in the Globalizing Society: One Place or None?* Berlin: Springer.

Indiana University Center on Philanthropy. n.d. *Learning to Serve, Serving to Learn: Shaping the Social Conscience of the 21st Century*. Indianapolis: Indiana University Center on Philanthropy.

Inglehart, Ronald. 1990. *Culture Shift in Advanced Industrial Society*. Princeton, NJ: Princeton University Press.

Jacoby, Barbara. 1996. "Service-Learning in Today's Higher Education," in *Service-Learning in Higher Education: Concepts and Practices*, ed. Barbara Jacoby, et al. San Francisco: Jossey-Bass Publishers, pp. 3–25.

Jacoby, Barbara, et al. 1996. *Service-Learning in Higher Education: Concepts and Practices*. San Francisco: Jossey-Bass Publishers.

Jenkins-Smith, Hank. 1990. *Democratic Politics and Policy Analysis*. Pacific Grove, CA: Brooks/Cole.

Kahl, Colin. 1998. "Population Growth, Environmental Degradation, and State-Sponsored Violence: The Case of Kenya, 1991–93." *International Security* 23: 80–119.

Kahne, Joseph, and Joel Westheimer. 1996. "In the Service of What? The Politics of Service Learning." *Phi Delta Kappan* 77: 593–599.

Kakönen, Jyrki, ed. 1994. *Green Security or Militarized Environment*. Brookfield: Dartmouth Publishing Company.

Kaplan, Robert. 1994. "The Coming Anarchy." *Atlantic Monthly* 273: 44–76.

Keck, Margaret, and Kathryn Sikkink. 1998. *Activists beyond Borders: Advocacy Networks and International Politics*. New York: Cornell University Press.

Kendall, Jane, et al. 1990. *Combining Service and Learning: A Resource Book for Community and Public Service*, volumes 1 and 2. Raleigh, NC: National Society for Internships and Experiential Education.

Kloss, Robert. 1994. "A Nudge Is Best: Helping Students through the Perry Scheme of Intellectual Development." *College Teaching* 42: 151–158.

Knorr, Klaus. 1977. "International Economic Leverage and Its Uses," in *Economic Issues and National Security*, ed. Klaus Knorr and Frank Trager. Lawrence: University Press of Kansas, pp. 99–126.

Kohl, Herbert. 1994. *"I Won't Learn From You" and Other Thoughts on Creative Maladjustment*. New York: The New Press.

Kolb, David. 1984a. *Experiential Learning: Experience as the Source of Learning and Development*. Upper Saddle River, NJ: Prentice Hall.

————. 1984b. "Learning Styles and Disciplinary Differences," in *The Modern American College*, ed. Arthur Chickering, et al. San Francisco: Jossey-Bass Publishers, pp. 232–253.

Kuehls, Thom. 1996. *Beyond Sovereign Territory: The Space of Ecopolitics*. Minneapolis: University of Minnesota Press.

Kupiec, Tamar, ed. 1993. *Rethinking Tradition: Integrating Service with Academic Study on College Campuses*. Providence, RI: Campus Compact.

Lapid, Yosef, and Friedrich Kratochwil, eds. 1996. *The Return of Culture and Identity in IR Theory*. Boulder, CO: Lynne Rienner.

Laski, Harold. 1930. "The Limitations of the Expert." *Harpers Monthly*: 101–110.

Leakey, Richard. 1994. *The Origin of Humankind*. New York: Basic Books.

Lee, Kai. 1993. *Compass and Gyroscope: Integrating Science and Politics for the Environment*. Washington, DC: Island Press.

Lee, Virginia. 1999. "Creating a Blueprint for the Constructivist Classroom." *The National Teaching and Learning Forum* 8: 1–4.

Lélé, Sharachchandra. 1991. "Sustainable Development: A Critical Review." *World Development* 19: 607–621.

Leo, John. 1996. "No Books, Please; We're Students." *U.S. News and World Report.* (September 16): 24.

Leopold, Aldo. 1949. *A Sand County Almanac and Sketches Here and There*. Oxford: Oxford University Press.

Lerner, Steve. 1994. "Life Studies: Student Greens Get Practical at the University of Wisconsin." *Amicus Journal* 16: 36–41.

Levine, Arthur, and Jeanette Cureton. 1998. *When Hope and Fear Collide: A Portrait of Today's College Student*. San Francisco: Jossey-Bass Publishers.

Levy, Marc. 1995. "Is the Environment a National Security Issue?" *International Security* 20: 35–62.

Lipschutz, Ronnie. 1989. *When Nations Clash: Raw Materials, Ideology and Foreign Policy*. New York: Ballinger.

Lipschutz, Ronnie, with Judith Mayer. 1996. *Global Civil Society and Global Environmental Governance: The Politics of Nature from Place to Planet*. Albany: State University of New York Press.

Lisman, C. David. 1998. *Toward a Civil Society: Civic Literacy Service Learning*. Westport, CT: Bergin and Garvey.

Litfin, Karen. 1997. "Sovereignty in World Ecopolitics." *Mershon International Studies Review* 41: 167–204.

Little, M., N. Dyson-Hudson, R. Dyson-Hudson, J. Ellis, K. Galvin, P. Leslie, and D. Swift. 1990. "Ecosystem Approaches In Human Biology: Their History and a Case Study of the

South Turkana Ecosystem Project," in *The Ecosystem Approach in Anthropology: From Concept to Practice*, ed. E. F. Moran. Ann Arbor: University of Michigan Press, pp. 389–434.

Little, P. 1988. "Land Use Conflicts in the Agricultural/Pastoral Borderlands: The Case of Kenya," in *Lands at Risk in the Third World: Local Level Perspectives*, ed. P. Little, M. Horowitz, and A. Nyerges. Boulder, CO: Westview, pp. 195–212.

Loeb, Paul. 1994. *Generation at the Crossroads*. New Brunswick, NJ: Rutgers University Press.

———. 1999. *Soul of a Citizen*. New York: St. Martin's.

Lonergan, Steve, ed. 1999. *Environmental Change, Adaptation, and Security*. Dordrecht, The Netherlands: Kluwer.

Lowi, Miriam, and Brian Shaw, eds. 2000. *Environment and Security: Discourses and Practices*. New York: St. Martin's.

Ma, Jason. 1999. "California Governor Proposes Service Requirement." *Indiana Daily Student*, Indiana University Bloomington, (July 22): 3.

Maalouf, Amir. 1994. *Samarkand: A Novel*. Trans. R. Harris. London: Little, Brown and Company.

Mackinder, Halford. 1944/1919. *Democratic Ideals and Reality: A Study in the Politics of Reconstruction*. Harmondsworth, U.K.: Penguin.

Mahfouz, Naguib. 1991. *Palace of Desire: The Cairo Trilogy II*. Trans. W. M. Hutchins, L. M. Kenny, and O. E. Kenny. Cairo: The America University in Cairo Press.

Maniates, Michael. 1993. "Geography and Environmental Literacy: Let's Look before We Leap." *The Professional Geographer* 45: 351–354.

———. 2002a. "Individualization: Plant a Tree, Buy a Bike, Save the World?" in *Confronting Consumption*, ed. Thomas Princen, Michael Maniates, and Ken Conca. Cambridge, MA: The MIT Press, pp. 43–66

———. 2002b. "In Search of Consumptive Resistance: The Voluntary Simplicity Movement," in *Confronting Consumption*, ed. Thomas Princen, Michael Maniates, and Ken Conca. Cambridge, MA: The MIT Press, pp. 197–236.

Maniates, Michael, and John Whissel. 2000. "Environmental Studies: The Sky Is Not Falling." *BioScience* 50: 509–517.

Mann, Sheilah. 1999. "What the Survey of American College Freshmen Tells Us about Their Interest in Politics and Political Science." *PS: Political Science and Politics* XXXII (June). Retrieved August 29, 2001 from the World Wide Web at www.apsanet.org/PS/ june99/ mann.cfm

Mansfield, William. 1998. "Taking the University to Task." *World Watch* 11: 24–30.

Markus, Gregory, Jeffrey Howard, and David King. 1993. "Integrating Community Service and Classroom Instruction Enhances Learning: Results from an Experiment." *Educational Evaluation and Policy Analysis* 15: 410–419.

Mathews, Jessica. 1989. "Redefining Security." *Foreign Affairs* 68: 162–177.

Matthew, Richard. 1996. "The Greening of American Foreign Policy." *Issues in Science and Technology* 12: 39–47.

———. 1997. "Rethinking Environmental Security," in *Conflict and the Environment*, ed. Nils Petter Gleditsch. Dordrecht, The Netherlands: Kluwer Academic Publishers, pp. 71–90.

———. 1998. "Environment and Security: Concepts and Definitions." *National Security Studies Quarterly* 4: 63–72.

———. 1999. "Security and Scarcity: Common Pool Resource Perspective," in *Anarchy and the Environment*, ed. Samuel Barkin and George Shambaugh. Albany: State University of New York Press, pp. 155–175.

———. 2000. "The Environment As a National Security Issue." *Journal of Policy History* 12: 101–122.

Matthew, Richard, and George Shambaugh. 1998. "Sex, Drugs and Heavy Metal: Transnational Threats and National Vulnerabilities." *Security Dialogue* 29: 163–175.

McCabe, J., and J. Ellis. 1987. "Beating the Odds in Arid Africa." *Natural History* (January): 33–40.

McCay, B. 1992. "Everyone's Concern, Whose Responsibility? The Problem of the Commons," in *Understanding Economic Processes*, ed. S. Ortiz and S. Lees. Lanham, MD: University Press of America, pp. 189–210.

McCay, B., and S. Jentoft. 1998. "Market or Community Failure? Critical Perspectives on Common Property Research." *Human Organization* 57: 21–29.

McDaniel, Thomas. 1994. "College Classrooms of the Future: Megatrends to Paradigm Shifts." *College Teaching* 42: 27–31.

McKeachie, Wilbert, et al. 1994. *Teaching Tips: Strategies, Research, and Theory for College and University Teachers*. Lexington, MA: DC Heath and Company.

McKibben, Bill. 1989. *The End of Nature*. New York: Random House.

——. 1998. *Maybe One: A Personal and Environmental Argument for Single-Child Families*. New York: Simon and Schuster.

Meadows, D., and B. van der Waals. n.d. *Games on Sustainable Development*. Durham: University of New Hampshire Laboratory for Interactive Learning.

Milbrath, Lester. 1989. *Envisioning a Sustainable Society: Learning Our Way Out*. Albany: State University of New York.

Minter, Deborah, and Heidi Schweingruber. 1996. "The Instructional Challenge of Community Service Learning." *Michigan Journal of Community Service Learning* 3: 92–102.

Mitchell, Ronald. 1997. "A Tragedy of the Commons Game," at darkwing.uoregon.edu/~rmitchel/tragedy/ (accessed August 29, 2001).

Mohammed, Nadir. 1994. "The Development Trap: Militarization, Environmental Degradation and Poverty and Prospects of Military Conversion." Addis Ababa: Organization for Social Science Research in Eastern Africa, Occasional Paper 5.

——. 1997. "Environmental Conflicts in Africa," in *Conflict and the Environment*, ed. Nils Petter Gleditsch. Dordrecht, The Netherlands: Kluwer Academic Publishers, pp. 137–156.

Morrison, Toni. 1987. *Beloved: A Novel*. New York: Knopf.

Murray, Bridget. 1998. "Data Smog: Newest Culprit in Brain Drain." *American Psychological Association Monitor* 29, at www.apa.org/monitor/mar98/smog.html (accessed August 29, 2001).

Myers, Norman. 1989. "Environment and Security." *Foreign Policy* 74: 23–41.

——. 1993. *Ultimate Security: The Environmental Basis of Political Stability*. New York: Norton.

Naqvi, Nauman, ed. 1996. *Rethinking Security, Rethinking Development*. Islamabad, Pakistan: Sustainable Development Policy Institute.

Nash, Roderick. 1989. *The Rights of Nature: A History of Environmental Ethics*. Madison: University of Wisconsin Press.

National Commission on Civic Renewal. 1998. *A Nation of Spectators: How Civic Engagement Weakens America and What We Can Do about It*. College Park: University of Maryland.

Oakshott, Michael. 1962. *Rationalism in Politics and Other Essays*. London: Methuen.

Ophuls, William. 1974. "The Scarcity Society." *Harpers Magazine* (April): 47–52.

Orr, David. 1992. *Ecological Literacy: Education and the Transition to a Postmodern World*. Albany: State University of New York Press.

——. 1994. *Earth in Mind: On Education, Environment, and the Human Prospect*. Washington, DC: Island Press.

——. 1999. "The Ecology of Giving and Consuming," in *Consuming Desires: Consumption, Culture, and the Pursuit of Happiness*, ed. Roger Rosenblatt. Washington, DC: Island Press, pp. 137–154.

Ostrom, Elinor. 1990. *Governing the Commons: The Evolution of Institutions for Collective Action*. Cambridge, England: Cambridge University Press.

Oye, Kenneth. 1992. *Economic Distribution and Political Exchange*. Princeton, NJ: Princeton University Press.

Palmer, Clare. 1998. *Environmental Ethics and Process Thinking*. Oxford: Oxford University Press.

Papp, Daniel. 1997. *Contemporary International Relations: Frameworks for Understanding*. Boston: Allyn & Bacon.

Parsons, Edward. 1993. "Protecting the Ozone Layer," in *Institutions for the Earth: Sources of Effective International Environmental Protection*, ed. Peter Haas, Robert Keohane, and Marc Levy. Cambridge, MA: The MIT Press, pp. 27–73.

Peet, R., and M. Watts, eds. 1996. *Liberation Ecologies*. London: Routledge.

Peluso, Nancy, and Michael Watts, eds. 2001. *Violent Environments*. Ithaca, NY: Cornell University Press.

Peters, P. 1987. "Embedded Systems and Rooted Models: The Grazing Lands of Botswana and the Commons Debate," in *The Question of the Commons: The Culture and Ecology of Communal Resources*, ed. B. McCay and J. Acheson. Tucson: University of Arizona Press, pp. 171–194.

Picardi, A., and W. Seifert. 1976. "A Tragedy of the Commons in the Sahel." *Technology Review* (May): 42–51.

Pierce, Morris. 1992. "Campus Energy Management Program," in *The Campus and Environmental Responsibility*, ed. David Eagan and David Orr. San Francisco: Jossey-Bass Publishers, pp. 31–43.

Ponting, Clive. 1991. *A Green History of the World: The Environment and the Collapse of Great Civilizations*. New York: St. Martin's.

Porter, Gareth, Janet Welsh Brown, and Pamela Chasek. 2000. *Global Environmental Politics*. Boulder, CO: Westview.

Postman, Neil. 1996. *The End of Education: Redefining the Value of School*. New York: Knopf.

Postman, Neil, and Charles Weingartner. 1969. *Teaching As a Subversive Activity*. New York: Dell.

Poundstone, Paula. 1997. "Lean, Green Fighting Machine." *Mother Jones* (March/April): 80.

Princen, Thomas, and Matthias Finger. 1994. *Environmental NGOs in World Politics: Linking the Local and the Global*. New York: Routledge.

Princen, Thomas, Michael Maniates, and Ken Conca, eds. 2002. *Confronting Consumption*. Cambridge, MA: The MIT Press.

Putnam, Robert. 2000. *Bowling Alone: The Collapse and Revival of American Community*. New York: Simon and Schuster.

Randal, Jonathan. 1989. "Third World Seeks Aid before Joining Ozone Pact." *Washington Post* (March 7): Sect. A, 16.

Randall, Michael. 2000. "A Guide to Good Teaching: Be Slow and Inefficient." *Chronicle of Higher Education* (December 8): Sect. B, 24.

Rawls, John. 1971. *A Theory of Justice*. Cambridge, MA: Harvard University Press.

Reeher, Grant, and Joseph Cammarano, eds. 1997. *Education for Citizenship: Ideas and Innovations in Political Learning*. Lanham, MD: Rowman & Littlefield Publishers.

Reinicke, Wolfgang. 1998. *Global Public Policy: Governing without Government?* Washington, DC: Brookings Institution.

Rich, A. 1979. *On Lies, Secrets, and Silence: Selected Prose, 1966–1978*. New York: Norton.

Rich, Bruce. 1994. *Mortgaging the Earth: The World Bank, Environmental Impoverishment, and the Crisis of Development*. Boston: Beacon.

Richelson, Jeffrey. 1998. "Scientists in Black." *Scientific American* 278: 48–55.

Risse-Kappen, Thomas, ed. 1995. *Bringing Transnational Relations Back In: Non-State Actors, Domestic Structures, and International Institutions*. Cambridge, England: Cambridge University Press.

Rosenau, James. 1990. *Turbulence in World Affairs: A Theory of Change and Continuity.* Princeton, NJ: Princeton University Press.

Roskin, Michael, and Nicholas Berry. 1999. *The New World of International Relations.* Upper Saddle River, NJ: Prentice Hall.

Rowlands, Ian. 1991. "Ozone Layer Depletion and Global Warming: New Sources for Environmental Disputes." *Peace and Change* 16: 260–284.

Saad, Somaya. 1991. "For Whose Benefit? Redefining Security." *Eco-Decisions* 2: 59–60.

Saltmarsh, John. 1996. "Education for Critical Citizenship: John Dewey's Contribution to the Pedagogy of Community Service Learning." *Michigan Journal of Community Service Learning* 3: 13–21.

Sanchez, Rene. 1998. "College Freshmen Have the Blahs, Survey Indicates." *Washington Post* (January 12): 1.

Sandel, Michael. 1996. *Democracy's Discontent: America in Search of a Public Philosophy.* Cambridge, MA: The Belknap Press of Harvard University.

Sarewitz, Daniel, and Roger Pielke, Jr. 2000. "Breaking the Global-Warming Gridlock." *Atlantic Monthly* 286: 54–64.

Savion, Leah, and Joan Middendorf. 1994. "Enhancing Concept Comprehension and Retention." *The National Teaching and Learning Forum* 3: 6–8.

Sax, L., A. Astin, W. Korn, and K. Mahoney. 1999. *The American Freshman: National Norms for Fall 1999.* Los Angeles: Higher Education Research Institute, University of California, Los Angeles.

Schultz, Steven. 1990. "From Isolation to Commitment: The Role of the Community in Values Education," in *Community Service as Values Education,* ed. Cecilia Delve, Suzanne Mintz, and Greig Stewart. San Francisco: Jossey-Bass Publishers, pp. 91–100.

Schwerin, Edward. 1998. "Transformational Research and Teaching: An Overview," in *Transformational Politics: Theory, Study, and Practice,* ed. Stephen Woolpert, Christa Slaton, and Edward Schwerin. Albany: State University of New York Press, pp. 91–117.

Sell, Susan. 1994. "Is Ozone the Exception?" Paper presented at the Academic Council on the United Nations System, the Hague, Netherlands (June 25).

Sennett, Richard. 1977. *The Fall of Public Man.* New York: Knopf.

Sessions, George, ed. 1995. *Deep Ecology for the Twenty-First Century.* New York: Random House.

Shapiro, Michael, and Hayward Alker, eds. 1996. *Challenging Boundaries: Global Flows, Territorial Identities.* Minneapolis: University of Minnesota Press.

Sheldrake, Rupert. 1991. *The Rebirth of Nature: The Greening of Science and God.* Rochester, VT: Inner Traditions International Ltd.

Shenk, David. 1997. *Data Smog: Surviving the Information Glut.* New York: HarperCollins.

Shulman, Lee. 1997. "Professing the Liberal Arts," in *Education and Democracy: Re-imagining Liberal Learning in America,* ed. Robert Orrill. New York: College Entrance Examination Board, pp. 151–173.

Simon, Julian. 1987. *The Ultimate Resource.* Princeton, NJ: Princeton University Press.

———. 1989. "Lebensraum: Paradoxically, Population Growth May Eventually End Wars." *Journal of Conflict Resolution* 33: 164–180.

Smith, C. 1984. "Local History in Global Context: Social and Economic Transitions in Western Guatemala." *Comparative Studies in Society and History* 26: 193–228.

Smith, Toby. 1998. *The Myth of Green Marketing: Tending our Goats at the Edge of Apocalypse.* Toronto: University of Toronto Press.

Soroos, Marvin. 1991. "Adding Green to the International Studies Curriculum." *International Studies Notes* 16: 37–42.

Soulé, Michael, and Daniel Press. 1998. "What Is Environmental Studies?" *BioScience* 48: 397–405.

Springer, Allen. 1996. "Unilateral Action in Defense of Environmental Interests: An Assessment." Paper presented at the International Studies Association annual convention. San Diego, CA (April 16–20).

Sprout, Harold, and Margaret Sprout. 1971. *Toward a Politics of the Planet Earth*. New York: Van Nostrand Reinhold.

Stammer, Larry. 1989a. "6 More Nations Agree to Sign Ozone Accord." *Los Angeles Times* (March 6): Sect. I, 8.

———. 1989b. "China and India Ask Aid to Meet Rules on Ozone." *Los Angeles Times* (March 7): Sect. I, 10.

———. 1989c. "Global Ozone Talks Described As Successful." *Los Angeles Times* (March 8): Sect. I, 6

———1989d. "Saving the Earth: Who Will Do Without?" *Los Angeles Times* (March 13): 17.

———. 1990. "Chinese Delegates to Seek Beijing's Approval for Pact to Protect Ozone." *Los Angeles Times* (June 29): Sect. A, 8.

Stone, Deborah. 1988. *Policy Paradox and Political Reason*. Glenview, IL: Scott, Foresman, and Company.

Strange, Susan. 1996. *The Retreat of the State: The Diffusion of Power in the World Economy*. Cambridge, England: Cambridge University Press.

Suliman, Mohammed. 1999. *Ecology, Politics, and Violent Conflict*. London: Zed Books.

Svinicki, Marilla. 1991. "Practical Implications of Cognitive Theories," in *College Teaching: from Theory to Practice*, ed. Robert Menges and Marilla Svinicki. San Francisco: Jossey-Bass Publishers, pp. 27–38.

Taylor, Bron, ed. 1995. *Ecological Resistance Movements: The Global Emergence of Radical and Popular Environmentalism*. Albany: State University of New York Press.

Taylor, Peter. 1995. "Building on Construction: An Exploration of Heterogeneous Constructionism, Using an Analogy from Psychology and a Sketch from Socio-economic Modeling." *Perspectives on Science* 3: 66–98.

———. 1997. "Dynamics and Rhetorics of Socio-environmental Change: Critical Perspectives on the Limits of Neo-Malthusian Environmentalism," in *Advances in Human Ecology*, ed. L. Freese. Greenwich, CT: JAI Press, 257–292.

———. 1998. "How Does the Commons Become Tragic? Simple Models As Complex Sociopolitical Constructions." *Science As Culture* 7: 449–464.

———. 2001. "Critical Studies of Environment, Science, and Society," at omega .cc.umb.edu/ ~ptaylor/ (accessed August 29, 2001).

———. 2002. "The Limits of Ecology and the Re/construction of Unruly Complexity." Unpublished manuscript.

Taylor, Peter, and R. García Barrios. 1995. "The Social Analysis of Ecological Change: From Systems to Intersecting Processes." *Social Science Information* 34: 5–30.

Terry, Lynda. 1996. "Junior Seminar Reshapes Campus Life." *Allegheny Monthly* (December). Meadville, PA: Allegheny College.

Thucydides. 1954. *The Peloponnesian War*. Trans. Rex Warner. Harmondsworth, U.K.: Penguin.

Tiberius, Richard, and Janet Billson. 1991. "The Social Context of Teaching and Learning," in *College Teaching: From Theory to Practice*, ed. Robert Menges and Marilla Svinicki. San Francisco: Jossey-Bass Publishers, pp. 67–85.

Tickner, J. Ann. 1992. *Gender in International Relations: Feminist Perspectives on Achieving Global Security*. New York: Columbia University Press.

Tripp, James. 1988. "The UNEP Montreal Protocol: Industrialized and Developing Countries Sharing the Responsibility for Protecting the Stratospheric Ozone Layer." *New York University Journal of International Law and Politics* 20: 742–743.

Turner, M. 1993. "Overstocking the Range: A Critical Analysis of the Environmental Science of Sahelian Pastoralism." *Economic Geography* 69: 402–421.

Tyson, James. 1989. "Why China Says Ozone Must Take a Back Seat in Drive to Prosperity." *Christian Science Monitor* (March 23): 1.

Ullman, Richard. 1983. "Redefining Security." *International Security* 8: 129–153.

United Nations Development Program. 1994. *Human Development Report 1994*. New York: Oxford University Press.

———. 1998. *Human Development Report 1998*. New York: Oxford University Press.

United Nations Environment Program. 1997. *Global Environmental Outlook*. New York: Oxford University Press.

VanDeveer, Stacy, and Geoffrey Dabelko. 1999. "Redefining Security around the Baltic: Environmental Issues in Regional Context." *Global Governance* 5: 221–249.

Van Dieren, Wouter, ed. 1995. *Taking Nature Into Account: A Report to the Club of Rome*. New York: Sringer-Verlag.

Vernon, Raymond. 1993. "Behind the Scenes: How Policymaking in the European Community, Japan, and the United States Affects Global Negotiations." *Environment* 35: 12–20, 35–43.

Victor, David. 2000. "Kyoto Is Dead, an Upbeat Requiem." *Grist Magazine*, at www.gristmaga zine.com/grist/heatbeat/debates011700-b.asp (accessed August 29, 2001).

Wackernagel, Mathis, and William Rees. 1996. *Our Ecological Footprint: Reducing Human Impact on the Earth*. Philadelphia: New Society Publishers.

Wæver, Ole. 1995. "Securitization and Desecuritization," in *On Security*, ed. Ronnie Lipschutz. New York: Columbia University Press, pp. 46–86.

Wagner, Jon. 1990. "Beyond Curricula: Helping Students Construct Knowledge through Teaching and Research," in *Community Service As Values Education*, ed. Cecilia Delve, Suzanne Mintz, and Greig Stewart. San Francisco: Jossey-Bass Publishers, pp. 43–54.

Walt, Stephen. 1991. "The Renaissance of Security Studies." *International Security Studies Quarterly* 35: 211–39.

Waltz, Kenneth. 1979. *Theory of International Politics*. New York: McGraw-Hill.

Wapner, Paul. 1996a. *Environmental Activism and World Civic Politics*. Albany: State University of New York Press.

———. 1996b. "Toward a Meaningful Ecological Politics." *Tikkun* 11: 21–24.

———. 1997. "Environmental Ethics and Global Governance: Engaging the International Liberal Tradition." *Global Governance* 3: 213–231.

Washington, James, ed. 1992. *I Have a Dream: Writing and Speeches That Changed the World*. New York: HarperCollins.

Weinstein, Claire, and Debra Meyer. 1991. "Cognitive Learning Strategies and College Teaching," in *College Teaching: From Theory to Practice*, ed. Robert Menges and Marilla Svinicki. San Francisco: Jossey-Bass Publishers, pp. 15–26.

Westing, Arthur. 1989. "The Environmental Component of Comprehensive Security." *Bulletin of Peace Proposals* 20: 129–134.

Wheeler, Nedra. 1995. "The Instructional Leader's Primer in Systems Thinking." Available from the ERIC Document Reproduction Service at edrs.com/ #ED415203.

Wilson, Edward. 1992. *The Diversity of Life*. Cambridge, MA: Harvard University Press.

Winner, Langdon. 1986. *The Whale and the Reactor: A Search for Limits in an Age of High Technology*. Chicago: University of Chicago Press.

———. 1992. "Citizen Virtues in a Technological Order." *Inquiry* 35: 341–61.

Wolf, Aaron. 1998. "Conflict and Cooperation along International Waterways." *Water Policy* 1: 251–265.

Wolf, E. 1957. "Closed, Corporate Peasant Communities in Mesoamerica and Central Java." *Southwestern Journal of Anthropology* 13: 1–18.

———. 1982. *Europe and the People without History*. Berkeley: University of California Press.

World Bank. 1999. *World Development Report 1998/99*. New York: Oxford University Press.

World Commission on Environment and Development. 1987. *Our Common Future*. New York: Oxford University Press.

Worster, Donald. 1985. *Rivers of Empire: Water, Aridity, and the Growth of the American West*. New York: Pantheon Books.

Young, Oran. 1994. *International Governance: Protecting the Environment in a Stateless Society*. Ithaca: Cornell University Press.

Zivi, Karen. 1997. "Examining Pedagogy in the Service-Learning Classroom: Reflections of Integrating Service-Learning into the Curriculum," in *Experiencing Citizenship: Concepts and Models for Service-Learning in Political Science*, ed. Richard Battistoni and William Hudson. Washington, DC: American Association for Higher Education, pp. 49–67.

Zlotkowski, Edward. 1996. "A New Voice at the Table? Linking Service-Learning and the Academy." *Change* 28: 21–27.

———, ed. 1998. *Successful Service-Learning Programs: New Models of Excellence in Higher Education*. Bolton, MA: Anker Publishing.

Index

Page references in italic refer to boxed text.

247

About the Contributors

Matthew Auer is associate professor of public and environmental affairs at the School of Public and Environmental Affairs at Indiana University. He has been recognized for excellence in teaching and recently received the Myres McDougal Prize from the Society for the Policy Sciences for his research and writing in global environmental governance. He advises the U.S. Agency for International Development, U.S. Department of Defense, U.S. Forest Service, and U.S. Department of Energy on a variety of environmental policy matters. He is also a member of the board of editors and a book review coeditor of the journal *Policy Sciences*.

William Ayers is a school reform activist, Distinguished Professor of Education, and Senior University Scholar at the University of Illinois at Chicago, where he teaches courses in interpretive research, urban school change, and youth and the modern predicament. He is the founder of the Center for Youth and Society and founder and codirector of the Small Schools Workshop. His book *To Teach: The Journey of a Teacher* (2nd ed., 2001) was named Book of the Year by Kappa Delta Pi and won the Written Award for Distinguished Work in Biography and Autobiography. His interests focus on the political and social contexts of schooling and the meaning and ethical purposes of teachers, students, and families.

Ken Conca is associate professor of government and politics at the University of Maryland, where he also directs the Harrison Program on the Future Global Agenda. In addition to several book chapters and journal articles, he is the author of *Manufacturing Insecurity: The Rise and Fall of Brazil's Military-Industrial Complex* (1997); the coeditor, with Geoffrey Dabelko, of *Green Planet Blues: Environmental Politics from Stockholm to Kyoto* (2nd ed., 1998) and *Environmental Peacemaking* (2002); and coeditor, with Thomas Princen and Michael Maniates, of *Confronting Consumption* (2002).

Geoffrey Dabelko is director of the Environmental Change and Security Project, a nonpartisan policy forum on environment, population, and security issues located in Washington, D.C., at the Woodrow Wilson International Center for Scholars. He is currently coprincipal investigator on the Environment, Development, and Sustainable Peace Initiative, an international effort to bridge the gap between Northern and Southern perspectives on environment, development, poverty, conflict, and peace. He is coeditor with Ken Conca of *Green Planet Blues: Environmental Politics from Stockholm to Kyoto* (2nd ed., 1998) and *Environmental Peacemaking* (2002).

B. Welling Hall is professor of politics and international studies at Earlham College. She serves as Section Chair of the International Law section of the International Studies Association. Her work on teaching international relations and on global environmental politics has appeared in *Alternatives*, the *Annals of the American Academy of Political and Social Science*, *PS*, *International Studies Notes*, and *International Studies Perspectives*. Following a fellowship at the Institute of Comparative Politology in Moscow, she edited *Women, Politics, and Environmental Action* (at www.earlham.edu/~wellingh/wpea/index.html). She is currently at work on an international law text for undergraduates.

Lamont Hempel is Hedco Professor of Environmental Studies and director of environmental programs at the University of Redlands. He specializes in U.S. and international environmental policy, with emphasis on issues of climate change, sustainable community development, air pollution, and coral reef protection. His publications include *Environmental Governance: The Global Challenge* (1996) and *Sustainable Communities: From Vision to Action* (1998).

Michael Maniates (editor) is associate professor of political science and environmental science at Allegheny College. He also codirects the Meadville Community Energy Project, a student-centered program fostering regional energy efficiency and sustainability, and administers the International Project on Teaching Global Environmental Politics, an electronic network of college and university professors exploring solutions to global environmental ills. He is coeditor, with Thomas Princen and Ken Conca, of *Confronting Consumption* (2002), and his work on the nature and future of undergraduate environmental studies programs recently appeared in *BioScience*. In 2000, he received Allegheny College's Thoburn Teaching Award for exemplary teaching.

Richard Matthew is associate professor of international and environmental politics in the Schools of Social Ecology and Social Science at the University of California, Irvine, and director of the Global Environmental Change and Human Security Research Office at UCI. He has worked closely with the International Union for the Conservation of Nature and the International Institute for Sustainable Development, as well as a number of U.S. government departments and agencies including Defense and State. His books include *Dichotomy of Power: Nation versus State in World Politics* (2002), *Conserving the Peace: Resources, Livelihoods, and Security* (2002), and *Environmental Insecurities* (forthcoming).

Thomas Princen is associate professor of natural resources and environmental policy in the School of Natural Resources and Environment at the University of Michigan, where he also codirects the Workshop on Consumption and Environment. He is coeditor, with Michael Maniates and Ken Conca, of *Confronting Consumption* (2002); coauthor, with Matthias Finger, of *Environmental NGOs in World Politics: Linking the Local and the Global* (1994); and author of *Intermediaries in International Conflict* (1992). Over the past thirty years he has taught at all levels of education, from kindergarten to graduate school, and from biology and reading to microeconomics, negotiation, and environmental policy. He was a Pew Faculty Fellow for International Affairs where he received intensive training in methods of active learning.

Nancy Quirk is a Ph.D. candidate in political science at Indiana University, Bloomington. Her dissertation on European Union environmental policy examines the emergence of voluntary regulatory approaches, such as the European Ecolabel and the EU's Environmental Management and Auditing Scheme. She has been teaching in the areas of European and international environmental policy.

Karl Steyaert is a Ph.D. student in anthropology and natural resources policy at the University of Michigan. He also is an educator and advocate fostering sustainable community development and sustainability education. Working with the Center for a New American Dream, he coedited, with Betsy Taylor and Juliet Schor, *Sustainable Planet: Roadmaps to the 21st Century* (forthcoming).

Peter Taylor is associate professor in the Graduate College of Education at the University of Massachusetts, Boston, where he coordinates the Program on Critical and Creative Thinking. His research focuses on the complexity of intersecting processes that produce environmental change, on the complexity of influences on the sciences that investigate such processes, and on ways to foster critical pedagogy and reflective practice that attends to those dual complexities. He coedited *Changing Life: Genomes, Ecologies, Bodies, Commodities* (1997).

Paul Wapner is associate professor and director of the Global Environmental Policy Program in the School of International Service at American University, Washington, D.C. His research focuses on environmental ethics, social movements, and international relations theory. He is the author of *Environmental Activism and World Civic Politics* (1996) and coeditor, with Lester Ruiz, of *Principled World Politics: The Challenge of Normative International Relations* (2000).

Howard Warshawsky is professor of political science and chair of the Department of Public Affairs at Roanoke College. He developed the college's multidisciplinary major program in International Relations and has served as its coordinator for the past two decades. His research and writing focuses on U.S. environmental diplomacy and comparative foreign policymaking.